66 OF THE MOST IMPORTANT VIDEO GAMES EVER!
(ACCORDING TO ME)

S. L. PERRIN

66 OF THE MOST IMPORTANT VIDEO GAMES EVER! (ACCORDING TO ME)

S. L. PERRIN

Copyright © 2021 S. L. PERRIN
All rights reserved.
ISBN: 9798736012268

S. L. PERRIN

66 OF THE MOST IMPORTANT VIDEO GAMES EVER!
(ACCORDING TO ME)

CONTENTS

INTRODUCTION	PAGE 7
PONG (1978)	PAGE 9
SPACE INVADERS (1978)	PAGE 14
PAC-MAN (1980)	PAGE 18
ZORK I (1980)	PAGE 21
ROGUE (1980)	PAGE 24
DONKEY KONG (1981)	PAGE 29
PITFALL! (1982)	PAGE 34
POLE POSITION (1982)	PAGE 37
RAIDERS OF THE LOST ARK (1982)	PAGE 40
E.T. THE EXTRA-TERRESTRIAL (1982)	PAGE 43
DRAGON'S LAIR (1983)	PAGE 46
MANIC MINER (1983)	PAGE 50
KARATE CHAMP (1984)	PAGE 54
TETRIS (1984)	PAGE 57
ELITE (1984)	PAGE 62
PAC-LAND (1984)	PAGE 67
KNIGHT LORE (1984)	PAGE 69
SKOOL DAZE (1984)	PAGE 72
SUPER MARIO BROS. (1985)	PAGE 76
GAUNTLET (1985)	PAGE 80
THE LEGEND OF ZELDA (1986)	PAGE 84
TURBO ESPRIT (1986)	PAGE 88
LABYRINTH: THE COMPUTER GAME (1986)	PAGE 91
METROID (1986)	PAGE 95
OUTRUN (1986)	PAGE 99
DRACULA (1986)	PAGE 102
DOUBLE DRAGON (1987)	PAGE 106
METAL GEAR (1987)	PAGE 109
THE KING OF CHICAGO (1987)	PAGE 113
SUPER MARIO BROS. 3 (1988)	PAGE 117
SIMCITY (1989)	PAGE 121
POPULOUS (1989)	PAGE 126
PRINCE OF PERSIA (1989)	PAGE 129

STREET ROD (1989)	PAGE 133
SWEET HOME (1989)	PAGE 136
MIDWINTER (1990)	PAGE 138
STREET FIGHTER II (1991)	PAGE 142
ZELDA: A LINK TO THE PAST (1991)	PAGE 145
MORTAL KOMBAT (1992)	PAGE 148
DUNE II: BATTLE FOR ARRAKIS (1992)	PAGE 152
SYNDICATE (1993)	PAGE 155
MYST (1993)	PAGE 158
DOOM (1993)	PAGE 162
FINAL FANTASY VI (III) (1994)	PAGE 166
RISE OF THE ROBOTS (1994)	PAGE 170
SENSIBLE WORLD OF SOCCER (1994)	PAGE 175
RESIDENT EVIL (1996)	PAGE 178
SUPER MARIO 64 (1996)	PAGE 182
TOMB RAIDER (1996)	PAGE 187
GOLDENEYE 007 (1997)	PAGE 191
GRAND THEFT AUTO (1997)	PAGE 196
GRAN TURISMO (1997)	PAGE 201
HALF-LIFE (1998)	PAGE 204
THE NEW SUPERMAN ADVENTURES (1999)	PAGE 208
SHENMUE (1999)	PAGE 213
ZELDA: MAJORA'S MASK (2000)	PAGE 217
THE SIMS (2000)	PAGE 220
THE ELDER SCROLLS III: MORROWIND (2002)	PAGE 224
GRAND THEFT AUTO III (2001)	PAGE 227
WORLD OF WARCRAFT (2004)	PAGE 231
LEGO STAR WARS: THE VIDEO GAME (2005)	PAGE 235
WII SPORTS (2006)	PAGE 239
BATMAN: ARKHAM ASYLUM (2009)	PAGE 243
ANGRY BIRDS (2009)	PAGE 248
RED DEAD REDEMPTION (2010)	PAGE 251
MINECRAFT (2011)	PAGE 255
HONOURABLE MENTIONS	PAGE 260
THANKS	PAGE 271
SOURCES	PAGE 272

66 OF THE MOST IMPORTANT VIDEO GAMES EVER!
(ACCORDING TO ME)

INTRODUCTION

Video games, they've certainly grown and evolved a fair bit over the years eh? From those early days of *Pong* and seeing two white sticks move up and down a single black screen, knocking a square back and forth that supposedly represented a ball, in a very early attempt at simulating a game of tennis. It was hardly Björn Borg v John McEnroe in the Wimbledon finals, but we loved it. From those early days, to now, with these huge open and explorable worlds, fully voice-acted characters, featuring cinematic style stories, crammed with immersion and player interactivity and all presented in full HD quality. The gaming world, as a whole, has changed a lot over the last nigh on five decades, so much so that when you put something like *Space Invaders* next to *Red Dead Redemption II*… You just can't help but be in awe of how different those two eras of gaming really are.

Still, without those very early pioneers of the gaming world, we wouldn't be where we are today. If I had a cap, I'd be doffing it profusely in respect. But as I don't own a cap (note to self: must buy a cap), I thought I'd write a book instead. A book that looks at *66 Of The Most Important Video Games Ever! (According To Me)*.

Now, before I really get into this, I'm not necessarily compiling a list and looking at the best or greatest games ever, that's a whole other book (note to self: write another book). There will be some glaring omissions in that regard. No, this is my very own, personal opinion on what I feel are the most important games ever, selected from almost fifty years of video games. The titles in this book come from a wide spectrum of genres, years, developers and countries. Some franchises get more than one entry, some only one, others don't even get that. Most of the games I have chosen are amazing trailblazers. Some are not very good, but could still be considered important in their own right for 'reasons'. See, it's not necessarily about the quality, acclaim or popularity of the titles in this book, but more a case of the importance to the gaming industry and how they have affected me personally as a gamer, from a young 'un right up to the cynical and cantankerous old bastard I have now become.

Now, I have set myself a handful of stipulations for this book. I'm mainly concentrating on the original release of each game, no ports or re-releases (except for the odd mention/reference) and the games I look at are on the original format they were released for and in and the year they were originally released. Unless it was a multi-format release, then I'm allowing myself to look at the format I first played the game on, or the version I am most familiar with. This list and views on said titles are also my own opinions, there will be a few behind the scenes facts and titbits thrown in too, but the main thing is the games in this list as here because I personally feel they have been important to the industry or even to me. If you think I've not included a game that you feel should be here… Then write your own damn book (insert cheeky winky face here to denote humour and don't leave this lazy note to self in for an all too easy and incredibly lazy joke). So, with that out of the way, here they are:

66 Of The Most Important Video Games Ever! (According To Me).

66 OF THE MOST IMPORTANT VIDEO GAMES EVER! (ACCORDING TO ME)

PONG

DEVELOPER: ATARI
PUBLISHER: ATARI
PLATFORM: ARCADE
RELEASED: NOVEMBER, 1972

For me, *Pong* is the first-ever video game. Yeah, yeah I know I'll have fellow gaming enthusiasts screaming at my words there. 'Actually! I think you'll find that *Spacewar!* from 1961 was the first-ever video game!', with more than a hint of snark thrown in for good measure too. I guess it really depends on how one chooses to define a video game. I mean, couldn't it be argued that 1958's *Tennis for Two* or the Noughts & Crosses (Tic-Tac-Toe) inspired *Bertie the Brain* from 1950 were possible contenders for the first-ever video game? Maybe a bit more digging could reveal even earlier video games? I'll let you argue amongst yourselves what you feel the first-ever video game was. I don't have time, I have a huge book to write.

Anyway, for me, for a video game to be included in this book, it has to meet certain criteria. It has to be playable, it has to have a wide appeal and it has to have been made specifically for mass consumption... It has to be a video game basically. As impressive and as ground-breaking as *Tennis for Two*, *Bertie the Brain*, and *Spacewar!* were, they were really more like experiments. Experiments that would go on to be considered the birth of gaming yes, but still just experiments nonetheless and not, in my eyes, true video games. And yes again, before the snarky comments come thick and fast. I do know that *Spacewar!* was adapted in 1971, complete with a coin-operated arcade cabinet and re-released to the public as *Computer Space*, making it the first-ever arcade machine... But it wasn't the original and as I said in the intro, no re-releases, ports, etc, only the original versions can be considered... Plus, it was a bit of a flop and hardly set the world on fire as a video game, as *Pong* did.

So, as I was saying, for me, *Pong* is the first-ever video game. This is really where it all began, this is where the video gaming industry truly kicked off proper. Designed by Allan Alcorn in 1972 as nothing more than a training exercise in programming, that was given to him by Atari co-founder Nolan Bushnell. Alcorn was said to have been 'inspired' by a version of Ping-Pong called *Table Tennis* on the first-ever home games console, the Magnavox Odyssey. In fact, *Pong* was so 'inspired' by Magnavox's game, that the company decided to sue Atari for patent infringement, a case they won. Along with stressfully suing other companies who had also made several games 'inspired' by that simple *Table Tennis* game on the Magnavox Odyssey console. Magnavox ended up making around $100 million from all of the litigation alone, in what would become the first-ever video game lawsuit. Then in 1985, Magnavox tried to take on Nintendo and well... Let's just say that Nintendo are still around today whereas Magnavox are long gone in terms of gaming. And I've gotten a little sidetracked.

So, back to the point, *Pong* was released in 1972 and it kick-started the whole arcade gaming trend and indeed, the entire video gaming boom. The original prototype (made using a $75 Hitachi black & white TV set) designed by Allan Alcorn was placed in a bar in August of 1972, a bar called Andy Capp's Tavern in Sunnyvale, California, quite literally over the road from where Atari's headquarters were located at the time. The *Pong* prototype was nestled in with a few other electronic entertainment machines such as a jukebox, pinball machines and even a (previously mentioned) *Computer Space* cabinet. Of all the machines in that bar, *Pong* quickly became the obvious favourite. It was easy to understand and play and according to pong-story.com Atari's co-founder Nolan Bushnell said of *Pong* that:

"To be successful, I had to come up with a game people already knew how to play, something so simple that any drunk in any bar could play."

And it was. It was *Pong's* simplicity that made it such a success, even in that early prototype form.

For a game that was so simple, it held quite a few interesting gameplay mechanics that added a little depth to that simplicity. Alcorn added the idea of splitting the paddle into eight separate parts. These different areas on the paddle would change the way the ball reacted when it was hit. For example, if the ball hit the middle of the paddle, it would bounce off at a 90° angle. Other areas on the paddle would make the ball reflect at other angles. This added a little strategy to the game. Then there was

66 OF THE MOST IMPORTANT VIDEO GAMES EVER! (ACCORDING TO ME)

the fact that the longer the ball remained in play, the faster it became. This made each game slowly increase in difficulty. Neither of these features were in that previously mentioned Magnavox Odyssey *Table Tennis* game and so, they gave *Pong* a bit of an edge over other similar games. Another feature was actually born from a technology limitation. If you have ever played *Pong*, you may have realised that the in-game paddles don't reach the very top of the screen. As Allan Alcorn explains in this interview with IGN, that limitation became a feature:

"The paddles on the original *Pong* didn't go all the way to the top. There was a defect in the circuit, I used a very simple circuit. I had to make the paddles, but they didn't go to the top. I could have fixed it, but it turned out to be important because, if you get two good players, they could just volley and play the game forever. And the game has to end in about 3 or 4 minutes otherwise it's a failure as a game. So that gap at the top, again, a feature. So that was sort of a happy accident."

Atari's Nolan Bushnell flew out to Chicago to meet with two of the biggest entertainment companies in the US at the time, Bally Manufacturing and Midway Manufacturing. Both companies had made plenty of money in the amusement games, slot machines and the casino line of business. Atari was still relatively small in 1972 and so Bushnell went to the business meetings with Bally and Midway to tell them of this amazing and massively popular *Pong* prototype, hoping to licence the game to one them for a lot of money in return. However, within a few days of the *Pong* game being in Andy Capp's Tavern, it began to display some technical issues and glitches. Allan Alcorn was called in to fix it, if he could. Finding no issues with the hardware itself, he was puzzled as to why the game was not working properly, despite there being no actual apparent problems with the machine, he decided to open the coin mechanism and found it overflowing with quarters. Apparently, the coin receptacle was so full, that the quarters fell onto the circuit board of the game and the metal then caused short circuits with the game's hardware, which in turn, made the game glitch. That was why Alcorn was called out to fix the problem and once the coins were emptied, the prototype was said to have worked fine again. At least, that is how the famous story of *Pong* goes. But perhaps that's a story worth looking into?

See I, and I'm sure you too have heard of the famed tale that the overflowing coin receptacle caused that early *Pong* prototype to fail. It is one of gaming's most famous stories. But I can't find any 100%, concrete evidence that this is true. In fact, I have found quite the opposite. Pong-story.com has a very detailed and lengthy article on the development and popularity of *Pong*. According to them, the story of the overflowing coins is a myth, as they state:

> "No, the game did NOT fail. No, the quarters DID NOT fill the coin recipient so as to fall on the circuit board and produce short circuits."

Yes, that early *Pong* prototype did fail and yes Allan Alcorn had to fix it. But not due to overflowing coins causing short circuits. In fact, there were two failings that needed to be fixed. The first one seems to be very vague as to exactly what the problem was. It was around two weeks after *Pong* had been installed in Andy Capp's Tavern when Alcorn was called out to fix the game and give the angry waiting players free games to keep them happy. The second time was a week after the first, when the paddles used as the controllers stopped working. This was because the prototype was made on such a tight budget that the cheap potentiometers used for the paddles simply broke. Allan Alcorn just had to replace the cheaper and now broken potentiometers with more sturdy and expensive ones and the game was up and running once more. Anyway, the point is that the classic *Pong* story of the overflowing coins seems to be false, or at least there doesn't seem to be any real evidence to back it up.

Now, I do need to add a little clarity to the story here. I have seen an interview where Allan Alcorn himself said he was called out to fix *Pong* because it was full of coins. But not that those coins caused any issues with the hardware itself. It was just so full that it couldn't take any more coins, that's it. No evidence that the coins were responsible for the game's hardware failing in any way as the old story goes.

Back to the story and once Nolan Bushnell learned of just how much money the *Pong* prototype was making and only in one bar remember, he thought it would be best to not sell the licence to another company and instead, felt that they could make more profit if Atari themselves made and distributed the machines. But, Atari lacked the financial backing to make that happen. After several failed deals and requests,

66 OF THE MOST IMPORTANT VIDEO GAMES EVER!
(ACCORDING TO ME)

Atari finally landed themselves a line of credit. They quickly began putting together assembly workers, hiring from a local unemployment office to help turn their simple *Pong* prototype into a real arcade cabinet to put into bars all over the US. However, the first machines had issues, the workers were not properly trained and could only manage to produce around ten machines a day, several of which failed quality testing and were unplayable. After some brainstorming, the whole process was streamlined and the workers were better trained, that was when the machines began to fly off the production line. By 1973, Atari began shipping *Pong* units to other counties. Before long, *Pong* was the biggest selling arcade game in the US, with other countries not too far behind either. Allan Alcorn recalls the game's popularity with IGN:

"We put the damn thing in a box over a weekend... At Andy Capp's Tavern, and geez, the thing was a hit from day one. This was completely unexpected. So obviously we start building these things. We manufactured about three-thousand upright coin-op *Pongs*. There were probably ten or twelve-thousand manufactured in total."

The success of *Pong* is what kick-started the whole arcade revolution, the one game that really birthed the entire video game's industry. While the arcade machines were selling like hotcakes, Atari engineer, Harold Lee, came up with the idea to make a home version in 1974. A simple and smaller version of its arcade bigger brother that you could plug in and play at home. In 1975, *Home Pong* was released and it too became a huge success. The arcade version of *Pong* was bringing in around four times what other coin-operated machines were managing to do at the time, while the home version sold just over a hundred and fifty-thousand units by Christmas of 1975. Soon after its success, the market was being flooded with *Pong*-clones from various manufacturers, but it was Atari who made the biggest impact and they would go on to be one of the biggest names in gaming for decades... All thanks to *Pong*, that simple game of electronic tennis, which was only originally made as a training exercise in programming.

S. L. PERRIN

SPACE INVADERS
DEVELOPER: TAITO
PUBLISHER(S): TAITO, MIDWAY
PLATFORM: ARCADE
RELEASED: JUNE, 1978

By the late 1970s, the arcade business was booming. More and more companies began making more and more games, to try and emulate Atari's success with *Pong*. Technology was advancing and the machines that were swallowing coins became ever more impressive. By 1978, the simplicity of *Pong* was pretty much a distant memory, no more black & white gaming with sticks sliding up and down the screen... The aliens had arrived.

We had some 'colour'. Okay, so it wasn't colour as you'd think by today's standards. The original *Space Invaders* was actually in black & white, but it had transparent coloured overlays to add strips of faux colour to the display. The game also had some pretty decent sound effects and of course, we finally had the shoot 'em up genre. I guess it could be debated just what was the first-ever shoot 'em up video game (go on say it, say *Spacewar!*), but you can not argue that the one game that defined the genre was the original *Space Invaders*. Designed by Tomohiro Nishikado and published by Taito, *Space Invaders* is unarguably one of the all-time most important games ever made. Nishikado not only designed the game, but he also helped create and develop the hardware on which the game would run. The title's main inspiration seems to have come from two places. The first was a mechanical arcade game made by Taito in 1972 called *Space Monsters*. The second was a nightmare that Tomohiro Nishikado has said that had about school children waiting for Santa Claus to arrive on Christmas, who are attacked by invading aliens... Maybe he ate some particularly strong cheese just before bed? Other influences for *Space Invaders* include the game *Breakout* and even the movies, *The War of the Worlds* and *Star Wars*. Tomohiro Nishikado himself talks about the game's influences in this interview with Retro Gamer:

"Back then, Atari's *Breakout* was very popular in Japan, and I was addicted to it myself. I especially liked the gameplay elements, such as a

66 OF THE MOST IMPORTANT VIDEO GAMES EVER! (ACCORDING TO ME)

sense of achievement at destroying the targets, and the tension that piles up when there's only one block left. I included these elements into a shooting game, then began creating the game on an arcade board featuring microprocessors that were just emerging in the US. Originally I wanted to create a shooting game with a lot more movements, but the idea had to be reworked due to the limited hardware available. The alien designs were inspired by the Martians from *The War of the Worlds*, I remembered watching the film version in my childhood. In addition, I heard that a film called *Star Wars* was becoming very popular in the US, so I decided to create a space-themed game."

The original concept of the game was for you, the player, to be shooting at human soldiers and the initial idea was to make a military-based game. However, Taito began to worry that killing humans would send out a bad message and possibly upset the gaming industry (how times have changed eh?). So the idea came about to make the targets the less possibly offending aliens instead, and thus born was one of the most famous gaming images ever. As those pesky *Space Invaders* descended toward the Earth, your ship had to shoot them all. As they reduced in numbers, they would speed up, making them increasingly harder to hit. I think one of the most commonly known facts about the game is that the whole speeding up of the aliens thing was not actually intentional. The aliens were always meant to maintain the same speed from the start to the end, no matter how many were taken out. However, due to the fact the hardware could render the graphics faster with fewer sprites on screen, the aliens would speed up with each one killed. It was one of the first examples of a bug making the game better, as Nishikado recalls:

"Originally I wanted to move [the] fifty-five invaders at the same time, but the hardware only let me move one invader every 1/60 second. As a result, invaders began to move faster as they decreased in number. But in the end, this actually added more thrills to the game. Techniques such as Wall of Death are all bugs. Unlike now, there was no strict debugging process in those days. Actually, I think I did the testing myself. If *Space Invaders* was developed now, it would go through many testers and I'm sure the bugs would be fixed. It was just a matter of luck that there were no freeze bugs!"

Plus, *Space Invaders* birthed a lot of gaming firsts too. It was the first game to give the player multiple lives, the first that had enemies shooting back, the first with destructible scenery (those shield things at the bottom of the screen). It was also the first to feature a continual soundtrack, those infamous descending 'duh-duh-duh-duh' notes which increased in pace as the attacking aliens sped up. A simple 'soundtrack' for sure, but one that is embedded into many gamer's minds forever and one that is one of gaming's most memorable.

Space Invaders was a gargantuan hit when it was released in Japan. So huge was its popularity, it has been said that it got to a point where the entire country was running out of coins, so Japan had to quadruple the production of the Yen to compensate. Though, that famous gaming fact actually makes no sense really. Just think about it for a second, how/why would Japan run out of coins due to an arcade game? The machines would've been emptied on a regular basis and those coins would've been put into banks, then all of the Yen would've been recirculated. One of many gaming facts/myths I aim to question and possibly correct in this book. Anyway, arcades were still in their infancy in the late-seventies when *Space Invaders* was released, but they always had a mix of various games to entice people to play. Yet, *Space Invaders* was so popular in Japan that they had to create arcades that only housed that one game. There is a bit of a dark side to the popularity of the game though, there were multiple reports of youths turning to crime to get money just to play *Space Invaders*. Muggings increased across the country and children even stole money from their parents to thrust into the coin slot. *Space Invaders* may have possibly caused the game industry's first-ever public controversy.

Due to its massive success in Japan, *Space Invaders* was soon licensed to be sold in other countries and that's when the big money really came in. By the end of 1978, the game had made around $600 million in Japan alone. By 1982, *Space Invaders* had made over $2 billion worldwide... And that's in early-eighties money too, around $7.8 billion today. At one time, *Space Invaders* was the highest-grossing entertainment product ever, it even managed to out-gross mega-hit movie, *Star Wars*.

1980 saw the first homeport of *Space Invaders* on the Atari 2600, where it became the first game to sell over one million copies, and it just kept

66 OF THE MOST IMPORTANT VIDEO GAMES EVER! (ACCORDING TO ME)

growing from there. *Space Invaders* is still going strong now too. The title has seen sequels, remakes, updates, collections and just good old-fashioned blatant rip-offs for years. Between its original release in 1978 up to the latest game in the franchise with *Space Invaders Invincible Collection* in 2020, the series has seen more than forty different releases spanning over six decades.

Space Invaders is simply one of the most important and influential video games ever made. The great, great, great, grandfather of the shooter genre. Hugely famous industry names such as Shigeru Miyamoto, Hideo Kojima, John Romero and John Carmack have all cited *Space Invaders* as the reason they got into video games and game design/development to begin with. So without it, we may never have seen the likes of *Zelda*, *Mario*, *Metal Gear*, *Doom* and so many other great titles…. Which are very likely to appear in this book (SPOILERS!).

S. L. PERRIN

PAC-MAN
DEVELOPER: NAMCO
PUBLISHER(S): NAMCO, MIDWAY
PLATFORM: ARCADE
RELEASED: JUNE, 1980

By the time the eighties had rolled around, arcades were a huge business. The likes of *Pong* and *Space Invaders* really laid the foundation for what games could be and developers began to push more creative ideas. Still, as great as games like *Pong* and *Space Invaders* were, they were ultimately very basic. A rudimentary version of tennis and shooting aliens were limited to simple and restrictive movements within each title. But what if instead of only moving up and down or left and right, what if you could do all four directions?

In 1979, 24-year-old Toru Iwatani was sitting down and enjoying a pizza in a restaurant when he first came up with an idea to create a game centred around eating. Iwatani took a slice from his pizza and ate it. He then looked down at his food, now with a slice taken, he thought the gap in his pizza looked like an open mouth and came up with a basic character design. Iwatani has also claimed that the design of *Pac-Man* came from rounding out and simplifying the Japanese character 'kuchi' (口), which means 'mouth'. Anyway, that was when Iwatani's game idea and character design began to gain some traction and was given the original title and name of *Pakkuman*. The name derived from the Japanese phrase 'paku-paku taberu', an onomatopoeic slang term for the sound made when the mouth is opened wide and quickly closed, like when someone quickly gobbles down food.

Previous arcade games back then really tried to attract a more of a teenage male-only demographic, but Toru Iwatani wanted to change all of that. He wanted to create a game that could appeal to anyone of any age, especially women. The original *Pakkuman* game was designed with bright pastel colours, cute characters and a simple, no-nonsense, pick up and play, almost non-violent gameplay mechanic (no blasting invading aliens here), so it would appeal to a much broader audience. Toru Iwatani explained his influence and ideas for the game with Time Magazine:

66 OF THE MOST IMPORTANT VIDEO GAMES EVER! (ACCORDING TO ME)

"While thinking about the word 'eat' when taking a piece of pizza, I saw that the rest of [the] pizza looked like a character, and that's how *Pac-Man's* iconic shape was created. I realized that although keywords such as 'fashion' and 'love' would appeal more to women, my opinion is that the word 'eat' is universally appealing and would attract their attention as well. That's why I went with this idea.

In the late 1970s, there were a lot of games in arcades which featured killing aliens or other enemies that mostly appealed to boys to play. The image of arcades was that they were darkly lit and their restrooms were dirty. This perception was similar in Japan. I wanted to change that by introducing game machines in which cute characters appeared with simpler controls that would not be intimidating to female customers and couples to try out, and couples visiting arcades would increase."

The maze-like/chasing gameplay had never really been seen before and it was certainly a far cry from the more shooty-shooty, pew-pew games that were taking arcades by storm back then. So much so, that when Toru Iwatani's *Pakkuman* game was finally released in Japan in 1980 (and given a name change to *Puck Man*), that it alienated gamers, the game just wasn't that big of a success when compared to other arcade machines at the time. Don't get me wrong, *Puck Man* wasn't a flop or anything, it just underperformed when compared to other games that were in the arcade back then. But then, it was released in America.

For its international release, *Puck Man* had a few changes. The game was sped up and the difficulty was increased too. The ghosts were given a name change. Then, of course, was the game's more (in)famous change, the title. Midway, who published the game for its western release, worried that unsavoury youths and vandals could very easily scratch away or partly cover the P in *Puck Man* on the cabinets to create a rather obscene name (fuck knows what though?). So, the game's title was changed to *Pac-Man*. See, while the game did just okay in Japan, it was an absolute monster hit in America, to the point where it made over one billion dollars in its first year alone. The popularity of the game in the US suddenly translated over to Japan and finally, it began to be a lot more successful there. They even officially re-titled the game and character to *Pac-Man* over in Japan too. In fact, *Pac-Man* became so popular worldwide that it's actually the highest-grossing arcade game of all time. Yes, it even sold more units and made more money than the mighty *Space Invaders*. And as far as I've managed to find out, *Pac-Man* still holds that distinction today too, forty-one years and hundreds of arcade games later. Given the state of the arcade business today, I'm pretty sure *Pac-Man* will always hold the record too.

Much like the previously mentioned *Space Invaders*, *Pac-Man* is also responsible for a lot of gaming firsts. The first-ever gaming mascot and a mascot that's still widely popular today. The first game to be designed and targeted (mainly) toward women and to have mass universal appeal. The first to feature cut-scenes (though it can be debated that *Space Invaders Part II* was the first). The first to feature differing AI, as each of the ghosts had their own personalities and traits. The first successful licensing in gaming, as *Pac-Man's* face was plastered on everything from pillowcases to bubblegum. It was also the first game to feature power-ups... Which reminds me, *Pac-Man's* famed eating of power-pellets to eat the ghosts was inspired by the famous cartoon *Popeye* and his spinach-eating.

Pac-Man has gone on to become a massive success, the original game has had numerous ports, sequels and spin-offs... One of which will pop up later in this very book. That little yellow dot is still a widely popular character today too. The original game's importance to the industry can not be overstated. It was truly ground-breaking, it opened up the world of gaming to a whole new audience and made games overall feel much more accessible to everyone. Iwatani himself even dared to liken his creation to The Beatles:

"It might be a bit of a stretch to use a Beatles comparison, but if the song *Yesterday* is looked at as **THE** standard musical number for music, then I think *Pac-Man* is **THE** standard for games. Thus, *Pac-Man* will be loved forever, and I'm proud of that."

That statement is almost as bold as John Lennon saying that The Beatles were more popular than Jeebus. Whether I agree or disagree with that statement, I just wonder what would've happened if Toru Iwatani had gone out for a burger instead of a pizza that night?

66 OF THE MOST IMPORTANT VIDEO GAMES EVER!
(ACCORDING TO ME)

ZORK I
DEVELOPER: INFOCOM
PUBLISHER(S): INFOCOM & PERSONAL SOFTWARE
PLATFORM: APPLE II
RELEASED: DECEMBER, 1980

```
WEST OF HOUSE
YOU ARE STANDING IN AN OPEN FIELD WEST OF A WHITE
HOUSE, WITH A BOARDED FRONT DOOR.
THERE IS A SMALL MAILBOX HERE.
>_
```

And thus begins one of the most iconic and important video games ever to be made. To give the game its full and proper title, *Zork: The Great Underground Empire - Part I*. It is often shortened to *Zork I*... Which I am very grateful for, as that made formatting the title for this chapter a lot easier. Anyway, *Zork I* was a text-adventure game, kind of like an interactive book of sorts. There were no bright pastel, *Pac-Man*-like cute graphics here. What you got was a black screen with white writing on it (or green, depending on your platform of choice). You would read the descriptions on the screen, then use the keyboard to type in commands to guide your character through the world.

Back in the early eighties, in terms of power, home computers were 'lacking', for want of a better word. The graphical capabilities of the machines were pretty much non-existent because the computers back then were not seen as things to play games on, they were used for work. So, programmers got around the no graphics issue by creating the text-adventure genre. Games that you had to read and seriously take in, rather than just look at. *Zork I* was created by Tim Anderson, Marc Blank, Bruce Daniels, and Dave Lebling, who bonded over their love for computers. MIT graduates who had all met at MIT's Laboratory for Computer Science, the quartet started work on the game in 1977. Originally for use on a DEC PDP-10 computer (Google Image search that bad-boy, it's huge and looks like something a James Bond villain would use circa 1964). Limited to basic commands, like 'open mailbox' (that's the first part of the game's walkthrough covered for you, you're welcome). You the player/reader must navigate the world by typing directions and instructions for your character to follow.

Now, *Zork I* wasn't the first game of its genre. Just for reference, *Colossal Cave Adventure* from 1976 is cited as the first text-adventure game. But, it was *Zork I* that catapulted the genre into the limelight. It was the game's word parser that set it apart from other titles of the same ilk. In other titles, the words used by the player were really very basic, often just simple verbs and two-word sentences. However, *Zork's* word parser was far more complex, adding adjectives, conjunctions, prepositions and more to the basic use of verbs. You could also create shortcuts to speed things up a tad. As an example, you could type something like: 'take all but rug'. This would allow you to pick up every collectable item in a location (except the rug), instead of repeatedly having to type: 'pick up [item]' and each individual collectable. It was simple, but it was *Zork's* clever word parser that led to far more intricate puzzles for you to solve and in turn, that offered a deeper level of gameplay overall.

Then there was the general writing of the game. *Zork* felt less stiff and contrived than other games in the genre, it had a real sense of humour and one that made the title a lot more fun to read/play. When you cross paths with characters like 'Lord Dimwit Flathead the Excessive', you get the idea of the level of silliness. The world created was rich, textured and vibrant, full of zany characters and witty writing. The lack of graphics really wasn't missed when you had such a brilliantly realised text-based world to lose yourself in.

It was in 1979 when the game was almost done. Up until then, the title was actually playable, even when unfinished. *Zork I* was playable via ARPANET (The Advanced Research Projects Agency Network), think of it as a really, really, really early progenitor to the internet. The game's creators, Tim Anderson, Marc Blank, Bruce Daniels, and Dave Lebling could actually see how people were playing *Zork*, where they were getting stuck, where it looked too easy, and then they could tweak and change the game, adding much-needed polish. Removing or adding words to the game's word parser to make it easier to use, but without

66 OF THE MOST IMPORTANT VIDEO GAMES EVER! (ACCORDING TO ME)

losing any of the game's challenge. When finished, *Zork* was a huge game for the time. In fact, it was so big that it had to be split into three parts. Then, when it was released proper at the end of 1980, it was ported to pretty much every computer ever. Well, perhaps 'port' isn't quite the right word to use. When a game is ported to other machines, it is often built from the ground up to accommodate each computer's individual architecture, and that's a lot of expensive and time-consuming work. So to cut costs and time, a virtual platform was created instead. This platform was called 'Z-Machine' and this platform allowed for Infocom's text games to be played on anything, as long as it could run the Z-Machine platform… And pretty much all of them could. A very clever little bit of programming that really helped to get *Zork* onto other machines with little to zero fuss.

Outside of its original release, *Zork I* has had a very impressive life. Sequels, prequels and spin-offs aplenty over the years. There have been around fifteen *Zork* games released between 1980 and 2009, with the last (so far) being *Legends of Zork*. The original game still has a life today, featuring as an Easter egg in *Call of Duty: Black Ops.* You can even play *Zork* on your Amazon Alexa speaker if you want. It's quite amazing how such a simple game with no graphics still has a life today in the modern gaming world. *Zork* was also one of the first, if not the first, to offer real-world help. After receiving so many letters from *Zork* players requesting assistance with certain puzzles, Infocom launched something called the *New Zork Times*. This was a monthly newsletter that gave out hints for the game. They even sold specially created hint books that were printed with invisible ink that could be revealed with a special marker. This way, the reader could get specific hints or solutions for a puzzle without having the rest of the game ruined for them. *Zork* pretty much created game guides, hints & tips.

Zork I, as a game, may not have created the narrative/story led text-based game, but it vastly improved and popularised it quite early on. It built on what already existed and pushed the technology as far as it could go at the time. The fact *Zork I* is still referenced and continues to influence today is why it's so damn important.

S. L. PERRIN

ROGUE
DEVELOPER: A.I. DESIGN
PUBLISHER: EPYX
PLATFORM: ???
RELEASED: ???, 1980

I've really been getting into roguelike/lite games recently. I just love the whole 'hard as nails' approach and getting sent back to the start for you to try again after hopefully, learning something from your previous attempt. These roguelike/lite games are fast becoming my go-to sub-genre right now. And this right here is where it all began.

I tried to find the original platform and release month for the game, but concrete details are almost non-existent, I found several contradictory claims of the first machine *Rogue* was released on, but nothing that I could 100% confirm. This is mainly because *Rogue* was very much overlooked when originally released. But, before I get into any of that, I guess I should quickly cover what *Rogue* is about. It's basically a dungeon-crawler type game with you playing as an adventurer, who has to find the Amulet of Yendor, found in the lowest level of the dungeon. Unlike the previous *Zork I*, *Rogue* is pretty much all-out action. But very much like *Zork I*, it also doesn't feature any 'graphics' so to speak. Well, let me rephrase that, the original release of *Rogue* didn't feature graphics, at least not in the sense you'd think of today. *Rogue's* action was displayed using basic ASCII characters. So basic they were that I could actually recreate a typical *Rogue* screen in this book… In fact, I will…

```
-----------                    ---------------------------
|         |                    |          M         |###
|  @      |########            ---------------------  #
|         |         ---------------    #                #
-----------    |            |          #                #
      #        |            |          #         ----------------
    ######     |            |########          |      E        |
               --------------                  |      ?        |
                                               ----------------
```

66 OF THE MOST IMPORTANT VIDEO GAMES EVER!
(ACCORDING TO ME)

Yup, that's how basic the graphics were for the game. With you playing as the '@' character and the enemies being displayed by simple letters, Z for zombie, S for spider and so on. While the rooms, paths and items of the dungeon were created with a mix of various ASCII characters. Certainly a far cry from the HD graphics we are used to today.

Anyway, *Rogue* was created by Michael Toy, Glenn Wichman and Ken Arnold. Originally, they wanted to make a graphic adventure-type game, but the limitations of the hardware in 1980 meant that was pretty much impossible. It was Michael Toy who came up with the idea of using a top-down, map-like view. One of the major influences for *Rogue* was the table-top game, *Dungeons & Dragons*, in fact, a lot of early adventure games exist because of *D&D*. Glenn Wichman recalls in an article from Edge:

> "In the very first version, the monsters and their strengths and abilities were very closely modelled on *Dungeons & Dragons*, but we quickly changed this to avoid getting in trouble with Gygax and Arneson (the creators of *D&D*)."

As mentioned, the game has you exploring a multi-level dungeon, killing monsters and trying to obtain the Amulet of Yendor, which is stored on the very lowest level of the dungeon. Yendor being Rodney spelt backwards... And who was this Rodney fella? As far as I can tell, he was no one. It was just a name the game designers thought sounded funny at the time.

So, this is how *Rogue*, as a game, works. It's kind of turn-based I guess, in that, whenever you move, so do the monsters on the level. You're mostly blinded by a 'fog of war' and have to explore each level to find the various rooms. Kill the monsters on the level, find weapons and items, earn XP and improve your stats (hit points, strength, etc). Find the exit to the next level where you'll face higher levelled monsters, rinse and repeat until you reach the bottom and find the Amulet of Yendor. After which, you then have to return to the surface as a hero, fighting your way back to the start. It was very basic stuff, but also quite revolutionary at the time too. As Michael Toy recalls, *Rogue* really pushed what could be done back then:

S. L. PERRIN

"Glenn and I were pounding away at keyboards on the UNIX time-sharing system at UC Santa Cruz. This was around 1980, and *Rogue* ran in something like 128K of memory, which was an order of magnitude more than any personal computer had. We were theoretically supposed to be attending classes and earning a degree, but instead, we spent most of our programming for fun."

I did say earlier that I couldn't find which platform the original *Rouge* ran on, and that is probably because it wasn't actually originally released on any platform really. It was just programmed into BSD (Berkeley Software Distribution) UNIX, a now long discontinued operating system. So it wasn't really released on a computer per se, it just kind of existed as a program in an operating system. Full disclosure, I never played the original *Rogue* back in 1980. The first version I played was on the Amiga in the mid-eighties. The thing about the Amiga version is that it actually had graphics, basic ones yes, but graphics nonetheless. Your character looked like a warrior/adventurer, the monsters looked like monsters instead of just being letters and so on. Yet even with the graphical upgrade, the gameplay itself was identical.

Anyway, I digress, what made *Rogue* stand out was the fact that it was procedurally generated. Every time you started a new game, everything was randomised. Each level of the dungeon, the monsters, items, everything was randomly placed in every new game. So you couldn't really make maps of the area as it would change next time you played anyway. This randomness of the game made *Rogue* pretty damn difficult, and it is the game's difficulty that most people remember about it. Everyone raving (or raging) on about the difficultly of the *Dark Souls* games today... Well, this is where it all started.

But, it wasn't just the procedurally generated aspect of the game that made it difficult, it was the fact that *Rogue* featured a permadeath game mechanic. There were no checkpoints, so saves, no continues. One life, and when that life was over... So was the game. Which all meant you had to start from the very beginning no matter how close you were to finishing the game. And as covered, every time you restarted, everything was randomised. The game created the now very popular roguelike and roguelite sub-genre, hence the name.

66 OF THE MOST IMPORTANT VIDEO GAMES EVER!
(ACCORDING TO ME)

Okay, so before I continue, I just want to differentiate between the two sub-genres of roguelike and roguelite. So, a roguelike game is exactly that, a game like *Rogue*. A title where when you die, you go back to the start with nothing. A roguelite is a lite version of the above. When you die and restart, you carry over something that helps with further playthroughs. Be it an upgrade, a character, a weapon, whatever. If the game lets you restart with something from a previous play attempt, then it's roguelite and not a roguelike.

In a strange way, the confinements of *Zork I* are what led to *Rogue's* more open and random nature. See, Michael Toy, Glenn Wichman and Ken Arnold, the trio behind *Rogue*, were big fans of text adventures like *Zork*, but they realised that once you knew how to solve the puzzles in those type of games, then there was very little to drag you back into them. So Toy, Wichman and Arnold wanted to create a game that made people want to come back to it again and again. This is why the whole permadeath and procedurally generated game mechanics existed, to make the player want to return. Really piss us off plenty first, yes but, return we certainly did.

That early version of *Rogue* had its fans for sure, but due to it not having a proper release and it being stuck on BSD UNIX, it didn't 'sell'. It was in 1983 when the idea to convert, update and actually give *Rogue* a proper and physical release came about. Pretty much every major computer had some version of *Rogue* released for it at some point in the early to mid-eighties. The Atari ST version from 1986 being one of the better graphically and user-friendly efforts. However, those physical releases didn't exactly rocket up the sales charts, this was mostly blamed on the rampant piracy of the day. Another downside was the graphics, even in the later updated versions, the graphics were lacking (the Amiga version was a visual joke for what the computer could do), this also led to poor sales. Then there was the fact that by 1983 when those updated versions of the game began to emerge, the whole roguelike gameplay was being done better in other titles, *Hack* and *The Dungeons of Moria* were two such titles. Overall, *Rogue* was a commercial flop.

It's really kind of strange to think of this game as being a flop when it is also so damn important. It's probably the most important game in this book that ended up being such a sales disappointment. *Rogue* created its own sub-genre, two if you want to get picky. A gameplay style and mechanic that is still used today. In fact, the whole roguelike/roguelite sub-genre is becoming increasingly more popular now. The indie game scene of today is really getting behind what *Rogue* began forty-one years ago, with titles such as the cave exploring *Spelunky* from Mossmouth. The platforming action-packed, Metroidvania-like *Dead Cells* from Motion Twin. Or even the very eighties themed, very awesome and my game of 2020, *HyperParasite*, from Troglobytes Games. So many (mainly indie devs) all owe a great debt to *Rogue*, its tough as old boots gameplay and back to the beginning style gameplay that is becoming so damn popular right now.

66 OF THE MOST IMPORTANT VIDEO GAMES EVER! (ACCORDING TO ME)

DONKEY KONG
DEVELOPER: NINTENDO
PUBLISHER: NINTENDO
PLATFORM: ARCADE
RELEASED: JULY, 1981

Pre-warning, this is not the only Mario-based game in this book, not by a long shot…

When a song from the awesome DJ Jazzy Jeff & the Fresh Prince exists, which is directly inspired by this very game, you know it's got to be important. But of course, that's not the reason *Donkey Kong* is in here, there's so much more to cover as to what makes this game so damn important. Before I get to that though, let's get all the obvious stuff out of the way first…

Yes, *Donkey Kong* was the first appearance of Mario and yes, he was called Jumpman then… And yes, he was a carpenter and not a plumber. But, I think that what is perhaps slightly more interesting is that Mario is actually the bad guy in the game. See, the plot for *Donkey Kong* has the titular giant ape kidnap Mario's lovely lady friend and our plucky carpenter has to save her in a *King Kong* kind of scenario. However, few people seem to question just why *Donkey Kong* kidnapped the fair lady to begin with. Well, according to the game's manual, it turns out that the titular Kong was Mario's pet, and Mario continually abused him. That's why the big gorilla kidnapped his lass, to teach Mario a lesson for all the previous abuse. Plus, think about it, why would the villain be the title character? Then, if you still need proof, go and play the sequel *Donkey Kong Jr.,* where you play as the younger Kong and have to rescue your father from Mario who's apprehended and imprisoned the elder Kong. See, these games existed before Mario became Nintendo's mascot and hero of so many titles, he actually began as a bad guy and an animal abuser. What a dick!

Anyway, *Donkey Kong* was the brainchild of the then-unknown, but now Nintendo legend that is Shigeru Miyamoto. Back then in the early eighties, Nintendo as a company were struggling, they had some moderate success in the gaming world, but nothing major. They did okay in their home country of Japan, but just couldn't get any of their games to make it big in the US. Nintendo tried to sell their latest game, *Radar Scope* to the Yanks and it failed. So the Nintendo warehouse held thousands of unsold *Radar Scope* cabinets, doing very little more than just gathering dust and costing Nintendo a fortune in unsold hardware. It was very early 1981 when Nintendo company president, Hiroshi Yamauchi, suggested that they re-purpose all of the unsold *Radar Scope* machines. That's when the young Shigeru Miyamoto stepped forward and said he could probably do something with all of the unsold units.

Back then, Nintendo tried to secure the license to make a game based on the *Popeye* comic strip characters, a game that Nintendo had already begun early pre-production on. That deal fell through, but not wanting to waste the work they had started, they thought they could perhaps tinker with the main *Popeye* characters and create something of their own. At the same time, Miyamoto had begun work on the plot for his new game. He settled on a love triangle kind of thing story inspired by *King Kong*. Miyamoto came up with the idea of having a human, fighting to save his girlfriend from a giant ape. After a few meetings, *Popeye* became the then-unnamed playable character (later labelled Jumpman, before becoming Mario), Olive Oyl became the unnamed girlfriend (later to be called Pauline) and the bad guy Bluto became the giant gorilla.

Shigeru Miyamoto worked feverishly on the game and even had to move into Nintendo-owned dwellings, which were opposite the Nintendo HQ at the time. Miyamoto recalls those early days in an article from Wired:

> "At the time, I was living in company-owned housing, just across the river from the office. So every day, I was just going back and forth between the office and the company housing. Thank goodness we had a company bathtub! It was really effective at letting me put my ideas in order."

Miyamoto has actually said that he came up with a lot of the ideas for *Donkey Kong* while in that bath. The character that would eventually become Mario was born from one of those bath sessions. So there you go, Nintendo's future and most famous mascot was created while Shigeru Miyamoto was naked and washing his balls.

66 OF THE MOST IMPORTANT VIDEO GAMES EVER!
(ACCORDING TO ME)

Now, it's the name of that giant gorilla and the title of the game where things get a bit cloudy. The original story goes that he (Kong) and the game was originally supposed to be called *Monkey Kong*, but it got 'lost in translation' from Japanese to English somewhere along the line, or that a fax was misread/smudged and Monkey became Donkey by accident. It's one of those long-standing gaming stories. But I couldn't find any concrete evidence of that being true at all. However, what I did find was that when naming the character, Shigeru Miyamoto wanted a name that that translated to silly, stubborn or goofy, he settled on the name Donkey after looking through a Japanese to English dictionary. An interview on the fan-site Miyamotoshrine.com (now defunct, I had to use an archive site to find it) that Miyamoto took part in about his career backs up the latter story:

> "For *Donkey Kong* I wanted something to do with Kong which kind of gives the idea of apes in Japanese and I came up with *Donkey Kong* because I heard that 'donkey' meant 'stupid' so I went with *Donkey Kong*. Unfortunately when I said that name to Nintendo of America nobody liked it and said that it didn't mean 'Stupid Ape' and they all laughed at me! But we went ahead with that name anyway."

So yeah, the long-standing *Monkey Kong* title rumour seems to be false as far as I can tell. Anyway, with the characters and plot of the game all worked out, Shigeru Miyamoto began developing *Donkey Kong* proper, only there was a bit of a tiny little problem... Miyamoto wasn't a game developer/programmer (still isn't). Back then, he was an industrial designer, he knew very little about the technical skills to program and develop a video game. Needing help, he just stuck with creating the concepts of the game and then consulted with Nintendo's more knowledgeable and experienced minds to actually make it all come together as a game, and come together it did.

One of Miyamoto's ideas for the title that didn't make it, was for it to feature digitised speech. Yes, if things had been different, then *Donkey Kong* would have had Mario (and others) speak, but there were hardware limitations that meant the sound didn't quite come out right. Shigeru Miyamoto talks about the abandoned speech elements of *Donkey Kong* with Wired:

"The lady stolen away by *Donkey Kong* was supposed to yell out, 'Help, Help!' And when Mario jumped over a barrel, she was supposed to yell, 'Nice!,' complimenting him. But some people within the company said, 'Doesn't the pronunciation sound a little weird?' So we tested it on a native English speaker, a professor. They said it sounded like she was talking about seaweed: 'Kelp, Kelp!' At that point in development, we couldn't fix it, so we took out all of the voices. 'Help!' was replaced with *Donkey Kong's* growl, and 'Nice!' was replaced with the pi-ro-po-pon-pon! sound. It's really good that we went with pi-ro-po-pon-pon. When you walk past an arcade and hear that sound, it's really catchy. So even though we took out the voices, it still had great results. From this experience, I learned the importance of having good sound effects."

And yes, 'pi-ro-po-pon-pon' is officially how it sounds when Mario jumps, according to Miyamoto-san himself. *Donkey Kong* was finished, but it needed a bit of market testing before Nintendo spent what little money they had on converting all those unused *Radar Scope* machines back in their warehouse. The aim was for Nintendo to break America, as they had been struggling with that market at that point. There was a reluctance from arcade owners to be put this new game into their arcades in the US, the Yanks just didn't see much potential in it, and it looked like Nintendo had failed. In fact, only two bars in Seattle agreed to take a *Donkey Kong* cabinet each on a trial period. After the first week, word began to spread of just how popular the game had become and more units were eventually ordered from eager punters. So, Nintendo set about re-purposing around two-thousand of those unused *Radar Scope* cabinets into *Donkey Kong* games and it officially went on sale in July 1981, when it became a huge success.

Everyone loved *Donkey Kong*, it offered a unique style of gameplay and started a new game genre, the platform game. Well, everyone loved it except for Universal Studios. I don't know if I really want to get into all of this as it's a very famous story within the gaming world. But, long story short and Universal tried to sue Nintendo in 1982, claiming trademark infringement because the game was too similar to their movie *King Kong*. It really kind of was to be fair, as previously mentioned, Shigeru Miyamoto has said that *King Kong* was a major influence. Anyway, Universal's main claim was that *King Kong* and *Donkey Kong*

66 OF THE MOST IMPORTANT VIDEO GAMES EVER!
(ACCORDING TO ME)

could be easily confused due to the name (but the fact they were two very different mediums wasn't mentioned). Universal also argued that the plot of the game involving a giant gorilla kidnapping a female, who had to be saved, was an infringement on their famous film. Enter Nintendo's counsel, John Kirby who argued that Universal themselves once had to prove that *King Kong* was actually in the public domain when they made their film, it was and still is. The novel the film was based on, written by Delos W. Lovelace, fell into the public domain when its copyright was never renewed. After which, the whole case fell apart and the judge ruled in Nintendo's favour.

Nintendo made a lot of money from that case, money that allowed the then struggling games company to grow. It also taught Nintendo a very valuable lesson, that IPs need to be protected at all costs. Ever wonder why Nintendo are so protective and litigious these days? It's because they learned the hard way that companies need to protect their own work when they went up against Universal. As a thank you, Nintendo bought John Kirby a luxury sailboat named Donkey Kong as well as universal (no pun) rights to use that name on all boats. Oh, and one of Nintendo's other famed mascots is named after Mr Kirby too. *Donkey Kong* is important for so many reasons, not just for introducing the world to the platform game and Mario, but also for that court case that helped Nintendo grow into the worldwide brand they are today. And for making court cases involving game companies a very serious business.

Just a quick aside to finish though. This claim that *Donkey Kong* was the first-ever platform game... Just how true is it? I mean, what about *Space Panic* from 1980? It didn't feature jumping, but it did feature platform-like gameplay with a character climbing ladders to different platforms. Then there's *Crazy Climber* also from 1980, a game that people like to say was a precursor to the platforming genre. Oh, and of course, there was *Jump Bug*, a title that I can't find an accurate release date for. December 1981 in the US, but the Japanese version was earlier... Quite possibly before *Donkey Kong* in fact. Plus, *Jump Bug* didn't just include platforming and jumping, but screen-scrolling too. Still, I'll leave that one open for debate as to whether *Donkey Kong* was the first platform game. For me, that claim certainly requires a big old question mark.

S. L. PERRIN

PITFALL!
DEVELOPER: ACTIVISION
PUBLISHER: ACTIVISION
PLATFORM: ATARI 2600
RELEASED: APRIL, 1982

Between you and me, I actually prefer the sequel, *Pitfall II: Lost Caverns*. But, I don't feel the sequel (as great as it is) is as important as a game, to be honest. Anyway, the home gaming market was really growing by the early eighties as more home machines became available and allowed us young gamers to play action-packed software at home. Developers really began to experiment with new ideas, taking what was making arcades so popular, but adding their own unique flair and pushing the boundaries of gaming. Those single-screen games, *Space Invaders*, *Pac-Man*, *Donkey Kong*, etc, they were certainly great and ground-breaking... But what if you could go beyond a single, static screen, what if screens could be connected, making an overall much bigger game?

Okay, so *Pitfall!* wasn't the first multi-screen platform game, that accolade goes to (the previously mentioned) *Jump Bug* from 1981, that one scrolled too. But, it was also on more advanced arcade hardware. However, it's *Pitfall!'s* impact that makes it so damn important. Created by programmer and co-founder of Activision (the first third-party game publisher), David Crane, who already had a few Atari games under his belt by the time 1982 rolled around. You played as Pitfall Harry and had to explore a jungle in search of numerous treasures. Jump, swing and climb your way to victory while avoiding rolling logs, campfires, snakes, bats, crocodiles, that really fucking annoying scorpion at the bottom of the screen... Oh and try not to fall into any pits. *Pitfall!* was the closest thing you could get to playing as Indiana Jones until... Well, a couple more chapters.

While working on the game, Crane really struggled with the title. Names like *Jungle Runner*, *Zulu Gold* and several others were considered for a while before being dismissed. Then, given the fact you (quite often) fall into pits in the game, began to resonate with him and a title suddenly stuck. Crane added the exclamation mark at the end of *Pitfall!* because he wanted it to stand out and seem more dynamic compared to other game titles that were on the shelves at the time, It really worked too. I wonder why I included an exclamation mark in the title of this book...

Pitfall! really was a technical marvel at the time. The Atari 2600 was cutting edge home entertainment back then, but it was still limited to what it could do compared to arcade hardware. Yet, David Crane managed to squeeze every inch he could out of its 160 x 192 maximum pixel resolution and the 128 bytes of RAM, while using the 4 kB ROM game cartridge to its fullest. What followed was a bright and vibrant, multi-screen game that was unlike anything else on the home market.

Just looking at the animation of Pitfall Harry running was truly stunning then, we had never seen a human being depicted so realistically and detailed in a video game before, maybe in the arcade yes, but certainly not in the home market. We normally had basic geometric shapes that we had to imagine were characters, but Pitfall Harry, he had arms, legs, a head and he was fully animated too. David Crane actually developed the tech to animate a human back in 1979, but he couldn't find a game to use his new animation. Then, four years later and he sat down with a pen and a piece of paper, as Crane himself explains in this excerpt from an interview with Edge:

> "I sat down with a blank sheet of paper and drew a stick figure in the center. I said, 'Okay, I have a little running man and let's put him on a path [two more lines drawn on the paper]. Where is the path? Let's put it in a jungle [draw some trees]. Why is he running [draw treasures to collect, enemies to avoid, etc.]?' And *Pitfall!* was born. This entire process took about ten minutes. About a thousand hours of programming later, the game was complete."

Look, I really don't want to bore you with all the amazing technical details of *Pitfall!* and just how David Crane managed to create a masterpiece of gaming through some very clever design and programming, all while struggling with the strict limitations of the Atari 2600. Mainly because Crane himself already did an amazing job of just that during a very lengthy, detailed but thoroughly interesting talk. Just go on YouTube and search for 'making *Pitfall!* 2600' for a fascinating look at just how *Pitfall!* was made. Seriously worth watching if you're into your classic gaming history. Anyway, *Pitfall!* was the best-selling game of 1982, spending a total of sixty-four weeks at number one on the best-sellers list and shifting over four million units in total. Oh, and the original advert for the game featured a young Jack Black in his first-ever acting role.

It wasn't the first platform game, no. It wasn't the first multi-screen game either. But, for the home market, for the Atari 2600 specifically, it was truly revolutionary and showed that games didn't have to be single-screen, that grander adventures could be made. *Pitfall!* went on to spawn a pretty successful franchise too. There were sequels such as the previously mentioned (and better) *Pitfall II: Lost Caverns*, *Pitfall: The Mayan Adventure*, *Pitfall 3D: Beyond the Jungle* and *Pitfall: The Lost Expedition* over the years, with some of those titles even hiding the original games in them as Easter eggs. Most recently, in 2012, *Pitfall!* made a come back as an endless runner type game for mobile devices, but since then, it's been quiet. There was even an animated *Pitfall!* TV show in 1984, as well as all sorts of licensed merchandise like board games, action figures, etc. *Pitfall!* was huge back then.

Pitfall! was also one of the first games to actually give the programmer(s) credit for their work, an idea Activision pushed to do and something that is now commonplace in today's gaming industry. It also pretty much began the whole achievement/trophy thing we have today. See, if you got a high-score in *Pitfall!*, took a photo for proof, and then send it to Activision, they would reward you with a stylish sew-on patch. A few of those early Activision games had this little feature.

Pitfall! really is amazing, even today I still find it playable and that Atari 2600 original version has a very special place in my heart. I don't think *Pitfall!* was the first game I ever played (1982 seems a tad late for when I first started playing games). My middle-aged and slightly jaded memory thinks it was *Combat* on the 2600. But *Pitfall!* definitely was the game that captured my imagination like no other back then and got me hooked on gaming at a young age. In fact, I'm gonna go play some right now.

**66 OF THE MOST IMPORTANT VIDEO GAMES EVER!
(ACCORDING TO ME)**

POLE POSITION
DEVELOPER: NAMCO
PUBLISHER(S): NAMCO, ATARI
PLATFORM: ARCADE
RELEASED: SEPTEMBER, 1982

Racing games were all the rage in the early to mid-eighties. There was this influx of high-speed thrills hitting the arcades as the racing genre grabbed the attention of gamers around the world. I used to love walking around arcades back then, they had a certain feel from the moment you stepped through the doors. Those flashing lights and the many, many sounds of the arcade were an adrenaline shot to the synapses. Quite often, you'd hear a game before you even saw it, and when you heard the immortal line, 'Prepare to qualify!', you just knew that *Pole Position* was nearby. It was never a clear voice sample, in fact listening to it now, it's really very distorted... But back then? That was amazing, very few arcade games featured speech sampled back then, I can only think of *Wizard of Wor*, *Gorf!* and *Karate Champ* right now. So when a game spoke, it caught your attention instantly.

But of course, it wasn't just the speech that made *Pole Position* stand out. The bright graphics, the engine noises and the sound of the start lights. Then there was the sense of speed. Man, this game was buttery smooth and just watching the attract screen got the heart racing. Then, if you could find one of the rarer sit-down cabinets... That was pure heaven.

Everything about the game felt 'real' then. It even featured an early example of real-world advertising in a game (the first?). The side of the track was peppered with billboards for various real-world products such as Pepsi, Canon, Martini and others. Some versions of the game even advertised other games, the American *Pole Position* (published by Atari) had billboards for other Atari games like *Centipede*, and *Dig Dug*. Adding to the authenticity was the fact that this title was also the first racing game to feature a representation of a real racetrack, as the game took place on the famed Fuji Speedway circuit. It has been said that the game felt so real that when Namco showed the game to the head of Atari for the first time, that he fell out of the arcade sit-down cabinet due to the speedy 3D graphics. No idea whether that is true or not, but it's funny if it is true. It kind of reminds me of the stories when people saw a train coming toward the screen in a cinema for the first time and panicked, worried the train would hit them.

Namco had previous experience with arcade racers in the past, their mechanical and impressive *F-1* from 1976 (as featured in the movie, *Dawn of the Dead*) is always worth mentioning. But, it was with *Pole Position* where Namco's sheer brilliance with driving games really came to light, a genre they really excelled at for decades. The creators of the game, Shinichiro Okamoto and Kazunori Sawano had to use two 16-bit processors to get the game running as fast it did. As for the title of the game? That actually came from *Pac-Man* creator, Toru Iwatani, he chose it purely based on nothing other than he thought it sounded cool.

Pole Position could be seen as the first proper racing simulation. By today's standards, it's about as far away as you can get from a true racing sim, but in 1982, we felt that 'realism'. In fact, Okamoto and Sawano, the two visionaries behind the development of the game, strived for authenticity from the start. They wanted the game to be as real to actual racing as it could, that's why a real racetrack was used, that's why the concept of having to qualify before racing was included. If you ever played this game in the arcade, then you'll also know it's not the easiest game to play, handling wise. It really does take a lot of skill to learn how to steer effectively… Yup, that came from the desire to make the game as simulation-like as possible too.

The viewpoint of the game was also meant to give the player a real sense of racing. Pretty much all racing games before *Pole Position* offered an overhead view. But shifting the view to behind the car got you closer to the action, close to the track and closer to the car. Originally, the intention was to have the view be first-person, viewed from the driver's eyes, but technical limitations proved to be troublesome and slowed down the pace of the game. Shinichiro Okamoto talked about his vision for the game with BEEP! Magazine:

> "There were three things I wanted to realize with *Pole Position*: first, I wanted a complete simulation that would allow a player to execute real driving techniques; second, I wanted the screen to be a 3D type view;

66 OF THE MOST IMPORTANT VIDEO GAMES EVER! (ACCORDING TO ME)

and third, I wanted the track to be based on the actual Fuji Speedway, and for that to be recognisable to players when they played. The difficult part was configuring and engineering the hardware necessary to realize such an ambitious concept. We used dual 16-bit processors, something unheard of for video games at the time. Getting the controls to feel realistic, and at the same time, match up with the gameplay, was also a very difficult challenge, but I feel we worked it into something enjoyable."

Of course, *Pole Position* went on to be a huge success. There were reports of long queues forming in and outside of arcades in Japan just for this one game. Plus, as with *Pac-Man*, due to the lack of violence and killing, *Pole Position* had a wider appeal to all ages and both sexes. So popular was the game that it was one of the top-selling arcade cabinets for two years. Even after the release of the official (and arguably better) sequel, *Pole Position II* from 1983, the original was still massively popular. The games evolved into the *Final Lap* franchise, with the latest in the series, *Final Lap Special*, being released in 2001. So, it's had a pretty lengthy run for a racing game franchise.

For me, *Pole Position* is one of those 'golden age of the arcade' games, one of those classics that innovated and influenced for decades. The sense of speed, the feel of 'real' racing and the genesis of the racing simulation in gaming.

S. L. PERRIN

RAIDERS OF THE LOST ARK
DEVELOPER: ATARI
PUBLISHER: ATARI
PLATFORM: ATARI 2600
RELEASED: NOVEMBER?, 1982

You know, I've only just noticed that these last few chapters have been very Atari centric, they really were the best of the best in the early eighties. Yes, it's back to the Atari 2600 once more with the first-ever movie licensed game. Just a few months (and two chapters) earlier, the amazing *Pitfall!* was the closest we ever got to being Indiana Jones, but now... We can really be the man with the hat, a very blocky, low-resolution version, but still Indiana Jones all the same.

Designed by Howard Scott Warshaw, a name that should send shivers down the spine of any older gamer, for one very big reason I will get into in the next chapter. As mentioned, *Raiders of the Lost Ark* was the first-ever movie licensed game. That itself is pretty important, but given the percentage of games made from famous movie IPs are utter shit, perhaps it really should be damned for opening that particular door? But I have a query, was this really the first-ever movie licensed game as it's often cited to be? Let's explore.

If you Google search 'first movie licensed game', then yes, it is the Atari 2600 game, *Raiders of the Lost Ark* that pops up, which all sources and many (if not all) gaming sites state was released in November of 1982. But there was *Star Wars: The Empire Strikes Back*, also released in 1982. Or what about *Alien* (a poor *Pac-Man* clone), again from 1982? Then there was *Tron: Deadly Discs*, which was released in... Yup, 1982. If *Raiders* was released in November of 1982 as sources claim, then I find it hard to believe all those other movie licensed games came out after it, that late in the same year. I'm not saying that it is impossible, just unlikely. Now, I've checked and double-checked and I've really struggled to find a definite release month of all of those games, so I'm not really sure which one came first. I did find an interesting little titbit that claimed the *Tron* game was released on the Intellivision sometime before the release of the film, to help promote the movie. And the movie was released in July of 82. So, if true, then *Tron: Deadly Discs* was

66 OF THE MOST IMPORTANT VIDEO GAMES EVER! (ACCORDING TO ME)

released earlier in 1982, beating *Raiders of the Lost Ark* to the market by several months. So does this mean that *Raiders* actually isn't the first movie based video game then as many believe?

But it doesn't end there because sources claim that Howard Scott Warshaw began working on the *Raiders of the Lost Ark* game in late 1981 and those Atari 2600 games didn't take very long to develop, sometimes only a matter of weeks. So maybe it wasn't released in November of 1982 as claimed, but early 1982 or very even late 1981 (though I found a source that claimed *Raiders* took around nine months to make, and that's before you get into actually manufacturing the game for sale, distribution of units, etc). Is it possible that the internet is wrong? Anyway, the point is that I'm not sure what the first-ever movie licensed game is, and the claim that it was this *Raiders* game may not be 100% true. I mean, there was even the game, *Star Trek: Phaser Strike* which was reportedly based on *Star Trek: The Motion Picture* and released for the Microvision hand-held console in 1979 to help promote the movie. Definitely before either 1981 or 82 and most certainly beating the *Raiders* game to the market before it had even begun development.

Well, I went off on a bit of a tangent there eh? Back to it. So, as stated, Howard Scott Warshaw started working on this game in late 1981. To get himself in the mood, he often role-played as Indiana Jones, as Warshaw himself explains in Classic Gamer Magazine:

"I had a ten-foot bull-whip that I got while doing *Raiders of the Lost Ark*, so I could get into character. When I'd take breaks, I'd go around the hallways, sneak up behind people and crack the whip. It was really loud. Like a gunshot."

When Howard Scott Warshaw wasn't being a dick by scaring people at Atari HQ with a bull-ship, he was working on creating a very unique game for the time. Warshaw wanted to make something a tad more complex, a little adventure title that forced you to think. Not necessarily an action-packed arcade-style game like pretty much every other Atari 2600 game at the time. But something more cerebral, one that got you exploring, thinking and puzzle-solving. A bit like being a treasure hunter or an archaeology professor... Kind of like Indiana Jones really.

Raiders was a world apart from other games around at the time, even the mighty *Pitfall!*. See, as great as *Pitfall!* was, it was still just one of those 'get a high score' type of games. With *Raiders of the Lost Ark*, there was no score. The game (loosely) followed the plot of the film and instead of trying to get the best possible score, you had to solve puzzles and explore areas of the game that were inspired by the movie, to find the Ark of the Covenant, all the way to an actual ending. Yup, *Raiders* had an ending, something unheard of back then. Given the fact most games were quite 'primitive' at the time, often just simple arcade fare that required simple controls, *Raiders of the Lost Ark's* controls needed something more complex to meet its more involved gameplay and given the fact the Atari 2600 joystick was only one button, that made things pretty tricky. So, for *Raiders*, you actually had to use both joysticks at the same time. The first one worked as an item/inventory select and the second was used to control Indy himself. Even the control method was revolutionary and showed some 'out of the box' thinking, as it opened the door to more in-depth gameplay options.

To be honest, I was a little too young in 1983 to really understand this game. For the time, it was vast and too complicated, there was trading in the market, hidden areas, tricky joystick movements and so much more to learn and master if you wanted to see the ending. It all went way over my head. I was used to playing *Space Invaders*, *Pac-Man* and the like, far more simple, single-screen games with simple mechanics. *Raiders* was a very different animal and it completely confused me. However, the game is actually one of my fondest gaming memories as a child, as I always remember sitting there watching my older brother as he played. He made notes, drew a map and slowly progressed through the game until the end. I remember being blown away that games could be like this back then. As with every game in this book, I have played it since.

So, *Raiders of the Lost Ark* may not have been the first movie based video game as claimed (it is certainly debatable), but it was the beginning of the adventure/exploration game genre. For the time, it was pretty open too as you could explore anywhere and not have to follow a specific set route. There is only really one right way to actually finish the game, but you were still free to explore at will. I guess you could say this was one of the first open-world games.

66 OF THE MOST IMPORTANT VIDEO GAMES EVER!
(ACCORDING TO ME)

E.T. THE EXTRA-TERRESTRIAL
DEVELOPER: ATARI
PUBLISHER: ATARI
PLATFORM: ATARI 2600
RELEASED: DECEMBER, 1982

Oh yeah, I'm doing this, I am saying that *E.T. The Extra-Terrestrial* on the Atari 2600 is one of the most important video game ever! Now, before you decide to close this book, spit on the cover, douse it in lighter fluid, to then throw a lit match on to it, just hear me out first. Also, if you are reading this on Kindle… I strongly suggest that perhaps, it would be in your best interests to **NOT** do that.

If you know your gaming history, then you really should already know that *E.T.* on the Atari is well renowned for being the 'worst game ever' and also know how it destroyed the game industry, by causing the much talked about video game crash of 1983. Well, that's not strictly true. See, the game crash had already begun in 1982 when this game was released and the cause of the crash was no single game either. It was more a case of the various companies that had flooded the market with inferior products at a time when people were not lining up to buy. Also, *E.T.* is far from being 'the worst game ever', in fact, it was actually quite innovative for its time all things considered.

Coming off the back of the success of the previously covered *Raiders of the Lost Ark*, Howard Scott Warshaw was handpicked by Steven Spielberg himself to make this game. Spielberg was/is an avid gamer and he loved the *Raiders* game, so he wanted another one. Warshaw was flown out to California at Spielberg's personal request to discuss making the game with the legendary film-maker himself. The following quotes used here are all taken from an interview that Howard Scott Warshaw did with the BBC:

> "I got down to Spielberg and I laid out the whole design, I told him, 'I think it's really important that we do something innovative. *E.T.* is a breakthrough movie and I think we need a breakthrough game."

But, Steven Spielberg was sceptical of the idea of creating something new and unique, he wanted something simple and familiar, he even pitched the idea of just doing a *Pac-Man* clone, something which Howard Scott Warshaw eventually managed to talk the famed movie director out of. Even before the project began, Warshaw was fighting the odds. Spielberg wanted something simple, Warshaw wanted a game with more depth like his previous *Raiders of the Lost Ark* game. Then there was the biggest problem of all, Atari and Spielberg wanted the game on shop shelves by Christmas of 1982 and Atari wanted to see the final product by the start of September at the very latest, so that they could get it mass-produced and in shops by the start of December. At the time, that September deadline was only five weeks away. Yup, Howard Scott Warshaw had only five weeks to make a game, and all on his own too:

"It was the hardest I've ever worked on anything in my life. I started working at the office but after a while, I realised there was a problem, I still have to go home to sleep and eat occasionally. So we had another development system installed in my house so that I would never be more than two minutes away from working on the code, except when I was driving. There was a manager who was assigned to make sure I was eating so that I'd be able to keep going. When it came to the end of the process, my reaction was, Wow, I did it!"

Yes, he did. He made a game in just five weeks and sent it off to Atari for mass production. It has always been said that *E.T. The Extra-Terrestrial* sold poorly, that's not strictly true. The game actually sold well, shifting one and a half million units by January 1983. Bearing in mind that the game only went on sale just a few weeks before in December 82, that's impressive sales for such a short time, especially for the early eighties. I wouldn't complain if I sold 1.5 million copies of this book in a little over a month... or ever. The main issue was the fact that Atari had overproduced the title and around three million game cartridges remained unsold. In fact, it has been said that Atari produced more copies of the game than there were Atari 2600 consoles that had been sold at the time (I'm not convinced that's true, to be honest). Shops sent all of the unsold game cartridges back to Atari and coupled with the overproduction of other games and hardware by Atari and other manufactures, the games crash in 1983 really kicked in.

66 OF THE MOST IMPORTANT VIDEO GAMES EVER!
(ACCORDING TO ME)

See, part of the reason the *E.T.* game was rushed into production was due to falling sales within the industry, the game crash had begun before the game even went into development. To combat the drying up of sales, Atari and Steven Spielberg thought a game based on the movie would also be a huge seller. *E.T. the Extra-Terrestrial* (the movie), had been a gargantuan hit over the summer and it was still in cinemas too, the film actually had a cinematic run of over a year. *E.T.* was everywhere in 1982, so yeah, it made sense that a game based on the flick would sell. And as covered, it did, Atari just overproduced it. So no *E.T.* on the Atari 2600 didn't cause the game crash of 83, as it had already begun and the game was just caught up in the furore. Then the whole landfill in the Alamogordo, New Mexico desert thing happened... And thus begun a famed gaming myth that was actually later proven true:

"Things just started to unravel. It's awesome to be credited with single-handedly bringing down a billion-dollar industry with eight kilobytes of code. But the truth is a little more complex."

Anyway, the game itself is far from being 'the worst game ever' either. Its rushed five-week development cycle certainly didn't help with the game and yes, it has its issues. But 'worst game ever'? Nope, there are far worst games coming up later in this book. The thing is that, most of the people who do damn this game were not around when *E.T.* was originally released, they are just jumping on the hate-bandwagon and the infamy the game has. Like Howard Scott Warshaw's previous *Raiders of the Lost Ark* game, *E.T.* was something different. It was open, there was a specific task to complete, but you could go explore the game's many screens at will. It was flawed sure, but still quite revolutionary in 1982.

Like *Raiders* before it, I'd happily argue that *E.T. the Extra-Terrestrial* was way ahead of its time. It's nowhere near as bad as people like to make it out to be and most definitely not worthy of the whole 'worst game ever' label. As for its importance to gaming? How many other games do you know that are regularly (incorrectly) blamed for destroying an entire billion-dollar industry, being the source of one of the greatest and true gaming myths in history and would also go on to create hatred for decades? *E.T. the Extra-Terrestrial* on the Atari 2600 has more than earned its importance and place in this book.

S. L. PERRIN

DRAGON'S LAIR
DEVELOPER(S): RICK DYER & DON BLUTH
PUBLISHER: CINEMATRONICS INCORPORATED
PLATFORM: ARCADE
RELEASED: JUNE, 1983

When walking around the arcades back in 1983, you would most probably hear the familiar 'duh-duh-duh-duh' of the *Space Invaders* aliens getting increasingly closer to the bottom of the screen. Or maybe the 'waka-waka-waka' of *Pac-Man* gobbling up pellets and ghosts would grace your ears. Perhaps it would be the announcer from *Pole Position* who was telling you to 'prepare to qualify', before the engine of the car roared into action. Those numerous, very welcoming and distinctly computerised audio cues that would grab your attention via their attract modes, enticing you to slide a few coins into the cabinet and play. But there was always one specific game that was bigger and louder than any other in the entire arcade, one that would bellow several decibels higher over the usual bleeps and bloops of the games of the eighty-eighties:

"*Dragon's Lair*. The fantasy adventure where you become a valiant knight, on a quest to rescue the fair Princess from the clutches of an evil dragon. You control the actions of a daring adventurer, fighting his way through the castle of a dark wizard, who has enchanted it with treacherous monsters and obstacles. In the mysterious caverns below the castle, your odyssey continues against the awesome forces that oppose your efforts to reach the *Dragon's Lair*. Lead on adventurer, your quest awaits!"

The announcer would boom in crystal clear and wonderful stereo sound. It was certainly an attention grabber. Even before you saw the game itself, you would always hear *Dragon's Lair*. The volume was often set so loud that sometimes, you'd even hear it from outside of the arcade. Then, when you did see the game playing, your jaw slammed to the floor in awe due to its gorgeous visuals. See, *Dragon's Lair* used LaserDisc technology to deliver Saturday morning cartoon-style… Errrrr 'graphics', I guess I'll have to call them. Nestled next to the likes of *Asteroids*, *Defender* and so on, with their typical early-eighties arcade sprites and

66 OF THE MOST IMPORTANT VIDEO GAMES EVER! (ACCORDING TO ME)

pixels, *Dragon's Lair* was like looking about twenty-five years into the future. The bright and bold movie-like animation was like nothing ever seen in an arcade before.

The truth is that I never even got to play *Dragon's Lair* back in 1983 in the arcade. The cabinet would always have a queue of people forming in front of it, with their pockets full of change... And that doesn't include the gawpers who would gather around the screen just to watch. Some cabinets even had extra monitors on top just so people could see the action. 7 or 8-year-old me just couldn't be bothered to wait to play, so I'd enjoy the many other delights the arcade offered instead. But I did get to play the arcade version a few years later when the novelty died off.

Okay, so before I carry on with this article, I have a slight confession to make. I've sat here for the last couple of hours, arguing with myself over whether I should even include *Dragon's Lair* in this book or not. I really don't like the game, but that is not the reason why I've been debating its inclusion, there are a few games in here that I don't like that have made the final cut. The reason for the debate in my own head is because, I really don't consider *Dragon's Lair* a true 'video game'. However, I just can not ignore its impact and importance to the industry though.

For those not in the know, *Dragon's Lair* is less a game and more like an interactive cartoon. The gameplay here is bare minimal, you don't actually control the hero, Dirk the Daring, directly. It's more a case of you directing him on a set route. For example, a door in the castle may open and you push the joystick toward the door, then the animation does the rest. An enemy might pop up, so you press the attack button, then the animation does the rest. A sword swings at your head and you pull the joystick down to duck, then the animation does the rest. It really is nothing more than *Quick Time Event: The Game*. It's more like playing around with the menus on a DVD/Blu-ray disc. In fact, you can actually get *Dragon's Lair* as a DVD/Blu-ray and 'play' it. Or you can even just watch the cartoon on YouTube too if you want. I guess that you never truly do play *Dragon's Lair* so to speak, you just kind of experience it.

But aside from its severe lack of any actual gameplay, it is a genuinely beautiful looking game. The reason why it's so damn pretty is thanks to ex-Disney animator, Don Bluth. Bluth not only worked on Disney films and shorts, but also directed and produced his own animated flicks. I love watching *Dragon's Lair*, because of Bluth's amazing art and animation. I just really dislike 'playing' it.

The idea to create *Dragon's Lair* actually came from Rick Dyer, who went to see the animated film, *The Secret of NIMH* (directed by Don Bluth), in the cinema with his wife sometime in 1982. Dyer loved the look and animation of the film and wanted to replicate it in video game form. He contacted Bluth and asked him to provide the art and animation for his game concept. Numerous ideas were thrown around, but it soon became clear that no hardware could pull off the cinematic animation style Dyer strived for. Then he discovered LaserDisc technology and soon realised his idea could work out.

A full script for the game was written with a plot, back-story and dialogue for Dirk the Daring himself. However, Don Bluth pointed out that recording all that dialogue could prove costly, especially when you consider having to record multiple versions for different countries and languages. As the LaserDisc technology being used was already expensive enough (around $1,000 just for the player alone and that's in 1983 money), the team knew they had to keep costs down. So the script was thrown out and Dirk was just given a few grunts, groans, screams and yelps instead, voiced in-house by the editor, Dan Molina. In fact, aside from the introduction, there is no dialogue in the game at all until the final level in the titular *Dragon's Lair* when Princess Daphne (also voiced in-house by Vera Lanpher) gives the player a few helpful hints.

Dragon's Lair was insanely popular when it was released and it soon became a worldwide phenomenon. The game was ported to around eighteen different home consoles and computers at the time, none of which had the LaserDisc technology. So of course, the various ports had to be massively stripped back from its original cartoon style, stripped back beyond recognition in many ways. Ironically, these lesser ports often had actual gameplay, something the original just didn't have, often bad gameplay yes, but still gameplay nonetheless. *Dragon's Lair* also became a pretty big franchise, comic books, an animated TV show and of course the sequel, *Dragon's Lair II: Time Warp* from 1991. *Dragon's Lair* is a game that is still fondly renumbered today. In fact, as I write

66 OF THE MOST IMPORTANT VIDEO GAMES EVER!
(ACCORDING TO ME)

this, Don Bluth is said to be working on a feature film prequel to the original game that will be on Netflix with Ryan Reynolds. Only it's not an animated feature, but a live-action flick instead. I think that will definitely annoy fans of the beautiful animation that *Dragon's Lair* is famed for. But thinking about it, they could make it an interactive experience akin to Netflix's *Black Mirror: Bandersnatch* and keep the 'gameplay' of the original game intact. It'll definitely be a shame to see that wonderful Don Bluth animation and art gone, but an interactive film could prove to be very popular. We'll have to wait and see.

As I've already said, I really don't like playing *Dragon's Lair* at all, but I do appreciate its importance. The first game to use QTEs and not Sega's *Shenmue* as people tend to claim. It was also the first-ever game to use LaserDisc technology, the forerunner to the CD format that dominated in the early nineties of gaming, and paved the way for the Blu-rays we use today. But, was *Dragon's Lair* really the first LaserDisc game?

No, no it wasn't. While Rick Dyer and Don Bluth were busy working on *Dragon's Lair*, Sega was working on a LaserDisc title of their own. Also released in 1983, but hitting the arcades in May of that year, several weeks before *Dragon's Lair*. *Astron Belt* is a third-person shooter where you control a sprite-based ship shooting enemies on a pre-filmed background. Gameplay-wise, it offers a bit more interactivity than *Dragon's Lair*... A little bit. So, while *Dragon's Lair* was not the first LaserDisc game, I think of the two, it is far more important. I mean, it is one of only three games that have been put on permanent display at the Smithsonian in Washington, DC. The other two have already been included in this book, *Pong* and *Pac-Man*.

S. L. PERRIN

MANIC MINER
DEVELOPER: MATTHEW SMITH
PUBLISHER: BUG-BYTE
PLATFORM: ZX SPECTRUM
RELEASED: MARCH/JUNE?, 1983

Ha! I had a right old game trying to find an actual release date for this one (thanks to those who helped me out over social media). See, Wikipedia claims the game was released in August of 1983, but I found an archived article that says *Manic Miner* won a golden joystick award in March of 83 and another one dated April 1984 that says the game was released 'a little over a year ago'. Either way, it seems the internet is wrong (again) and *Manic Miner* possibly came out early-ish 1983. Then, another source claims it was first reviewed in March of 83, but not released to the public until June of 1983 at the Earls Court Computer Fair. Truth be told, I don't know exactly when *Manic Miner* was released, so let's just say around March to June of 1983.

Anyway, up until now, this book and indeed the gaming industry in general, has been very Japanese and American orientated. The game crash of 1983 begun to really hit hard by Spring, 1983. However, it only really affected North America, a few ripples in Japan sure, but it was the gaming industry in the US where the game crash really destroyed the industry. Here in the UK, it really passed us by, because, by the early eighties, we had a pretty strong and very stable gaming industry building for a while. It was those teenage bedroom programmers and young wannabe entrepreneurs setting up publishing houses, with a vision to make as much money as possible, that really gave birth to the British gaming industry. (Contains non-paid advertisement) Look, I already wrote a fantastic book looking at the interweaving stories of the British gaming industry, go onto Amazon and search for *MicroBrits*.

One of those great British teenage bedroom programmers was Matthew Smith and he programmed one of the most important games ever made, *Manic Miner*. Inspired by the 1982 game, *Miner 2049er*, an early example of the platform genre. *Manic Miner* has you playing as Miner Willy, who is trapped underground and needs to escape by making his way to the surface. Taking place on over twenty caverns (screens), Willy

66 OF THE MOST IMPORTANT VIDEO GAMES EVER!
(ACCORDING TO ME)

has to jump his way to the end of each level, avoiding enemies while collecting specific flashing items to open the way to the next screen, before his oxygen runs out. Simple and basic, but bloody great fun, all topped off with a big slice of very Python-esque humour.

Matt Smith already had a few games under his belt before he took on the job of creating *Manic Miner,* which took just eight weeks, using a TRS-80 Tandy computer. Oh, and he was only 17-years-old at the time too. I don't want this to turn into a Matt Smith biography, but to not mention his genius would be criminal. Due to the ZX Spectrum's unreliability and penchant for crashing... A hell of a lot. Smith hated programming on it. So he would use a TRS-80 Tandy computer to code on, then just transfer the data to the ZX Spectrum. The only issue was that technology didn't exist back then to transfer data from one machine to the other so easily, so Smith invented it. Creating and using his very own, custom-made Veroboard which he could plug into the Speccy and the TRS-80. After finishing programming a game on the Tandy computer, he would (to use his own word) 'squirt' the code over to Clive Sinclair's rubber-keyed machine for testing. Again, he was just 17-years-old at the time. Do you know what I was doing aged 17? Drinking piss-poor (probably) illegally imported cheap beer, bought from a dodgy off-licence and being socially awkward around girls, while trying to cover up my zits. While I was doing that, Matt Smith was making gaming history.

There's a lot to talk about with *Manic Miner*. How about the fact it was the first Spectrum game to feature in-game music? A rather impressive (for the time) version of *In the Hall of the Mountain King* would chime away as you played. Oh, you may not recognise the name, but you definitely know the tune. Then there was the intro to the game itself, that iconic title screen with the piano playing *The Blue Danube*... Though to be fair, that particular tune was a bit ear-bleeding, even then. Still, just getting music to play on a game during gameplay on the ZX Spectrum took some serious coding talent. I really could write a chapter or three just about Matt Smith's coding genius. But there are still many, many more games and several more decades to get through yet.

Each of the levels of *Manic Miner* was very specifically designed to test the player as much as possible. Pixel perfect jumps were needed and

Matt Smith tested the hell out of each and every one to ensure they could be done. Each of the twenty levels had their own unique look and flavour and some even featured several rather 'legally questionable' enemies, but thankfully copyright laws were not quite as serious back then as they are now. Some levels contain numerous *Pac-Man* sprites, there are two levels that have a direct *Donkey Kong* reference… the fully copyrighted *Donkey Kong*, not the public domain *King Kong*. But let's not go down that route again. There's even a level that takes place on Endor (The Endorain Forest) complete with Ewoks walking around too. Perhaps one of the most famous levels of the game is the one that features a cheeky (but respectful) reference to another bedroom coder legend, Jeff Minter.

Manic Miner was just so damn creative, packed full of little details that make each of the levels such a joy to experience… If you can get to see them that is. If there is one thing that the game is very well known for, then it is its punishing difficulty. Even now in 2021 (almost four decades later) as I write this, I've still never finished the game, only managing to get to level fourteen, the Skylab Landing Bay screen, which itself is a reference to the Skylab space station crash of 1979. Oh yeah, *Manic Miner* tackled famed news stories as well as possible copyright infringement.

Manic Miner went on to spawn a few sequels. There was *Jet Set Willy* and *Jet Set Willy II* (the ending of which, brings the trilogy full circle). Plus there have been numerous fan-made games, remakes sequels and spin-offs. Even today, *Manic Miner* and the character of Miner Willy holds a very special place in many older (British) gamer's hearts, they are still referenced and very much celebrated now. Yup, Japan and America may have had their *Pac-Man* and Mario in the early-eighties, but we Brits worshipped a big white Willy. Due to how *Manic Miner* and sequels were coded, it became easy for fans to make their own Miner Willy games. There's a whole sub-genre of *Manic Miner* games that still exist now. It all dates back to 1985 when a fan of the game called Mark Jeffries made the first *Jet Set Willy* editor. From that point on unofficial sequels began to turn up, it was the beginning of the fan-made movement that's so popular today, before the term 'fan-made' even existed.

66 OF THE MOST IMPORTANT VIDEO GAMES EVER! (ACCORDING TO ME)

Manic Miner is what really kick-started the whole British gaming industry for me, not the first British game, but certainly the one that made an impact that is still felt today. It wasn't the first platform game either, but it was the one that showed just how well the genre could work on the home computers... With a genius coding it.

Manic Miner's creator, Matt Smith is notoriously hard to get to talk about his work... Or anything really. He even disappeared for a long while (he's had more than a few personal demons to deal with) with many people believing he had died and other such stories. He didn't die, he just wanted to get away from people and the industry for a while. Occasionally he pops up again and says a few words before disappearing once more. Still, finding interviews with Smith is rather like searching for the holy grail. Yet, he has spoken about his career and work during some of his very rare public appearances. One such interview can be found on the old gaming TV show, *Thumb Bandits* from 2002. Presenter Iain Lee talks to Matt Smith and says about making *Manic Miner* that:

> "Five years after I did it, I was a washout. Ten years after I did it, I was history... But it's coming up to twenty years now and I'm a legend."

No Mr Smith, I have to respectfully disagree with you there, you are wrong. You've always been a legend, you just never (sadly) knew it at the time. 6031769.

S. L. PERRIN

KARATE CHAMP
DEVELOPER: TECHNŌS JAPAN
PUBLISHER: DATA EAST
PLATFORM: ARCADE
RELEASED: JUNE, 1984

It's back in the arcades once more, and those sounds and sights of the attract screens really worked. *Karate Champ* (*Karate Dō* in Japan) was one such game. It had a very memorable theme tune, then the demo would start, and like the previously mentioned *Pole Position*, *Karate Champ* featured speech samples, as the judge of the fights would declare 'half/full point'. It was one of those game you always heard before you saw it as you wandered around the arcade looking for something to play. Granted, it wasn't as loud as *Dragon's Lair*, but you could hear and recognise *Karate Champ* before seeing it.

Okay, before I get into this. *Karate Champ* is often cited as the first-ever fighting game... According to the internet and numerous gaming sites. And yes, I'm sure the internet is wrong again. See, *Karateka* for the Apple II computer was released around the same time, with some sources claiming that *Karateka* actually came first. It seems like it's a bit of a hot debate over which was first, *Karate Champ* or *Karateka*. Just for the record, *Karateka* was released in December of 1984 (I checked), six months after *Karate Champ's* original release. There is a reason for the release date confusion though, which I will cover soon. Still, there was a fighting game before both of them. Back in 1982, the piratical themed *Swashbuckler* was released for the Apple II home computer, beating both *Karate Champ* and *Karateka* to the market by two years. So that was the first... Or was it? Cos you also need to take into consideration Sega's *Heavyweight Champ* from 1976, which is the earliest fighting game I've managed to find and (I think) the first-ever beat 'em up.

Anyway, back to *Karate Champ*. It wasn't just the sights and sounds of the game that stood out, as the cabinet itself had an interesting feature... Two joysticks. Now, I don't mean it had one joystick for each of the two players, it had two joysticks for one player. The controls were this dual-stick thing. The left stick would control the movement of your character, including blocking, while the right stick would be used for the punches

66 OF THE MOST IMPORTANT VIDEO GAMES EVER!
(ACCORDING TO ME)

and kicks. Then using a combination of both, you could pull off fancy roundhouse kicks, flying kicks and so much more. The controls for *Karate Champ* really were amazing, and once you got to grips with them, you could kick some serious pixel arse using twenty-four different moves... Which at the time really was pretty impressive.

The gameplay would be recognisable to anyone who had ever played a one on one beat 'em up before. Best of two rounds with the basic aim to knock the other character out. However, unlike most modern games of this genre, there was no health meter. *Karate Champ* used a more realistic point system, with the first to score two full points being the winner of that round. Different movies/hit would score either a half or full point, so theoretically, a round could be won in just two moves. Between the rounds, you would take part in various bonus stages. Dodge/hit objects being thrown at you from off the screen. Break various blocks like tiles, ice blocks and concrete. And the most famous bonus stage, punching a charging bull in the face, just like a real-life karate champion... if that champ was Chuck Norris. There was no real plot to the game, just you fighting one AI-controlled opponent after another, you just keep going until you finally get beaten.

Now, there was an alternate version of *Karate Champ* released the same year, a few months after the original version. *Karate Champ: Player vs Player* (*Taisen Karate Dō: Bishōjo Seishun Hen*) was pretty much the same game, but with a few tweaks. See, this is where I think the whole previously mentioned dispute over which was the first-ever fighting game between *Karate Champ* or *Karateka* originates. This alternate version is the more famous one of the two versions, in fact, *Karate Champ: Player vs Player* is the game that the international release (outside of Japan) of the game was based on, as well as all of the home ports. As, this other version was released a few months after the original, but still in the same year, 1984, which brings it more in line with the release of *Karateka*. So, my theory is that people get the later version of *Karate Champ* mixed up with the earlier original one and think they are the same game, leading to the later release of *Karate Champ: Player vs Player* being incorrectly used as the original game... If that makes sense? Not that it matters anyway, as I already covered that neither *Karate*

S. L. PERRIN

Champ nor *Karateka* were the first-ever beat 'em up game anyway, making this whole paragraph a waste of time for me to write. So to save yourself a lot of effort, don't bother reading it okay? You may as well just skip that entire paragraph that you just read, you can thank me later.

Anyway, *Karate Champ: Player vs Player* (just known as *Karate Champ* elsewhere) had a few tweaks and improvements over the first version. The game now had a plot... Kind of. You are fighting for the affections of a female in each round and each round takes place in a different location around the globe. The original version took place in one locale (when you pass the opening dōjō bit), that locale being a karate tournament and the background never changed, aside from when you had to Chuck Norris a bull in the face with your fist. This new version had backgrounds based on Japan, New York, Holland and others. Kind of like being a 'world warrior' I guess...

Yes, let's get this out of the way. *Karate Champ* may not have been the first-ever fighting game, but it was the one that kick-started and popularised the genre. In fact, the mighty *Street Fighter II* (which is in this book... SPOILERS!) was majorly influenced by *Karate Champ*. It has been said that the white and red karate gis worn by the characters in this game are the reason Ryu and Ken wear those same colours in *Street Fighter II*. Even the touring of the world from *SF II* is said to be based on *Karate Champ*... Not that Capcom's classic beat 'em up was the first to 'borrow' that concept. See, there was a game called *The Way of the Exploding Fist* from 1985 (*World Karate Championship* in the US) which was accused by Data East, the publisher of *Karate Champ* in America, as ripping off their game. Long story short, Data East took Epyx (the American publisher of *World Karate Championship*) to court, a case which Data East lost as the judge ruled that a company could not claim ownership over a sport like karate. Also, John Tobias, one of the creators of the *Mortal Kombat* games (also appearing later in this book... Also SPOILERS) has cited *Karate Champ* as a major influence. So, while *Karate Champ* was not the first-ever beat 'em up game, it can not be denied that it certainly is the one that made the most impact and went on to influence the entire genre for decades to come.

66 OF THE MOST IMPORTANT VIDEO GAMES EVER!
(ACCORDING TO ME)

TETRIS
DEVELOPER: ALEXEY PAJITNOV
PUBLISHER(S): MIRRORSOFT/SPECTRUM HOLOBYTE
PLATFORM: ELECTRONIKA 60/IBM PC
RELEASED: JUNE, 1984

Tetris was created by Alexey Pajitnov, a young speech recognition researcher, working in the Computer Centre of the Soviet Academy of Sciences in Moscow. Pajitnov loved puzzles and developed a few basic ones to be used on the institute's Electronika 60 computer. One of his favourite puzzles/board games as a child was called *Pentominoes*, a kind of jigsaw-like puzzle using specific shapes (look it up). Now, the Electronika 60 computer was extremely primitive. Other parts of the world had some pretty impressive computers in the early eighties, but by comparison, at the time, the Electronika 60 was utter pants. Yet, in Russia's (then the Soviet Union) struggling and crumbling economy, it was cutting edge hardware. The Electronika 60 couldn't display graphics of any kind, only alphanumeric characters. 'Basic' is just too basic a word to use to describe how basic the Electronika 60 really was, but it was really basic, basically.

Alexey Pajitnov thought back to his childhood and that *Pentominoes* game that he loved to play, he wondered if there was any way to modernise it and turn it into a computer game. First, he had to whittle down the more 'complex' pentomino (five-piece) shapes into easier to program tetrominoes (four-piece). In only six days, Pajitnov had designed the first version of his game that he called *Generic Engineering*, the game had a simple goal, to fit the tetrominoes shapes into a box. The problem was that *Generic Engineering* as a game was too simple, too boring and offered no real challenge. Once the player worked out how to fit the shapes into the box... That was it, no reason to play again. Alexey Pajitnov knew he needed to make his game more challenging and try to get people wanting to play it multiple times. He took the idea of fitting shapes into a box and stretched the box. He also came up with the idea of instead of just having to put shapes in a box like a jigsaw puzzle... What if the shapes dropped from the top to the bottom of the screen and you the player had to use reactions to slot them into place as they fell?

This idea opened up Alexey Pajitnov's *Generic Engineering* game, it made the game fast-paced and more frantic. It also added replay value as the shapes could be placed in numerous, non-sequential different orders, making each new game different from the last. However, Pajitnov found another issue with his new idea, that being that the shapes would fill up the screen fast and make the game end way too soon. Then it hit him, why not make the row of shapes disappear from the screen if a horizontal line is completed? This gave the shapes more room when they fell and added another layer to the game as the player had the goal of trying to keep the shapes from filling the screen in a test to see how long they could last. That was it, Alexey Pajitnov hit gold. As simple as his new game was, it was just as addictive, all he needed was a name. The shapes used, tetrominoes, were made up of four pieces, the Greek for four is tetra, plus Pajitnov loved tennis… **Tetra-tennis,** so he came up with the portmanteau of *Tetris*. There was no scoring system, no sound, no 'levels' and no real graphics, just those basic alphanumeric characters used to display the frame that the main gameplay took place in and the tetrominoes shapes. I feel another primitive graphical diagram coming on…

66 OF THE MOST IMPORTANT VIDEO GAMES EVER!
(ACCORDING TO ME)

Yeah, that's basic alright, but that's how *Tetris* looked on that primitive Electronika 60 computer. Alexey Pajitnov may have had his game, but the problems had only just begun. See, *Tetris* only worked on the very prehistoric Electronika 60 computer and it really couldn't exist outside of the Soviet Academy of Sciences, where Pajitnov worked and where he had designed his game. He knew he had to port it to get the game into the hands of more people. Alexey Pajitnov got help from Vadim Gerasimov, a 16-year-old wunderkind known for his impressive computer skills. It took a few weeks and it wasn't easy because the entire program had to be re-written from the ground up. Still, Gerasimov managed to make *Tetris* work on the IMB PC, not only that, it was improved upon too. It had actual graphics instead of alphanumeric characters... And with some basic colour too. A scoring system was added making the game even more playable as it got people wanting to beat their own scores. It even featured the ability to save high scores. Then, levels were added as the game got increasingly faster whenever enough lines had been completed, which all added to the challenge and playability. All Alexey Pajitnov had to do now was sell his game... Which, in the Soviet Union of the eighties, was far easier said than done.

The biggest problem was the fact that the game was made at the government-owned Soviet Academy of Sciences and on their computer, which technically meant that *Tetris* was government property. So *Tetris* couldn't be legally sold but, there was nothing stopping Alexey Pajitnov from giving his game away to friends for free. The game soon began to spread through Russia as people copied and shared *Tetris* with others. The game started to spread outside of the Soviet Union. In Hungary, *Tetris* became huge and this opened a possible door to get the game published properly. The Hungarian game publisher, Novotrade began to make clones of *Tetris* and the game soon reached an even bigger audience.

Enter Robert Stein, who was a software salesman for Andromeda Software based in London, he saw *Tetris* while on a trip to Europe. Stein loved the game and set about tracking down the developer with the sole aim to get the game officially published. After some investigating, Stein tracked the game's creation back to the Soviet Academy of Sciences in

Moscow and asked for permission to publish *Tetris* proper. The director of the institute told Stein that the game didn't belong to them and that he would have to make a deal with the Soviet Union government, which he did by sending a fax. Word (and the fax itself) eventually got back to *Tetris'* creator, Alexey Pajitnov, who by now had actually given up on selling the game. While Pajitnov made the game, he had no authority to negotiate any kind of a deal over it. Alexey Pajitnov expressed great interest in having *Tetris* published, but could not cement a deal, out of fear of being disciplined (to put it mildly) by the Soviet Union government. He replied to Robert Stein's fax saying:

"Yes we are interested. We would like to have this deal."

Bearing in mind that Pajitnov's English wasn't that great and that he was also bound by the Soviet Union government's strict rules. Stein, who didn't know or understand that, while Pajitnov had created *Tetris*, he didn't actually own it, nor could he negotiate deals, saw the reply as an official agreement to publish *Tetris*. So Robert Stein approached Mirrorsoft in the UK to release the game.

Cutting an already very long story short, this was the start of a huge misunderstanding and Stein sold *Tetris* to both Mirrorsoft in the UK and Spectrum HoloByte in the US. At the time, Robert Stein had not officially secured a deal with the Soviet Union government who actually owned the game, believing that the game's creator's broken English fax was good enough. Look, the whole deal was a mess that will take up way too much time to cover here. All you need to know is that eventually, *Tetris* saw a proper commercial release. There was interference from the Soviet government, Stein didn't have the deal he thought he did and as for the creator of *Tetris* himself, Alexey Pajitnov, he didn't see a penny of the money the game eventually made, and it made an absolute fuck-tonne of it over the years too.

Tetris went on to become ~~one of~~ the most ported and best-selling games in the world. It helped make Nintendo's Game Boy such a popular handheld and dominating console. As simple as *Tetris* was/is, it's truly remarkable how popular it became. From such a strange and confusing origin, to one of the world's most influential games ever made. The story of *Tetris* is as long as it is interesting. The game had no real

66 OF THE MOST IMPORTANT VIDEO GAMES EVER!
(ACCORDING TO ME)

graphics, whereas other games at the time did, no story, no hero to play as. For all *Tetris* was, it wasn't your typical video game. Yet it became a massive phenomenon.

As for Alexey Pajitnov? As I said, despite making the worldwide popular *Tetris*, he didn't earn a single penny from any of its multiples of millions of sales of the game from around the globe. Years later in 1996, he co-founded The Tetris Company and he now owns the rights to the entire *Tetris* brand. After many years of nothing, Pajitnov now makes plenty of money on every single *Tetris* game or any *Tetris* related merchandise ever made/sold, deservedly so too.

S. L. PERRIN

ELITE

DEVELOPER(S): DAVID BRABEN & IAN BELL
PUBLISHER: ACORNSOFT
PLATFORM(S): BBC MICRO & ACORN ELECTRON
RELEASED: SEPTEMBER, 1984

While *Manic Miner* was most definitely a slice of British coding genius, *Elite* was on a whole different level. The entire reason this book exists is because of *Elite*. See, I was writing an article for my blog, looking back on my personal gaming history, the computers/consoles I played on and the games I've enjoyed for forty-odd years. This game was the first thing that came to mind over anything else. That got me thinking specifically about games that have impacted my life... Which turned into important games. I then sat there making a list of games that I felt were important and the next thing I knew, I was writing this book.

As I sit here tapping away on my keyboard, I now realise that I'm about to do *Elite* a massive injustice. Due to the number of games I have to cover here, I'm limiting myself to how big/small each chapter has to be to fit them all in. And to be honest, *Elite* deserves a whole damn book, not just a short-ish chapter sharing the limelight with so many other important games.

David Braben and Ian Bell met at Cambridge in 1982, where they were studying physics and maths respectively. Both were computer aficionados and they wanted to make a space-themed game like no other. Braben sat down and created a fairly basic demo featuring a 3D wire-frame spacecraft, with a scrolling star-field, and he did it on an Acorn Atom computer (a primitive and less powerful precursor to the BBC Micro). That simple demo is what encouraged David Braben and Ian Bell to converse about the strict limitations of current game design back then. *Elite* was really born from the frustration that games of that mid-eighties period were just too restrictive, as well as being influenced by *2001: A Space Odyssey*, *Star Wars* and *Hitchhiker's Guide to the Galaxy*.

The pair originally took their game idea to Thorn EMI, hoping to find a publishing deal. The company turned them down flat saying that their new game concept had no clear goal, no high-score to beat, no levels to

66 OF THE MOST IMPORTANT VIDEO GAMES EVER! (ACCORDING TO ME)

play through and that it couldn't be finished in ten minutes with three lives as was pretty much the norm for a game then... And it couldn't, because *Elite* was something the gaming world had never seen before. After being turned down by Thorn EMI, Braben and Bell took their game idea to Acornsoft who loved the concept and a publishing deal was made. That was when the idea really began to grow.

The fact their game idea wouldn't feature a traditional score to beat meant they needed something else to drive the player forward. That 'something' was the thing that the eighties was mostly driven by... Money. But what can you use the money for? Upgrades for your spaceship. But why would you need to upgrade your ship? Because people were out to kill you. So why were people out to kill you? Because you would be carrying valuable cargo. *Elite* really was a game built on simple ideas that were layered on top of other simple ideas.

It's kind of hard to describe what *Elite* really is. Of course, it is a shoot 'em up, perhaps not in the 'normal' sense, but there is plenty of shooting action. Yet, *Elite* really is so much more besides. It's a bit of an RPG too. But mainly, it's a trading game... In space! I've honestly never liked the whole 'trading game' moniker that *Elite* has been given. Don't get me wrong, it's a very accurate label, but it just makes the game sound a lot more boring than it actually is. Here, I'll let David Braben himself have a go at describing *Elite*, as he did in this interview with The Guardian:

> "In life, I like to look behind the set. I like to see how the world works. For me, that's what the original *Elite* was. It wasn't a space game first and foremost. It was an open-world game that gave the player freedom. Freedom to explore, and freedom to lose themselves. That was because I'm the kind of person who doesn't want to be limited in a game to linear 'A or B' choices. I want to explore and play and see how things turn out if I do them my own way. That's how *Elite* came about."

The main focus of *Elite* is to rise through the ranks from lowly trader to an *Elite*. Just how you do this really is very open. You start with a paltry one-hundred credits and a meagre, lightly armed junker of a trading ship. You are then free to build your bank balance, upgrade and even buy new spaceships in any way you see fit. Trading goods is the most obvious and 'easy' way to gain that much-needed coin. But there are so many other methods available, become a space pirate, work for the military, mine asteroids and even become a bounty hunter. Earn credits and buy better weapons for your ship, a bigger cargo hold and more. The basics and premise behind *Elite* are wonderfully simple, even in 1984. But it was how everything came together to create one of the most immersive and deeply imaginative games ever created.

But it's not just the depth and variety of gameplay that *Elite* offers which is so impressive, there's an entire galaxy to explore. Right here, I just want to remind people that this game came out in 1984. We had seen games evolve from single screen to multi-screen and even scrolling, which was impressive enough and usually in the arcades too. Home computer games were far more restrictive and a far cry from what the arcades were doing at the time. But now, now we had a fucking universe to play in. This was mind-blowing, jaw-dropping stuff... And in 1984. Truth be told, the game was bigger than one universe. *Elite* actually contained eight universes, and then each of those universes contained around two-hundred and fifty planets to discover and explore. That's an immense playing field for any game today, never mind one from over thirty-five years ago. *Elite* was one of the first games to feature procedural generation too... After *Rogue*.

Look, this is another one of those examples where I could write several chapters just on the amazing coding that made the game possible. The programming genius behind *Elite* is immensely creative and impressive, let's just leave it at that. Just look into the BBC Micro, the home computer *Elite* was first released on. Even for the time, that was a very primitive and a technically limiting computer, compared to others on the market in 1984. Pushing around four or five colours on screen at any one time, no sprite-based hardware and a with only 64k of memory too. The BBC Micro was actually built more for work and education. Games were just not what the computer was made for. The BBC Micro would struggle to play a half-decent port of something like *Pac-Man*, yet there it was in 1984 offering a title that on the surface, seemed impossible that it even existed. Still, setting the game in space was a major help to get around the limitations the BBC Micro had as a computer, as David Braben recalls:

66 OF THE MOST IMPORTANT VIDEO GAMES EVER! (ACCORDING TO ME)

"The space setting was chosen because it was the only one we could render on the technology at the time. The clue is in the word 'space'. It was a big open area with dots in it and some ships. That was what we could get working on the BBC Micro and similar machines at the time."

Elite's wire-frame/3D graphics were another talking point. 'Pioneering' is perhaps the best word to use here, planets, space stations, other ships and even a moving star-field provided the backbone of the visual journey *Elite* would take gamers on.

Elite was a smash hit as it really captured the imagination of us gamers back then. The game was ported to pretty much every major home computer at the time, it even had a NES port... And it's pretty damn great too. Of course, more games followed, *Frontier: Elite II* and *Frontier: First Encounters* (*Elite III*) were released in 1993 and 95 respectively. Rumours began to surface over a possible *Elite IV* in 1998, but nothing ever came of it. Until 2014 when David Braben unleashed *Elite Dangerous* onto the world. A game that, as of writing, is still being updated, expanded and added to. *Elite* has definitely had an impact and its influence can still be felt today. Games like the *Wing Commander* series, *Privateer*, *EVE Online*, *Everpsace*, *No Man's Sky* and pretty much any space combat/trading game owes something to *Elite*. Then, even the entire open-world genre of games which has definitely been influenced by *Elite's* non-structured approach to gaming. Without *Elite*, I doubt we ever would've had *Grand Theft Auto* and the many open-world titles that it inspired.

It is often debated what was the first-ever open-world game. Much like how I will argue that *Pong* was the first 'proper' video game (see the first chapter), I will happily argue that *Elite* was the first 'proper' open-world game in much the same way too, even if it can be debated there were other open-world games before it. For me, *Elite* isn't so much an important video game, more so that I personally believe that it's **THE** most important video game ever made. From the day *Elite* was released, it showed just how open the world of gaming could be and it changed the path gaming would take from that day to this. Over thirty years since its release and *Elite* is still influencing developers, and it'll probably do the same for another thirty years too. *Elite* showed that games could be so much more than just a guy jumping around a screen, or a yellow dot moving around a maze. It showed that games are only really limited by a coder's imagination and that even the most strict of technical restrictions could be overcome. Or as David Braben once put it:

"So many things have shifted since I made the original *Elite*, thirty years ago. They're good things, they aren't all about hardware, and they've allowed us to do so much more than could be done back in 1984. But ironically, things are also returning to how they were back then. There's a freedom today as developers are able to do what we like."

That's exactly what *Elite* gave the gaming world, freedom. Not just freedom to the player, but also freedom to those who make games now to push the boundaries and make games that could break all of those restrictive moulds that existed back then. As I said, *Elite* is **THE** most important video game ever made.

**66 OF THE MOST IMPORTANT VIDEO GAMES EVER!
(ACCORDING TO ME)**

PAC-LAND
**DEVELOPER: NAMCO
PUBLISHER(S): NAMCO, MIDWAY
PLATFORM: ARCADE
RELEASED: OCTOBER, 1984**

Just a few years after his original introduction to the world, *Pac-Man* returned for a game that really blew people away. Gone was the original game's single-screen maze-like gameplay. Now, the loveable, ravenous yellow dot was in a side-scrolling platform game.

Pac-Man had become pretty huge since the first game's release, as mentioned in that chapter, it was the first game to have any merchandise and was video game's first true licensing success. Part of that popular *Pac-Man* licensing was a kid's Saturday morning cartoon produced by the famed Hanna-Barbera animation studio. *Pac-Land* was based on that very cartoon. It featured the same colourful art style and presentation. The original *Pac-Man* didn't really have a plot to speak of, you just ran around a maze, eating dots and tried for a high score. *Pac-Land* actually had a story... Kind of. Playing as *Pac-Man*, you leave your family behind and go on a quest to deliver lost fairies to Fairyland. Okay, so the story is hardy of J. R. R. Tolkien depth and length, but it was a story.

As mentioned, the maze-like gameplay of the original is gone and now we have a side-scrolling platformer. Programmed by Yoshihiro Kishimoto who had to create all-new animation techniques to portray *Pac-Man*. See, back then, sprites usually only had around three to five frames of animation, but Namco wanted more. They loved the Hanna-Barbera animated show, as it was getting great viewing figures at the time, so Namco wanted the game to be just as animated as the show was. Easy by today's standards sure, but back in 1984, that kind of animation in a game was unheard of (unless you used LaserDisc tech). Kishimoto had to work hard, he and the Namco team had to develop hardware that could house such animations in an arcade game. All told, *Pac-Man* in the game had twenty-four different animation frames, quite a jump from the usual three to five frames used in early/mid-eighties arcade games. Plus, that animation didn't include Pac's facial expressions and extras needed for the various hats that the popular yellow dot wears through the game. Those twenty-four frames were just for *Pac-Man's* walking cycle and jumping animation.

Also, all of that extra work was just for one character in the game, *Pac-Land* also had to feature the cartoon's vibrant art style and other animations. For the time *Pac-Land* was truly ground-breaking from an animation and art-style point of view, it looked and felt like the animated show. It even had the proper music. The game also featured multi-layered backgrounds, parallax scrolling (something that wouldn't really become commonplace in gaming until the 16-bit era) and multiple sprites on screen at once, all with no flickering and no slowdown either. Arcade game-boards back then just couldn't do that, that was why all-new hardware had to be created and the Namco Pac-Land arcade board was born, a board used on several famed Namco games from that point on.

Then there was the arcade cabinet itself... No joysticks. I mean, *Pac-Land* was a fast-paced, action-platformer and all platform games used a joystick as a control. *Pac-Land* did something different, inspired by Konami's *Track & Field* from 1983, *Pac-Land* decided to use buttons instead. One button to go left, one to go right and another for jump. It was a different approach, but one that really worked too. The controls were incredibly intuitive and felt great... Until those damn springboards!

Pac-Land was a game full of innovation, one that pushed what an arcade platformer could do in 1984. Some of the later levels really test your skills as more and more enemies begin to appear (still with no flicker or slowdown), jumps get trickier and more dangerous. Levels throw up new ideas, like paying in pitch black with only about an inch of sight in front of you. *Pac-Land* was simply amazing back then. It has its haters now (what game doesn't?), but we are talking about a game that was a direct influence on so many platform games that followed, including the mighty *Super Mario Bros.*, keep reading...

66 OF THE MOST IMPORTANT VIDEO GAMES EVER!
(ACCORDING TO ME)

KNIGHT LORE
DEVELOPER: ULTIMATE PLAY THE GAME
PUBLISHER: ULTIMATE PLAY THE GAME
PLATFORM: ZX SPECTRUM
RELEASED: NOVEMBER, 1984

I adore the British game industry, particularly the early to mid-eighties period. While the Japanese and American gaming industries were certainty impressive and innovative, we Brits were truly revolutionary. Games like the previously covered *Elite* were literal game-changers. Not so much for breaking new ground, more like completely obliterating it. As I said in that *Elite* chapter, I think it is **THE** most important game ever made and Ultimate Play The Game's *Knight Lore* isn't far behind it.

The company's co-founding and programming brothers, Tim and Chris Stamper were the ones behind this masterpiece. *Knight Lore* was actually the third game in the popular Sabreman series of games, yet it was actually programmed and finished first, which if anything, just makes the game's stunning (for the time) isometric 3D engine and graphics even more impressive. In fact, it had been said that the reason this game was released later, despite being finished first, was because the Stamper brothers felt that if they had released it first, that it would've just embarrassed everything else on the market at the time. According to Stuart Hunt's in-depth T*he Ultimate Hero: A Complete History of Sabreman* article from Retro Gamer, Tim Stamper said:

> "We just had to sit on it because everyone else was so far behind."

Ant Attack from 1983 on the Speccy was the first-ever isometric game released on the home computers (just in case you were wondering) and as impressive as it was, *Knight Lore* was a whole other level. Graphically and technically, it made *Ant Attack* look positively ancient by comparison. Ultimate created, what they called, the Filmation game engine and it was this engine that gave the game (and other Ultimate titles) such a striking look and style. Sprites would move in front of each other without clashing, which I know sounds all so underwhelming now, but if you knew the ZX Spectrum back then, you knew just how much graphic/colour clashing was one of the computer's very ugly traits. So, to play a game that not only didn't have the Speccy's famed clashing, but one that also didn't have it in glorious isometric 3D was truly radical.

Knight Lore also offered a unique dual style gameplay mechanic. See your character, Sabreman, had been bitten by a wulf (wolf), which means you turned into a werewulf. This is where the day/night cycle of the game came into play. By day, you were intrepid explorer Sabreman, but by night, you transformed into the werewulf. This lycanthropy actually changed the character's permanence as in wulf form, you could jump higher. This would come in very handy when solving certain puzzles. But being in the wulf form did have a downside, that being that you were more vulnerable to certain enemies and hazards. This dual play style really was innovative at the time and added layers to the gameplay.

I guess this here would be a good point to yak on about how the game actually played? Well (as mentioned) you play as Sabreman who suffers from a touch of lycanthropy. You have to find items hidden around a wizard's castle to cure you of your werewulf curse, and all in forty in-game days and nights. Each of *Knight Lore's* very impressive one-hundred and twenty-eight rooms were packed with enemies, hazards and various puzzles for you to solve, each pushing your platforming and lateral thinking skills to the limit.

That Filmation game engine that Ultimate Play The Game created and used for *Knight Lore* would go on to be used for other isometric games from the developer. All of which were equally as visually impressive as *Knight Lore* was, even if they didn't play quite as sublime or didn't manage to come across as important.

I can only apologise for the lack of content in this chapter. See, back when Ultimate was riding high, the Stamper brothers were notoriously quiet when it came to talking to the gaming press. Finding info on games from thirty-odd years ago is difficult enough, digging up interviews and behind the scenes info from a studio that really didn't do interviews thirty-odd years ago is infinitely much more difficult. I mean, it did take me three hours of searching just to discover that single line Tim Stamper quote I used earlier. The lack of info all makes this chapter seem 'weaker' when compared to others, which really is a shame because

66 OF THE MOST IMPORTANT VIDEO GAMES EVER! (ACCORDING TO ME)

Knight Lore is such a hugely important game, especially to the British gaming industry. Those isometric 3D graphics were astounding back in 1984, the gameplay was tough, as all Ultimate game were and the impact the game had can not be overstated. Sometimes it's just hard to put into words what really needed to be experienced first hand when it happened.

Knight Lore wasn't the first isometric game, but it was the first to really offer depth and an explorable game world that swallowed the gamer whole. The game definitely feels very dated today and something like 1987's *Head over Heels* offers a much more 'refined' gameplay experience by comparison… but *Head over Heels* (as good as it is) didn't innovate, *Knight Lore* did.

S. L. PERRIN

SKOOL DAZE
DEVELOPER(S): DAVID REIDY & HELEN REIDY
PUBLISHER: MICROSPHERE
PLATFORM: ZX SPECTRUM
RELEASED: DECEMBER, 1984

At least I think this was released in December 1984. I made that assumption from two archived game magazine reviews that I managed to find. Still, whatever month *Skool Daze* was released, it's most definitely one of the most important games ever made... And yes, very distinctly British too. Before I get into all the behind the scenes stuff, I'll just give the game and the general gameplay a quick going over.

So, *Skool Daze* sees you playing as a schoolboy called Eric (though the name could be edited). The basic plot of the game is that you have to try to get the combination to the school safe and retrieve your report card.... And that's it. As simple as the game sounded, it was actually very involved, creative and unique gameplay-wise. See, *Skool Daze* was another one of those very early open-world titles that helped to not just trailblaze the genre, but gaming as a whole. Being set in a very British public school, you had to attend classes, enjoy break-times, interact with other pupils and the teachers and so much more. The combination to the safe that you had to find would be revealed when you made the numerous shields placed around the school flash... And how did you make them flash? By hitting them, either use your slingshot to ricochet a projectile to hit the shields or you could even knock down a pupil/teacher and use their unconscious bodies to jump and reach them instead. However, if you got caught misbehaving, you would be given lines (think Bart in *The Simpsons* intro) the more you misbehaved, the more lines you'd be given. Too many lines (up to ten thousand) and it was game over. Yeah, it's all a bit 'WTF?', but trust me, the eccentricity and irrelevance all add to the game's humour and appeal.

Skool Daze was the idea of the husband and wife team, David & Helen Reidy. David would write the code for the game down on paper and then Helen was the one who would have to type all of that code into the computer... Hundreds and hundreds of lines of code. The basic idea for *Skool Daze* actually came from Helen who was (at the time) a school

66 OF THE MOST IMPORTANT VIDEO GAMES EVER!
(ACCORDING TO ME)

teacher. As well as drawing inspiration from *Just William*, a short story collection written by Richmal Crompton and classic British comic *The Beano*, particularly *The Bash Street Kids* comic strip. David Reidy also drew from his own experiences as a schoolboy, as he revealed in this interview with Retro Gamer magazine:

> "What I remember best are the things between lessons. Kicking balls around corridors, playing conkers, firing a catapult. Making fun of teachers. Making fun of other kids. And that was basically how I wanted *Skool Daze* to be. There'd be a major task to perform, but if you wanted to spend all your time beating people up, you could. Just like school."

It was that freedom that David alluded to there that really made *Skool Daze* stand out as a game. Yes, there was that main goal of trying to get that safe combination, but you didn't have to do it if you didn't want to. Just walk around the school, go to the classes… Or don't go to classes, sit on the stairs (which would annoy the pupils and teachers), write messages on the backboards, hit pupils and teachers with your slingshot and fists. David and Helen Reidy were the main duo behind the game, but they also drafted in help from Keith Warrington who was brought in to handle the graphic designs. Yet, Keith had never worked on a video game before as he was more used to working with pencils and paper, and he had to learn fast as he recalls:

> "I remember Dave saying that he'd got this new game idea. The graphics were going to be a bit… More than the other games. So he asked if I'd be interested in doing them. I was game for anything. I was mostly unemployed, and I had the time. So I thought I'd give it a bash. I sat down with Dave and basically learnt everything, what pixels were, all that, from him. I didn't have a Spectrum to start with. It was easiest to do line drawings over squared paper, then block in the squares to make it pixelated. I just kept blocking in and rubbing out until I had something that looked decent when I stuck it on the wall at the far end of the room. For the animations, I used tracing paper to draw alternate legs and arms. Then I'd hand the whole lot over to Dave. After a while, though, I just thought, 'This is ridiculous'. So I bought a Spectrum to do it all properly. But I still often found it easier to return to the graph paper."

And about those graphics, for the time, they were extremely well detailed and varied too. See, programmers use certain tricks to get around workloads, they'll reuse assets and sprites over and over to avoid having to program things if they could get around it. Yet the graphics, the pupils and teachers used in *Skool Days* were all unique. They all had their own look and style. Even the characters themselves each had their own personalities. The teachers were all different, not just the same sprite reused, a different sprite created for each of the teachers. They all acted differently too, Mr Wacker (the headmaster), Mr Rockitt (science teacher), Mr Withit (geography teacher) and Mr Creak (history teacher) were all individuals. They all had the same goal as antagonists of the game, it was their job to stop Eric from trying to get that safe combination. But they all had distinct and separate personalities too. As an example, Mr Wacker being the headmaster was the main teacher you needed to watch out for. He was fast, never missed a thing and had eyes like an eagle. But then you had Mr Creak, the older history teacher. He was slower and got confused easily, so you could misbehave in front of him and possibly get away with it.

That variation also filtered through to the pupils... Well three of them anyway. You had Boy Wander (the tearaway), Angelface (the bully) and Einstein (the swot). I always remember Einstein would be the one that would tell the teachers if you ever did get up to any shenanigans, he was a prick. But Angelface the bully was worse, he'd punch you in the face and disappear, then the teachers would give you lines for lying on the floor while he got away scot-free. David looks back on those characters he created:

> "All the characters are those comic book stereotypes, because by and large, all schools are the same. There's always you. There's always the popular people, who you hate, of course. There's always a bully. There's always a swot. And *Skool Daze* was about giving people characters they would recognise. And making it funny, and enjoyable to play. Which, of course, meant making it a little bit evil."

Another thing that was great about the characters was that you could rename them. Not just Eric the main schoolboy, but everyone. This was something I always loved doing whenever I played *Skool Daze*. Naming the in-game teachers after my own real teachers at the time... And then

66 OF THE MOST IMPORTANT VIDEO GAMES EVER! (ACCORDING TO ME)

hitting them with the slingshot (take that Mr Ferguson!). If any of my friends had pissed me off at school, I knew I could go home, load up *Skool Daze*, rename the pupils and punch them in the face. *Skool Daze* wasn't just a great game, it was a brilliant frustration and stress reliever too.

The sequel, *Back to Skool,* came in 1985. It was more of the same, but with a lot of new features. The addition of a girl's school, new usable weapons and items, more characters, including a girlfriend for Eric called Hayley and even more gameplay features. You could even 'commit suicide' by jumping out of a window. The truth is that *Back to Skool* is arguably the better game, a far better one you might say. Still, it was the original that really set the standard. There were even plans to make a third game in the series that never came about. Given the working title of *Eric and Hayley's Decathlon*, it was going to be more sport-themed as David recalls:

"It may not have even gone out under that title, but a few things were planned. It involved a lot of sheep. Helen and I had moved to the country by then, so after the mice and frogs in *Back to Skool*, we had to have sheep being let loose and running in and out of the school. But generally, it was going to be a pastiche of *Daley Thompson's Decathlon*, with ten 'sporting' events and various scenes holding it together. Events like Throwing the Hibiscus."

That *Skool Daze* influence can still be felt in the open-world genre today. I mean, the kings of the open-world genre, Rockstar Games themselves even had a stab at the game when they made *Bully*, which was basically a modern remake of the original *Skool Daze*. There have been several fan remakes over the years too. I recommend giving *Skool Daze Reskooled* on Steam a go if you want a trip down memory lane.

S. L. PERRIN

SUPER MARIO BROS.
DEVELOPER: NINTENDO
PUBLISHER: NINTENDO
PLATFORM: FAMICOM, NES
RELEASED: SEPTEMBER, 1985

And here we are, after his entanglements with a giant gorilla as Jumpman in *Donkey Kong*, Mario is introduced into gaming proper in his very own game (shhhh, don't mention the original *Mario Bros.* from 1983, it really messes up my point). Thanks to the success of *Donkey Kong,* Nintendo's Shigeru Miyamoto became the go-to guy for new game ideas. He teamed up with Takashi Tezuka to bring Mario running and jumping onto the home market.

The platform genre was doing well in both the arcade and at home. Namco's *Pac-Land* really proved just how exciting the genre could be and Miyamoto wanted to replicate that for the home market. He set out to design a fast-paced platformer for the Famicom console that felt like it came right out of the arcade. His initial concept design didn't even have Mario in it, all it featured was a 16x32 pixel square block that could move and jump. Due to the popularity of the single-screen arcade game *Mario Bros.*, it was Tezuka who suggested using Mario and Luigi for this new title. Knowing they couldn't call the game *Mario Bros.* as the arcade game already had that title, they were stuck for a name. It was as Miyamoto's concept design grew and when he added the famed mushroom power-up when the idea to add 'super' to the title came about and *Super Mario Bros.* was born. In fact, quite a lot came from that simple mushroom idea, as Shigeru Miyamoto recalls in this interview with 1Up.com:

> "The first game prototype we had going wasn't very good because you couldn't see very far ahead of you. People wanted to have more of the world visible on-screen, but I didn't want to make Mario any smaller than he was. So we decided to build the world on the scale of a smaller Mario, then make him larger in the final version. That's the moment we struck upon the idea of starting Mario out small and letting him get bigger later. Since the game's set in a magical kingdom, I made the required power-up item a mushroom because you see people in folktales

66 OF THE MOST IMPORTANT VIDEO GAMES EVER!
(ACCORDING TO ME)

wandering into forests and eating mushrooms all the time. That, in turn, led to us calling the in-game world the 'Mushroom Kingdom,' and the rest of the basic plot set-up sprung from there."

As the game grew, new ideas were added, some removed. Originally, Shigeru Miyamoto wanted the Italian plumber brothers to fly a ship and early on in development, the game almost became shoot 'em up, but the idea was quickly dropped. Those hidden bonus areas in the clouds found in the final game are a remnant of the shoot 'em up concept. In the original arcade *Mario Bros.* game, Mario and Luigi could be hurt if they landed on the turtles, this was changed for this game so they could jump on as many turtles as they like, a trait that would soon become synonymous with Mario. Then there was the big bad guy, Bowser. Originally, Miyamoto had the idea to make him an ox, but when Takashi Tezuka felt he should look more like a turtle, he became the king of the turtle-like creatures and the whole Koopa race was born. Miyamoto recalls how the classic, iconic and now, very familiar controls of *Super Mario Bros.* were also very different originally:

"During much of development, the controls were A for shoot bullets, B to dash, and up on the control pad to jump. The bullets wound up becoming fireballs later. In the end, we realized that being able to shoot all the fireballs you want while running gave Mario too much of an advantage, so instead we had it so you shoot only one fireball when you start running. That freed up the A button, and we made that the jump button. I really wanted to have A be the action button and make you press up to jump, but it definitely worked out better for Mario in the end."

Up to jump, isn't that blasphemous? Anyway, once Shigeru Miyamoto and Takashi Tezuka were happy with the final design for the game, they then sat down with a small programming team and got them to work. But it wasn't all plain sailing as the team found a few problems that needed working out. The storage limitations of the cartridges was an issue and some sneaky coding tricks had to be implemented to save space. Did you know that the bushes found in the background of the game are the same sprite as the clouds, just coloured differently? Quite a few sound effects did double duty too, to help save as much space as possible. Even the Goomba enemy was carefully designed as a single and static image that is just flipped back and forth, this gives the impression that it's actually animated when it's not. All sorts of tricks were used to save space to help cram in more and more levels.

The opening level, World 1-1 was very carefully designed to work as a tutorial, even when game tutorials didn't really exist then, and the amazing thing is that you didn't even realise it as you played. That first level's design philosophy was highly unique at the time and created specifically to teach the player the basics of the game very quickly. That first Goomba you see is a very simple kill for a reason, but you could just as easily avoid it. However, if you didn't kill/avoid it and it killed you, then there was no great loss to your progress and you could try again. This quickly got the player used to the jumping and attack mechanic. The first mushroom power-up was placed just-so, as to teach the player that they are helpful and not another enemy. See, the Goombas had a similar, rounded design to them as the mushrooms did, so the player just learning that the Goombas are bad, would most probably try to avoid the mushroom when it appeared. But the blocks were placed in the exact right place that when you would instinctively jump to try and avoid the mushroom, the block would force you back down into its path and make you pick it up. There were also the first three green pipes, each one made slightly higher than the last. This taught the player that holding the jump button made Mario jump higher. Then there was the use of the run/jump combo to clear bigger gaps. And even if you had played the level and gotten used to the new features quickly, there was replay value added via the hidden secrets and areas.

Yes, I know this all seems rather trivial and obvious now, but back then, this was all pretty new stuff. We hadn't really played platform games like *Super Mario Bros.* before, or at least, no platform games so well crafted. Plus, Mario wasn't the huge gaming icon that *Pac-Man* was then so we had to learn about his world. Playing *Pac-Land* for the first time, for instance, we knew that the ghosts were bad and how eating power pellets worked as power-ups, we knew this because we had played *Pac-Man* before it. *Super Mario Bros.* was new and while not Mario's first game, it did introduce a lot of what would become Mario lore for the first time. We had to learn how to play this game and that opening level

66 OF THE MOST IMPORTANT VIDEO GAMES EVER!
(ACCORDING TO ME)

was the perfect introduction. World 1-1 of *Super Mario Bros.* could be a contender for the greatest ever opening level to any game ever made, because it was just so perfectly designed, crafted and realised to teach you so much in such a short space of time.

Now, I can't talk about this game and not mention sound designer Koji Kondo. The man created Mario's main theme tune, a tune that has gone on to become famed in the world of gaming, perhaps the most famous piece of gaming music ever? Aside from that iconic Mario theme (titled *Ground Theme* or *Overworld Theme*), Kondo also created all the music for the game, including that awesome underground tune.

Super Mario Bros. kick-started the whole *Super Mario* franchise, which itself became the core of the entire Mario video game legacy and even for Nintendo as a company. *Donkey Kong* may have been Mario's first appearance, *Mario Bros.* may have been the first proper Mario game. But it was with *Super Mario Bros.* where it all really began and when Mario became a cultural icon. Plus there's the whole story of how the NES and this game, in particular, helped revive the entire game industry after the game crash of 1983, well in North America anyway. Now, that's got to be quite important, right? All that, and *Super Mario Bros.* is still a thoroughly enjoyable game to play today, thirty-six years after its original release.

S. L. PERRIN

GAUNTLET
DEVELOPER: ATARI
PUBLISHER(S): TAITO, ATARI
PLATFORM: ARCADE
RELEASED: NOVEMBER, 1985

"Wizard (or your choice of character) needs food… Badly!"

That's all I need to hear and the memories come flooding back. Just seeing the *Gauntlet* arcade cabinet back then was pure joy, the thing was an absolute beast. Those four joysticks gathered around the monitor, the bright and action-packed artwork displaying the four main characters, engaging in battle with demons and even Death himself. It was awesome. I can even vividly remember where I was when I first saw and played *Gauntlet* in the arcade. Barmouth, Wales, used to have three arcades just on the seafront. *Gauntlet* was in the smallest of the three, it was kind of in the middle of the arcade with a *Paperboy* cabinet sitting in front, against the back wall.

Early on in the game's development, it was given the working title of *Dungeons*. Being hugely inspired by the table-top RPG game, *Dungeons & Dragons* and the Atari 8-bit computer game, *Dandy* from 1983. Ed Logg, an Atari game designer and co-designer of classic titles such as *Asteroids* and *Centipede* was the main man behind *Dungeons* and was aided by a very small team. Just a few months before the game was set to be released, Atari realised that the name *Dungeons* was unavailable due to 'legal reasons', so a new name was needed and *Gauntlet* was unleashed into the arcades in the winter of 1985.

Using a top-down view, *Gauntlet* was an early example of what we would now describe as a dungeon crawler game. The main goal was painfully simple, all you had to do was make it to the exit of a level to advance to the next, rinse and repeat. But under that simple goal, *Gauntlet* housed some really engrossing gameplay. Along the way, you'd cross paths with various enemies, ghosts, grunts, demons, sorcerers and more… Even Death. Find treasure for points, keys to unlock doors, magic potions and food to keep your character alive. So far, so basic really. It was the characters where the game added depth.

66 OF THE MOST IMPORTANT VIDEO GAMES EVER! (ACCORDING TO ME)

Gauntlet offered simultaneous four-player action. Yeah, games in the arcade back then had two-player options, but four-player was something else... Like, twice as many players! Not only that, this wasn't one of those competitive titles like so many others were back then, this was cooperative. You really had to work together as a team to get the most out of *Gauntlet*. As for the characters themselves, there was Thor (red) the warrior, Thyra (blue) a valkyrie, Merlin, (yellow) the wizard and Questor (green) an Elf. But these characters were more than just different names, colours and sprites, they had their own strengths and weaknesses too. Thor was strong, could withstand and cause more damage but his magic usage was poor and he was slow. Thyra was a good all-rounder and had the best armour so could take more damage. Merlin was the weakest of the four with below average damage and speed, but his magic was the best. Then there was Questor who was very fast, decent magic, but he had much poorer armour and was susceptible to taking a lot of damage.

You had to master and use each of the four character's strengths and weaknesses to get the most out of *Gauntlet*. Players had to work together to try and conquer the games one-hundred-plus levels. Just running around, grabbing food and potions alone, while ignoring your teammate's needs really didn't work. That kind of gameplay and greed was a sure-fire way to an early grave. Sure, you could play the game in single-player, but you had better bring a few pockets full of coinage if you wanted to last more than a handful of levels. Strategy was key to playing *Gauntlet* properly. Use the mazes to your advantage to create bottlenecks to force ghosts and demons into a crossfire with one or all of your team. Have the warrior up front and working as a tank due to his extra strength. Merlin the wizard and Questor the elf as back up ready with their stronger magic, just in case. With valkyrie as the go-between, offering support to the other three. This really was a team game, learn to be cooperative or none of you will make it. I had never played a game like it before, as other games were always competitive, one versus another and not co-op. The fact it was simultaneous four-player really added a lot that other arcade games just didn't have back then, *Gauntlet* was unique...

S. L. PERRIN

Well, it was kind of 'unique' anyway. Remember when I said that *Gauntlet* was inspired by another game, in particular, the Atari 8-bit computer game, *Dandy*? Well, that 'inspiration' caused a bit of a furore in the guise of yet another legal disagreement (there's been a few of those in this book already). See, when *Gauntlet* became such a big hit, the designer of *Dandy*, John Palevich, threatened a lawsuit due to the staggering similarities between the two games. The case never went to court though as it was settled before a lawsuit could be filed. Anyway, you may think the settlement was a huge cash one as *Gauntlet* was such a big success... No. Palevich was awarded with an original *Gauntlet* arcade cabinet while the creator of the game, Ed Logg, had his name removed from the credits from all later ports and releases of *Gauntlet* as the original game designer following the dispute. Of all the legal cases surrounding gaming, this is probably one of the most low-key and civil ones. I mean, *Gauntlet* made plenty of money, yet here's a legal settlement that involved no cash and just the handing over of an arcade cabinet.

Before it was officially unleashed into the arcades, Atari was unsure if *Gauntlet* would be a success, so they did a very limited test release in the summer of 1985. They gave an early, pre-release cabinet to an arcade for free. The arcade was not allowed to promote the game and they had to share the coin drop numbers with Atari, so they could try and measure the popularity of the game before its release. As the game's main designer, Ed Logg was desperate to see if his game was going to be a hit, so he went along to watch the test himself. When he arrived, he found that representatives from Sega were taking photos of the cabinet and making notes of the game itself. The test unit was quickly pulled to avoid anyone stealing their ideas. Ironic all things considered.

Gauntlet was perfection in an arcade cabinet. As I sit here writing this, I can clearly hear the game in my head. Those digitised speech samples, the 'yowl!' as you get hit by a lobber, the metallic 'boing' when using a transporter, the ear-piercing shrill as Death drains your health with every passing second. One of the most important games ever made due to its compulsory co-op play, varying characters with their own strengths and weaknesses and just for being so damn playable. Even though we didn't realise it back then, *Gauntlet* was perfectly designed to eat our coins.

66 OF THE MOST IMPORTANT VIDEO GAMES EVER! (ACCORDING TO ME)

Endless dungeons (they just repeat after so many, the game doesn't have an end) and an always reducing timer cleverly hidden via health that you could top up with more coins... Think of it as an early example of a 'pay-to-win' game. If there is one arcade cabinet that I would love to own, then it is an original *Gauntlet* one.

Still, the game's development was not without its problems. *Gauntlet* was originally set to be released in late 1983 or early 1984. However, there were some lay-offs at Atari at the time and several people found themselves unemployed, so there were fewer people to work on the game. One of those people was Robin Ziegler, who was originally working on *Gauntlet* with Ed Logg. Then there was the complexity of the game itself, new hardware had to be created, *Gauntlet* was the first Atari game to feature speech, so it needed a voice chip that had to be designed. That's before we get into the actual four-player cabinet itself, something that had never been done before. It needed a bigger screen and a completely new cabinet design so all four players could get a good view of the screen when playing. Atari couldn't cut corners and save some money by re-purposing and updating some of their other unused cabinets, this beast had to be completely designed and built from the ground up. Even Ed Logg himself was pulled off the game development at one point to work on a LaserDisc game based on the famed *Road Runner* cartoon. Quick aside, that *Road Runner* game was made and released in 1985, but all the initial LaserDisc work was removed, though a prototype cabinet with the LaserDisc tech does exist (YouTube it). After which, Logg finally got to return to finishing *Gauntlet*.

Gauntlet was said to have had ads shown in cinemas at the time. I've searched the interwebs and couldn't find any solid proof of this, except for a brief mention in an archived Game Developers Choice article. Still, if true, I think that could be a first. Though I did find an animated ad for the arcade version from 1985, but I couldn't find out if it was for TV, the cinema or just general advertising used to entice arcade owners to buy the game for their arcades. Anyway, *Gauntlet* went on to spawn a very successful franchise with sequels, re-releases, remakes and reboots. The most recent *Gauntlet* game was released in 2014. Still, nothing was ever as good as the original, though *Gauntlet II* was very close.

S. L. PERRIN

THE LEGEND OF ZELDA
DEVELOPER: NINTENDO
PUBLISHER: NINTENDO
PLATFORM(S): FAMICOM, NES
RELEASED: FEBRUARY, 1986

Shigeru Miyamoto and Takashi Tezuka teamed up once again, after the success of *Super Mario Bros.,* to make one of the most important games ever... That's why it's in the book. In fact, Miyamoto and Tezuka worked on *Super Mario Bros.* and *The Legend Of Zelda* concurrently. Being conscious of not wanting to repeat themselves, they ensured the two games were polar opposites. *Super Mario Bros.* was to be a linear, sequential, A to B type game, but *The Legend Of Zelda* would be open and allow the player to explore. The main inspiration for *Zelda* came from Miyamoto's childhood, remembering playing in fields or exploring the forests and caves in and around Kyoto where he grew up, Miyamoto wanted to recreate that feeling of boyhood wonderment in game form. It has been said that *The Legend Of Zelda* is Shigeru Miyamoto's most personal game.

The basic story was always a paper-thin one, our hero, Link, must go up against the main villain, Ganon and his many monsters to rescue a princess, the titular *Zelda*. It really was typical and basic 'rescue the gal' stuff. But the bare-bones story wasn't what we gamers loved about *Zelda*, it was its world and mechanics the game offered. Though *The Legend Of Zelda* is far from being the first action-RPG-adventure game, it was the one that pretty much perfected the idea the first time around. The land in which the game takes place, Hyrule, was full of dangers, mysteries, puzzles and characters to interact with. It gave us players a multifaceted game world to play in, to explore and to discover.

Shigeru Miyamoto actually began to become concerned that players would not understand the openness and freedom that *The Legend Of Zelda* offered. He worried that the exploration aspect could possibly confuse players who were used to much more linear and single path games like *Super Mario Bros.*, as he revealed in an interview with Super Play Magazine:

66 OF THE MOST IMPORTANT VIDEO GAMES EVER!
(ACCORDING TO ME)

> "I remember that we were very nervous because *The Legend of Zelda* was our first game that forced the players to think about what they should do next. We were afraid that gamers would become bored and stressed by the new concept."

His fears kind of came true too when Miyamoto presented an early build of the game to Nintendo bosses. The suits complained that the game was confusing, too difficult to understand. Now, at this point, Shigeru Miyamoto had two options. One, pander to the bosses and make the game easier or more linear. Two, ignore the bosses and throw in a new challenge, Miyamoto went for the latter. He would watch people playtest the early version and soon realised that it wasn't the game that was confusing and difficult, but more a case of the players not understanding the type of game it was. See, originally, Link started out with his sword from the very start, so players would run off, sword in hand, and just go killing enemies thinking that was the point of the game, an arcadey-like action game. Shigeru Miyamoto soon learned that people didn't realise you had to explore the map and interact with characters to progress through the game. So he went away and added a new start, an easy-to-understand instruction where the player had to pick up the sword first. That opening screen at the very start of *The Legend of Zelda* where Link runs into a nearby cave and finds the old man that gives him the sword was enough to trigger players to understand that exploring, talking to NPCs and solving puzzles was the key.

Due to the vastly different style of game, when compared to others on the market at the time, other problems arose. Take Shigeru Miyamoto's previous title, *Super Mario Bros.*, as an example. In that game, you can finish it in around forty minutes or so, no speed-running, no shortcuts, a general play-through of the game can last less than an hour. With *Zelda* though, due to its openness, exploration, backtracking and so on, you're looking at several hours. If you really know what you're doing, then yes, you can probably get through the game in a couple of hours or so. But for first-time players who had to learn the game right from the off, that playtime was dozens of hours. Saving in games is commonplace now, but back in 1986, it was pretty much unheard of, which was why *The Legend Of Zelda* original release in Japan was on the new Famicom

Disk System. An add-on for the Famicom that used floppy disks called 'Disk Cards' which were cheaper to produce than the standard cartridges. This new format also allowed for various game enhancements, including writeable mass storage, meaning that games could be saved. *The Legend Of Zelda* was a launch title for the Famicom Disk System and went on to be a huge seller in Japan.

Two years later and *Zelda* saw a release in America, but technology had moved on by then and the save feature of the Famicom Disk System (never released outside of Japan) became obsolete, as an internal battery could be added to game cartridges to enable saves. In fact, the American release of *The Legend Of Zelda*, that iconic golden cart, was the first-ever home console game to feature a save feature built-in... Or so that's what many gamers have been told for years anyway. Yup, it's time, once more, to right an incorrect and often cited gaming fact. As mentioned, the American release of *The Legend Of Zelda* is said to be the first game that featured an internal battery backup that allowed the player to save their progress. But after some digging around and researching, I'm not so sure that it was. It seems that *Hydlide II: Shine of Darkness*, which was released the year before *Zelda* on the NEC PC-6001, before seeing a port to the MSX, had a battery backup save feature first. *Hydlide II* is a game that was clearly a massive influence on *Zelda* in many ways. As an aside, *Hydlide II* also featured a health regeneration mechanic. You stood still and your health would slowly regain itself, kind of like most games today. So then, does that make *The Legend Of Zelda* the second game to feature an in-built battery save? Errrrr, no. It seems that there was another, *Morita Shogi* for the Famicom. A take on the popular Japanese chess game was released just a few months before *Zelda* hit the market. As games of chess could go on for hours, days, even weeks, *Morita Shogi* allowed you to save your game at any time and pick it up again later. Was *The Legend Of Zelda* the first video game with battery backup saves? As far as I can tell, no, it's actually, at least, the third game that had that feature. Yet, you do a interwebs search for 'first game with battery backup' and tell me what pops up.

Anyway, back to the point. *The Legend of Zelda* originally had a subtitle for the Japanese version, a subtitle that never made it to the western release. To give the game its full and original title, it was called *The*

66 OF THE MOST IMPORTANT VIDEO GAMES EVER! (ACCORDING TO ME)

Legend of Zelda: The Hyrule Fantasy. Shigeru Miyamoto explains why that subtitle was dropped for the American release in this interview with Nintendo.com:

"It's a bit like *Final Fantasy*! We might've looked like copycats!"

Even though *Zelda* came first and even influenced *Final Fantasy* in several ways, Miyamoto didn't want the two games getting confused for one another outside of Japan or people thinking that Nintendo had copied Square's first *Final Fantasy* game.

Zelda's mix of exploration, adventure and use of items and weapons to progress soon became a staple of, not just future Nintendo games, but the entire action-adventure and RPG genre in general. The impact this title has had on the gaming world can not be overstated. It was the first Nintendo game to sell over one million units too. *The Legend Of Zelda* has created a magnificent legacy over its thirty-five years with sequels, ports and spin-offs a-plenty, a franchise that is still going strong today. But also a game that paved the way for so many other titles across the entire gaming world. Whilst action-adventure games were not exactly new at the time, they were pretty much unheard of on consoles yet, *The Legend Of Zelda* opened the floodgates to a new genre of games for console owners.

S. L. PERRIN

TURBO ESPRIT
DEVELOPER: MIKE RICHARDSON
PUBLISHER: DURELL SOFTWARE
PLATFORM: ZX SPECTRUM
RELEASED: MAY, 1986

This is perhaps, one of the lesser-known games in this entire book and another slice of Great British development and design too, but also a game that is most definitely important and massively influential. The basic plot of *Turbo Esprit* has you playing as a special agent who has to track down and stop an international drug cartel. You drive the titular (Lotus) *Turbo Esprit* around various cities and have to ram or shoot the bad guys to stop them. So far, it all sounds very much like Taito's classic *Chase H.Q.*, only two years before that even existed. But it gets much, much more interesting. See, it is the game's approach and freedom that really marks this one as so important. I mean, yes you had a mission to carry out, sure, but you didn't have to do it. You had the freedom to drive around any of the cities that the game offered however you wanted. Ignore the main story and just go explore. Each city felt alive too, pedestrians walked the streets, traffic lights actually worked (not that you had to obey them), other cars on the roads created traffic and stuck to the speed limit, indicators on the cars worked and so much more. Then best of all, it was in (pseudo) 3D as the buildings of the city flew by you.

Not only did this cops 'n robbers driving game pre-date *Chase H.Q.* by two years, this relatively unknown open-world crime-based and driving focused game actually beat the mighty *Grand Theft Auto* to the market by eleven years too. Just like the original *GTA*, it also featured multiple cities to drive and play around in. The locales included in *Turbo Esprit* were Wellington, Gamesborough, Romford and Minster. The game's designer and programmer, Mike Richardson, recalls why he chose those places in an article from Eurogamer:

> "I called one Wellington because that's where I live in Somerset. I was a bit stuck after that. Gamesborough was because it had the word 'game' in it and Romford because it has the acronym ROM. But Minster? I have no idea!"

66 OF THE MOST IMPORTANT VIDEO GAMES EVER! (ACCORDING TO ME)

Originally released on the ZX Spectrum before seeing ports to both the Commodore 64 and Amstrad CPC 464. It took Mike Richardson ten months to develop *Turbo Esprit*, which in the mid-eighties was a huge amount of time to make a game on a microcomputer. Still, all of that hard work can be seen on the screen. To experience this game in 1986 was mind-blowing. *Turbo Esprit* even had backing and help from Lotus themselves, as the ads for the game boasted 'technical assistance from the car's makers'. But that boast was not exactly 100% truthful (you really need to watch it when people make boasts like that as they can be very misleading). Now, as the game's developer, Mike Richardson, did get to take a trip to the Louts factory, he took pictures of the then-latest model of the car and even got to give it a test drive too, but he never got any support or 'technical assistance' from Lotus other than that. It seems that Lotus were just happy that their car was getting, what was basically, free advertising in the game. Even Robert White, the founder of publisher, Durell Software, admits as much:

> "To be honest it's all pretty hazy now, but we certainly didn't have a licence and we didn't get any technical support. They [Lotus] probably told us we could do anything that might promote them, but the 'technical assistance' claim was hokum I'm afraid."

Still, Richardson's trip to the Louts factory was worth it in the end as he managed to recreate the car pretty damn faithfully. From the title screen with a very decent looking Lotus Turbo Esprit to the in-game car model and even a very accurate interior and dashboard of the car which was used for the game's HUD. It's this level of detail in *Turbo Esprit* that really is impressive, even now. The previously mentioned working traffic lights, pedestrians, indicators on the cars, and so on. But there were more, windscreen wipers on the cars worked, random roadworks would block the roads, you even had to keep an eye on your fuel and top up at a garage when running low. Plus, everything was working independently of the player's actions. It was a real, living and breathing city. All those details, those little nuances that Rockstar's *Grand Theft Auto* franchise is famous for today, well *Turbo Esprit* was doing it over a decade earlier. Seriously, YouTube *Turbo Esprit* on the ZX Spectrum (or Amstrad as it looked better) and watch it being played. Bearing in mind that this was 1986 and on a home computer with only 48k of memory. It's unreal. Like *Elite* before it, *Turbo Esprit* is a technical marvel that really was ahead of its time and amazing that it even existed when it did. Even today, Mike Richardson considers Turbo Esprit one of the favourite games he ever made:

"It was the most technical game that I wrote during the Spectrum days, and was really technically the pinnacle of them all with things that I hadn't done before such as sprite masking, compact sprite mask storage, area fill and the internal map model in memory. But I'm very proud of all the Spectrum games I wrote. I really miss those times."

When it was released, *Turbo Esprit* was critically acclaimed. Respected Speccy magazine, Sinclair User, called it one of the best games ever made. Whether Mike Dailly of DMA Design (later to become Rockstar North) ever played *Turbo Esprit* or even knew of its existence when he came up with the idea that would eventually lead to *GTA*, I don't know. Though I find it hard to believe that he wouldn't have been aware of it, seeing as he and the rest of the guys that would go on to form DMA Design were very much into gaming then, and that they were building their company back in 1986. Either way, you can't deny just how much of an impact it had on the gaming world and how important *Turbo Esprit* really is… Even if you've never heard of it before now.

66 OF THE MOST IMPORTANT VIDEO GAMES EVER!
(ACCORDING TO ME)

LABYRINTH: THE COMPUTER GAME
DEVELOPER: LUCASFILM GAMES
PUBLISHER: ACTIVISION
PLATFORM(S): COMMODORE 64, APPLE II & MSX
RELEASED: JUNE, 1986

So, I had already written the first and second drafts of this book when I had a break and put this whole thing on the back burner for a while. I decided to re-visit some of my favourite childhood films to see if they still stood up today. I put on a few childhood classics and found myself watching the Jim Henson/Lucasfilm classic flick, *Labyrinth*. I was about halfway through the film (and really enjoying it too) when it hit me. There was a game based on the film, I remember playing it on my Commodore 64. Plus, it was a pretty damn important game too, cos... Well, I'll be covering that as I go. So, I got back into it and added this chapter while working on the third draft. Funny how ideas can just pop in your head like that eh?

I think it would be fairer to say that *Labyrinth: The Computer Game* was inspired by the movie, more so than being based directly on it. It was beardy Star Wars geek, George Lucas himself who requested a game of the film too, though according to all accounts, he really had very little to do with the making of the game itself. I mean, it was 1986, so Lucas was probably too busy (very wrongly) thinking that *Howard the Duck* would make a good film. Anyway, *Labyrinth* doesn't follow the plot of the film exactly, you don't play as Sarah trying to rescue her baby brother from Jareth the Goblin King either. What you actually have to do is create your own character. It's a very simple character creation, all you do is pick your name, gender and favourite colour. The game then generates a character from your basic choices. The idea of creating your own character, which was meant to represent you as the player, instead of playing as Sarah from the film, was a way to hopefully bring you closer to the game and give you a greater connection to the story. David Fox from Lucasfilm Games recalls with IGN:

"As a film *Labyrinth* felt like the whole thing was an adventure. So we thought that if you could play the game as yourself, and then have you go off on your own adventure, then that would work. And we did that by also staying fairly close to the characters and things that happen in the movie. Being an adventure game, I knew I didn't want to do a text-parser, so I came up with a slot machine user interface."

Once you had created your character, the game then begins proper. You find yourself in a very familiar-looking text-based type of adventure title, very *Zork*-like. But something was different. Unlike other text-adventure games of the day, there was no typing here. Instead of having to write out 'go north, 'pick up (item)', etc, you were given two separate word wheels, as David Fox alluded to in the above quote. The one on the left housed the verbs, while the right wheel had the nouns. The various screens of the game would be context-sensitive to fit with the use of those two word wheels and to make navigation and actions easier to input. The removal of the command-line interface for text-based adventure games like this was revolutionary, and good enough reason to be in this book, there's more to come, which I'll get to later.

Anyway, when the game starts, you find yourself in the real world and walking around the streets. You'll soon come across a cinema that is showing the *Labyrinth* movie, so you go in to watch it. Before the film starts, you chat to some of the other patrons and they talk about the movie, one being a super-fan who's seen the flick eighty-three times. The conversation turns to David Bowie playing Jareth, the Goblin King. It all gets very meta for a while and even brings up plot points of the film that the game is inspired by that you are playing.

The (in-game) film begins and this text-adventure game suddenly changes to a graphic-adventure one. There's Jareth on the screen in full 8-bit glory talking to you... And I mean YOU, as in the character you are playing as (hence the character creation at the start). Jareth addresses you by your name and says how you have become his thrall. In order to be freed, you have to enter the labyrinth, get to the castle in the heart and defeat Jareth, all in thirteen hours. This really is one of the best and most clever starts to a game ever. Text-adventure games were massively popular in the early eighties, but dying out by the mid-eighties, and there was this shift over to graphic adventure games going on at the time. So to start out as one dying genre, to then change into another more popular one was brilliant. It all felt very... Well, it felt very *Labyrinth* really.

66 OF THE MOST IMPORTANT VIDEO GAMES EVER! (ACCORDING TO ME)

Then there was the way the game included your (admittedly simple) details into the game that added a whole new layer. Jareth talking to YOU and breaking the fourth wall, all while supposedly watching the film that the game you are playing is inspired by. It was pure madcap genius writing and unlike anything we had ever experienced in a game before.

Then when the game starts proper (again), after the faux text-adventure intro and when you're actually in the labyrinth itself, in full-on glorious graphic-adventure game mode, it all just kicks up a notch once more. You walk around interacting with and talking to the characters from the film, trying to solve puzzles, just like in the film and the use of the word wheels instead of the more standard command-line interface just worked. *Labyrinth: The Computer Game* raised the standards of the text and graphic-based adventure games from that point on. But there is the most important factor of this game to cover next, this was the first-ever adventure game title from Lucasfilm Games.

See, after *Labyrinth: The Computer Game*, Lucasfilm Games (later to be called LucasArts) went on to dominate the graphic adventure sub-genre of games. They followed this game up with titles such as *Maniac Mansion*, which introduced another new interface for graphic adventures, Script Creation Utility for Maniac Mansion (SCUMM). A system that would go on to still be used today in graphic adventures. More games followed from Lucasfilm Games, *Loom*, *The Secret of Monkey Island* (no I'm not doing an insult sword fighting reference) and of course, *Indiana Jones and the Fate of Atlantis*, the greatest graphic adventure game ever made. Plus many, many other titles in the genre.

Lucasfilm Games became kings of the graphic adventure genre and their influence and impact can still be felt today. Those classic Lucasfilm adventure titles are still fondly looked upon as the best by adventure game aficionados. While that other big adventure game studio, Sierra, was stuck with an ancient word parser, Lucasfilm Games were changing the genre and gaming in general. It all started right here with *Labyrinth: The Computer Game* and all thanks to that revolutionary new verb and noun wheels that changed the landscape of adventure games from that day forward, as David Fox recalls:

"That was kind of the forerunner for what Ron [Gilbert] ended up using in *Maniac Mansion*. We figured that if you didn't have to figure out what word the parser is expecting, and instead provided a limited set of words that still let you do a lot of things, it's not at all constraining and you forget about the UI really fast."

Not only was *Labyrinth: The Computer Game* an utterly brilliant game in its own right that changed adventure games forever, along with birthing the mighty Lucasfilm/Arts adventure game sub-genre, it was a (rare) great movie tie-in as well. Added little titbit to finish on for you, the game actually became a bigger commercial success than the film too.

**66 OF THE MOST IMPORTANT VIDEO GAMES EVER!
(ACCORDING TO ME)**

METROID
DEVELOPER: NINTENDO
PUBLISHER: NINTENDO
PLATFORM(S): FAMICOM, NES
RELEASED: AUGUST, 1986

What's this, a Nintendo game in this book that's not from Shigeru Miyamoto? I'm quite shocked myself. *Super Mario Bros.* was an all-action platformer, while *The Legend of Zelda* was more of an open-exploration type of a game. But what would you get if you blended the two together and wrapped it up in a gloomy sci-fi setting? *Metroid* (a portmanteau of the words 'metro' and 'android') is what you get.

Metroid was actually a co-development project by Nintendo's own Research & Development No. 1 Department and Intelligent Systems Co., Ltd, the latter being a very close affiliate of Nintendo. The game was produced by Gunpei Yokoi, who created the whole Game & Watch system, (debatably) invented the cross-shaped D-pad, which is still used today by pretty much everyone, as well as being the designer of the original Game Boy hand-held console too. To put it bluntly, he was pretty fucking big at Nintendo. One of the game's artists, Yoshio Sakamoto, talks of one of *Metroid's* major influences with Retro Gamer and whether *Metroid* really fit what Nintendo was doing at the time:

> "I think the film *Alien* had a huge influence on the production of the first *Metroid* game. All of the team members were affected by H.R. Giger's design work, and I think they were aware that such designs would be a good match for the *Metroid* world we had already put in place. To be honest, I've never really been clear on what is or isn't the 'Nintendo look', but as far as we were concerned, we were just projecting another image from within Nintendo, another face of Nintendo, if you like."

So yeah, *Metroid* was hugely inspired by Ridley Scott's seminal horror-sci-fi classic movie, *Alien*, especially H. R. Giger's wonderfully grotesque, yet beautiful creature designs. *Metroid* was a game that pulled from various sources to make one of the finest and most important games ever. The game may have used the previously released,

S. L. PERRIN

The Legend of Zelda's openness, exploration and weapons/items concept that aided the progression style of gameplay, but it removed the friendliness and cheery-like nature of *Zelda*. Instead, favouring a far bleaker style of desperation and a deep feeling of solitude vibe. The atmosphere felt in *Metroid* was unlike anything else on the market at the time. It really was quite a daring move to make a game feel so downbeat and desperate, a game that was so 'not Nintendo'. Games were about escapism, the sunny and happy world of *Super Mario Bros.* was the perfect antidote to a hard day at school. Then there was *Metroid* and its stark, darker edge that opened the doors for so many other titles that came after it. A bleaker tone to console gaming was born.

So, the plot. Space Pirates have stolen samples of the *Metroid* creatures, a parasitic life-form that can drain the life from any organism and kill it. The Space Pirates plan on turning the *Metroid* creatures into biological weapons to kill all living beings who challenge them. Playing as Samus Aran, a lone bounty hunter tasked with infiltrating the Space Pirate's base. You have to find and destroy the Mother Brain, a biol-mechanical life-form that controls the Space Pirates, to stop their nefarious plan.

Even the plot of *Metroid* is dreary and grim. Up to now, especially with Nintendo games, it was all about rescuing the maiden (princess) fair. Then along came this game and set up biological terrorist Space Pirates, human-killing alien organisms and more. It was a much more cinematic approach to creating a plot, a more grown-up slant to a medium that was aimed towards a much younger audience at the time. As I said before, very much inspired by 1979's *Alien* film, and that was hardly kid-friendly was it? Given the fact that games are much more immersive than movies and that you control the action yourself, as opposed to just sitting there watching a film, you feel much more in tune with what was going on. *Metroid* was one of the first (perhaps the first) games to really capture that feeling of engulfing the player in an atmosphere and even offering a more artistic sense of purpose in a video game of this type. Yeah, we had text-based adventures before this, but they really felt like interactive books, yet *Metroid* was more like a true interactive movie. As Yoshio Sakamoto stated in a blog post on siliconera.com:

"*Metroid* first came into being as our desire to create a game that took place in a gloopy, alien-like world."

66 OF THE MOST IMPORTANT VIDEO GAMES EVER!
(ACCORDING TO ME)

And they did just that. But it wasn't just the darker, H. R. Giger inspired graphics and more grown-up approach to storytelling that made the game stand out, as there were the sounds and music of the game too from composer Hirokazu Tanaka. The title screen of *Metroid* offers a memorable and truly haunting opening, featuring a minimal, desolate piece of music that just sets the tone perfectly, before you even press the start button. I think music theorist and composer Andrew Schartmann put it best in his book, *Maestro Mario: How Nintendo Transformed Videogame Music into an Art* when he said:

"Tanaka's greatest contribution to game music comes, paradoxically, in the form of silence. He was arguably the first video game composer to emphasize the absence of sound in his music. Tanaka's score is an embodiment of isolation and atmospheric effect, one that penetrates deeply into the emotions."

It really does too, you can tell that this game will be something special before you even play it, just from that opening title screen. The in-game music, when most of the action takes place, is much more upbeat than that 'silent' and foreboding opening tune though and it drives you to keep playing, it almost works as an antithesis to the game's darker tone and style. Those *Zelda*-like fanfares when you pick up a new weapon or item, the heart-pumping music during the boss fights and more. It's all just so beautifully orchestrated and oozes atmosphere from the opening title screen right up to the ending credits. But how did Hirokazu Tanaka feel about his music in the game? Well, he talked about the *Metroid* score with Gamasutra:

"I had a concept that the music for *Metroid* should be created not as game music, but as music the players feel as if they were encountering a living creature. I wanted to create the sound without any distinctions between music and sound effects. The image I had was, anything that comes out from the game is the sound that game makes. I suppose some of the players felt it was little bit too heavy. Back then, many people said the game music for *Metroid* was too serious. However, I believe I succeeded in emphasizing the characteristic of *Metroid* by synchronizing the theme of the music with the theme of the gameplay where a player must escape from an underground maze."

I feel that's a really convoluted way of saying that the musical score of *Metroid* was awesome. And yes, I guess I have to talk about the now famed ending. *Metroid* actually featured five different endings, one of the first games to feature multiple finales. Depending on how fast (or slow) you did finish *Metroid*, you would see one of the five resolves. Plus there was the surprise reveal that under that spacesuit, Samus Aran was female all along. Not the first female protagonist in a game, but certainly one that was an interesting revelation at the time. Interesting titbit time, the English manual for the game actually refers to Samus as 'he'. Whether this was intentional as to keep the secret that Samus was female all along or just a translation error is not known, but I'm guessing translation error.

For want of a better word, *Metroid* just felt so 'alive', a wonderful melding of specific gameplay elements that are still used today. With the addition of the great *Castlevania* franchise, *Metroid* went on to create its own genre of gaming, the portmanteau of the Metroidvania sub-genre. There just wasn't a game like *Metroid* back then, a title that dragged you into its very specific gloomy style and engulfed you with it. A game that was dripping in atmosphere and one that oozed substance too. *Metroid* felt like you were playing a sci-fi-horror flick. It placed you in a dark maze of a game and offered you little to zero help. You just had to play it, explore, try new things until you found what worked and what didn't. A true slice of genius game design in every aspect, graphically, audibly and of course, gameplay-wise too.

Even now, debates are made for and against as to whether games can or should be considered art. For me, *Metroid* was gaming's first proper argument for them being a true art form and melded that feeling of cinematic feels and gaming excitement really damn well.

66 OF THE MOST IMPORTANT VIDEO GAMES EVER! (ACCORDING TO ME)

OUTRUN
DEVELOPER: SEGA
PUBLISHER: SEGA
PLATFORM: ARCADE
RELEASED: SEPTEMBER, 1986

Nintendo had Shigeru Miyamoto and Sega had Yu Suzuki. Remember when I mentioned in previous chapters how, when walking around the arcade, you could hear certain games before you even saw them? Well in *OutRun's* case, you don't even have to be in an arcade. Any *OutRun* fan should be hearing composer, Hiroshi Kawaguchi's *Magical Sound Shower* in their head about now as they read this chapter.

Game designer, Yu Suzuki had already created some of the best Sega games with *Space Harrier, Hang-On* and *Enduro Racer* to name a few of his hits, the last two both being bike racers. Suzuki wanted to make a new racer inspired by one of his favourite films, 1981's *The Cannonball Run*. He wanted to capture the excitement and scenery of the film and America in general. Suzuki then had a realisation, America is just too big of a place, one that features a lot of wonderfully scenic and very open, but ultimately boring roads. So, he then set his sights on Europe as inspiration for *OutRun's* setting instead and went on a two-week tour. As Yu Suzuki himself recalls in an interview with Retro Gamer:

> "I felt that I should first actually follow such a course myself, collecting information with a video camera, a still camera, and other equipment. I started out from Frankfurt, where I hired a rent-a-car, and I installed a video camera on the car. I drove around Monaco and Monte Carlo, along the mountain roads of Switzerland, stopping in hotels in Milan, Venice and Rome, collecting data for a fortnight."

Driving around Europe in a BMW 520, Suzuki began to take videos, photos and copious notes of many of the places he visited. It was while he was in Monaco when Yu Suzuki found the star for his new game, a Ferrari Testarossa, which had only been in production less than two years before. Suzuki fell in love with the Testarossa from that point on and upon returning to Japan and Sega's headquarters, he began work on

OutRun. He asked Sega for a Ferrari Testarossa to use as the model for reference, a task that was harder than you realise as there was only a tiny amount of them in the whole of Japan at the time. It took several weeks to track down a Testarossa in Japan, and even then, all Suzuki and his team could do was take photos and record the sounds of the car. Yu Suzuki did ask Sega to buy a brand-new Ferrari Testarossa for him to use as a 'reference', but they refused... Nice try though.

Still, with all of the research from his European trip, Yu Suzuki had the basis for his new game. He didn't want to make a racing game like others, games that would focus on making the driving as thrilling as possible. Instead, Yu Suzuki wanted to make a racing game that focused on the 'pleasure' of driving over the thrill of it. The big and open roads, the eye-catching scenery, the sun shining overhead in *OutRun* were all very conscious decisions made for the game to make it as appealing to the eyes as possible. However, his ideas began to grow too big for the game itself and several of Suzuki's ideas never made the final cut:

> "I was only able to put around half of the things I wanted to do into *OutRun*. Because of budget and development time limitations, some of the content I'd planned had to be squeezed or cut. I'd made preparations for eight individual characters and I wanted to include various events at each checkpoint, which would have made the player experience a story, something like *The Cannonball Run* film. I also wanted to give players a choice of supercars to drive, so that they could enjoy differences in car performance."

It's a damn shame Yu Suzuki's original ideas didn't make it into the final game, multiple characters and cars, a story, etc. Still, what we got was rather amazing regardless. Playing *OutRun* back then was like nothing else. We may have had driving games before it, but *OutRun* just felt so different and original. Yu Suzuki's idea of making a game that celebrated the joy of driving over racing thrills really hit the spot. Just seeing *OutRun* being played with its sun-kissed environments, buttery-smooth gameplay and those unbelievable scaling sprites (super-scaler technology as it is known) really had an effect on me as a young gamer. But to actually play the game was a whole other level. The sense of speed was insane, the freedom of the open road was exhilarating and the awesome music just topped off an already amazing gaming experience.

66 OF THE MOST IMPORTANT VIDEO GAMES EVER! (ACCORDING TO ME)

If you were lucky enough to find one of the deluxe, sit-down arcade cabinets, then you were in for a real treat. It featured force feedback on the steering wheel, but best of all, it also had hydraulics. The sit-down cabinet featured a (stripped-down) car model that you could sit in and it would react in time to the action on screen, not just move and tit when turning, but also dip when the car went over bumps and hills, plus the steering column would shake if you crashed. This particular arcade cabinet really was a thing of beauty and is the very best way to play this masterpiece of a game. If anyone wants to donate one to me…

OutRun has itself quite a legacy too with plenty of sequels over the years, as well as the original making special appearances in other Sega games like *Shenmue* and the *Yakuza* franchises. For me, *OutRun* really is something special, even today. It's just timeless, still just as playable now as it was over thirty years ago. That red Ferrari, those blistering graphics and Hiroshi Kawaguchi's heart-thumping, toe-tapping music. *OutRun* is just a beautiful blending of elements that have been perfectly mixed. Yu Suzuki created one of the most important video games ever and opened the door for many more arcade races to come. Even today, when people play an arcade racer, it's often compared or likened to *OutRun*.

Dude wearing sunglasses, blonde girl by his side and a blood-red Ferrari. *OutRun* was the eighties defined in video game form. The sense of power, adrenaline and exhilaration was unmatched. No arcade could ever truly be complete without an *OutRun* cabinet, it's just one of those classics that needed to be there. Is there such thing as the perfect arcade game? I'm not sure, but *OutRun* is pretty damn close to it. Just to finish, did you know that despite starring the beautiful Ferrari Testarossa, that *OutRun* was never officially licensed or endorsed by Ferrari?

S. L. PERRIN

DRACULA
DEVELOPER: ROD PIKE
PUBLISHER: CRL GROUP
PLATFORM: COMMODORE 64
RELEASED: SEPTEMBER?, 1986

I have to admit that I'm not 100% sure about the release month for this one (again). I've had to go off an archived review and my own jaded memories to form a rough time frame. Still, that's not really all that important, why it is in this book is the main event.

What *Zork I* put in place back in 1980, in terms of text-adventure games, was beginning to die out six years later. The text-based game was making way for the more advanced graphic adventure game genre, thanks to *Labyrinth: The Computer Game*. Yet, some studios were still knocking out those 'old-timey' text-based adventure games. Over the years, text-based adventure games had been based on everything from superheroes (*Questprobe Featuring The Hulk*) to classic literature (*Lord of the Rings: Game One*) and more. Still, there was one area that the text-based adventure game had not yet sunk its fangs into... Until now.

East Anglian, Rod Pike developed a text-based adventure game for the British publisher, CRL Group, back in early 1986 called *Pilgrim*. It was a very average adventure game, to be honest, nothing really worth shouting about and it was pure text too, with no graphics. Those simple text-based adventure games like *Zork I* had evolved into having, at least, some basic graphics to help tell the story by 1986. However, due to the lack of any graphics in *Pilgrim*, it was given pretty mediocre to poor reviews in the gaming mags. What the game lacked in terms of visuals, it certainly made up for with its atmosphere though. *Pilgrim* may have been an average text-based game at best, but it most certainly oozed mood and style from every word. Rod Pike managed to really bring atmosphere to the text-based adventure. As CRL founder Clem Chambers remembers in an interview with Eurogamer:

> "*Pilgrim* was a dark and Gothic piece, and we therefore logically thought, let's ask Rod to do a horror game."

66 OF THE MOST IMPORTANT VIDEO GAMES EVER!
(ACCORDING TO ME)

The horror game genre was still relatively new in the mid-eighties, the few titles that did exist were usually action-based games and even so, they were never really horror games. Games inspired by horror IPs, sure, but not actual games that featured genuine horror and they would usually feature more cartoony-like presentation and graphics. But if they could get it right and make a horror game with the bleak, Gothic tone of *Pilgrim*, and one based on a great book, then CRL could really have something that would stand out.

The timing couldn't have been better either as by 1986, the whole 'video nasties' thing was going on here in the UK. Just a very quick history lesson. The video nasty thing was a period when the British Board Of Film Classification (BBFC) were heavily censoring or even outright banning a lot of horror films due to their content. And so, decent horror entertainment was pretty hard to come by for a while. However, there was one area where the BBFC didn't hold much sway, Video games. So in theory, a game could be as bloody and gory as it wanted to be and quench the thirst of horror fans who were being starved of their entertainment back then. Now, while the BBFC didn't have to rate video games, that didn't mean they couldn't rate video games, and while they could rate them if submitted... They couldn't actually censor or ban them like they were doing with horror films at the time. That was when CRL's Clem Chambers came up with the idea of making a game so bloody and graphic, that if they did submit to the BBFC, they could give it an adult rating, but would not be able to ban it as a 'video nasty', as it's not a video. All while hoping that the adult rating would do wonders for sales of the game too.

Plus, seeing as text-based adventure game were far quicker and easier to design than an action game (lack of animations, reliance on simple to type up text, etc), that meant the game could be produced relatively quickly and easily. So that was it, Clem Chambers got Rod Pike to make a gruesome horror game based on the immortal, Bram Stoker's *Dracula*. Only unlike Pike's previous text-only game, *Pilgrim*, this text adventure game would have graphics... And gory ones at that. All just to get an age rating from the BBFC. With the game basically an interactive version of Stoker's novel, all Pike really had to do was adapt what was already there. Then, once that was done, the artists at CRL worked on the graphics, vampires with blood dripping from their fangs and faces, grizzly death scenes when your character died... Which, given the game's difficulty, was much more prevalent than your average video game. Once the game was completed, CRL took it to the BBFC and hoped for an adult classification. The thing was that the BBFC had no idea about video games, they just rated films. So one of the head guys at CRL (Michael Hodges, CRL's game development leader) had to go through the game at BBFC headquarters, showing them (mainly) the bloody images. Once they saw what the game could do, the BBFC began to worry that the title could find its way into the hands of children. Exactly what CRL wanted, well that and the obvious publicity the game would bring.

The BBFC's biggest issue was with the death scenes, seeing as your character would be displayed in glorious C64, 8-bit pixels in various graphic demises. Having your throat slit, being impaled on spikes, eyes pecked out by a bird, eaten by rats and so much more. Though we are talking Commodore 64 graphics here, they were still highly detailed and full of gore, and they certainly got the attention of the BBFC. They gave the game an age rating of 15. In fact, the BBFC said of the game that:

> "Because the way in which the player loses is always by dying, it was felt to be unsuitable for persons under fifteen who might find it frightening to lose several times in solitary play prior to bedtime."

So CRL got what they wanted... But not quite. They were aiming for the highest rating the BBFC gave back then, an 18 certification. So the slightly lower age rating was a tad disappointing even though that rating made people want to buy it and the publicity it brought really did help too, as CRL hoped from the start.

Still, CRL knew they were onto something, and so they made more games in the same bloody vein. A title based on *Frankenstein* followed, also given a 15 rating by the BBFC. That higher age rating just didn't seem possible with a video game and yet, CRL still craved it, like a vampire craving virgin blood. That craving was quenched with the next two games in the series. *Jack the Ripper* and *Wolfman* released in 1987 and 1988 respectively were both given that coveted 18 age rating. CRL

66 OF THE MOST IMPORTANT VIDEO GAMES EVER! (ACCORDING TO ME)

finally had what they wanted. Looking back, Clem Chambers is more than happy with CRL's *Dracula* being the first-ever video game to be age rated:

> "I still feel very happy about it. It meant we had a hit and that meant we could make payroll. Payroll was the drumbeat we worked to because you were only ever thirty days away from disaster when you were self-funded as CRL was. I don't think anyone ever had a nightmare having played one of our games.
>
> You know, I once met Sir Christopher Lee and told him I'd spent my whole childhood having nightmares about him, he just looked me in the eyes and said 'Fairy tales, dear boy, fairy tales.' And compared to Sir Christopher Lee and his fangs, our games didn't even move the dial."

Most people seem to think that 1992's *Mortal Kombat* was the first video game to be given an age rating (more on this later). Not true, it was this simple but effective text-based adventure game from 1986 that was the first. Not only that, *Dracula* really opened the doors for what horror games could get away with on the screen too. From this point onward, horror games were created proper. Your *Resident Evils*, *Silent Hills*, *Dead Spaces* and so on, it all began right here in Blighty. Plus, this was a game that really got me into reading and writing at a young age too, more so than going to school ever could. So if you're enjoying this book, this game is the reason why it exists… That's got to be pretty important, right?

S. L. PERRIN

DOUBLE DRAGON
DEVELOPER: TECHNŌS JAPAN
PUBLISHER: TAITO
PLATFORM: ARCADE
RELEASED: JULY, 1987

Back in 1986, Technōs Japan developed the scrolling, street-gang based beat 'em up, *Renegade*. Published by Taito for the arcade, the game was partly inspired by the 1979 film, *The Warriors*... Well, at least it was for its Western release. The original Japanese version (*Nekketsu Kōha Kunio-kun*) was actually about a high-school delinquent. Anyway, *Renegade*, which was designed by Yoshihisa Kishimoto, was a big hit, and obviously, a sequel was on the cards.

Taking the basics of *Renegade* and building on them, Kishimoto got to work on the sequel. The idea of co-op play was included (so it could make more money), larger levels were added and the idea to pick up and use weapons was thrown in too. It got to a point where this sequel, while still very much a scrolling beat 'em up, was drifting away from what *Renegade* was. So the game was given a new name and would go on to become its own franchise, *Double Dragon*.

I suppose that I may as well quickly cover what happened to *Renegade*/*Nekketsu Kōha Kunio-kun* while I'm here. Well, that itself split into two separate franchises. *Renegade* became its own series with sequels on the home computers. While *Nekketsu Kōha Kunio-kun* (despite being the same game, just the Japanese version) spawned its own separate franchise, the *Kunio-kun* series of games... Which itself had many of its own spin-offs and sequels and more too. I honestly can't think of another game series in history that is as confusing as *Renegade*/*Nekketsu Kōha Kunio-kun*/*Double Dragon*.

Anyway, back to the topic of this chapter, *Double Dragon*. Playing as one, or both (in co-op) of the Lee brothers, Billy and Jimmy. You have to set out to take on the Black Warriors gang, who are ruling the streets. Members of the gang pay an unwanted visit to the Lee brother's home and kidnap Billy's Girlfriend, Marian. Yup, it's 'yer basic 'rescue the girl' plot as Billy and Jimmy punch, kick and (mostly) elbow their way through dozens and dozens of bad guys, making their way to the Black Warriors gang hideout, to take out the big boss-man and save the fair lady Marian.

We already know by now that *Double Dragon* was not the first scrolling beat 'em up, but it most certainly was the one that put the genre on the map and added a lot of variety and depth to the games back then. A huge arcade smash, before being ported to pretty much every home computer and console. I mean, there's even an Atari 2600 version! *Double Dragon* really enthralled the 11-year-old me at the time. The big and bold sprites, the smooth animation and crunching sound effects. Oh, then there was that kick-ass, heart-pumping soundtrack. I still remember seeing that big, bald bad-guy, Abobo, smash his way through the brick wall near the start of stage one (just after the poster featuring a VW Beetle). I was genuinely in awe. *Double Dragon* had a slick, yet 'grimy' feel to it. The game looked, sounded and played brilliantly. Yet, there was all the street-gang stuff going on, the dominatrix-like female enemy with the big whip and a bigger cleavage. There was certainly a deliberate element of sleaze added to the game. If you manage to get to the end of the game and save Marian, there's even a sneaky panties shot (removed from the home versions). Technōs were definitely aiming for a specific style.

Of course, I have to mention the ending if you play in co-op, as it seriously raises a lot of questions. When both brothers risk their lives to save the girl, you are pitted to fight each other to the death to see which one of the two gets to take her home. Now just think about this ending for a second. According to the story of the game, Marian is Billy's girlfriend, so why are the brothers having to fight over who gets her? Then, if Billy does win, he just killed his own brother to get to keep the girl he was with anyway. But if Jimmy wins, he just killed his own brother to get with a girl who is clearly a whore and will just go for the last person standing, regardless of who it is. Doesn't matter how you try to slice this one, that is one seriously fucked up ending to a game eh? Committing fratricide to save a whore who doesn't care who she's with.

Technōs as a developer had a good run, but they are no more, despite the amazing success of *Double Dragon*. Yoshihisa Kishimoto, creator of the franchise recalls their demise with Polygon:

> "*Kunio-kun* and *Double Dragon* became franchises after their initial success. Technōs wanted to continue them because both franchises made money, and as a result, I wasn't able to create many other original projects while working there. I got tired of making games for the same franchises. Also, over the years the company made a lot of money and started spending it on real estate and even bought a racing team, so it was spending less and less on game development. Ultimately, I got fed up with the way it was handling its finances."

Double Dragon went on to spawn a very successful franchise. Sequels and remakes for thirty years from the original in 1987 to the most recent *Double Dragon IV* from 2017... Oh and a so-called 'film' too. Even with that three-decade pedigree, I'm still drawn to the first game over all the others. There was just something about it that worked and even now, the original *Double Dragon* holds a very special place in my heart as it was the first arcade game that I ever finished... With heavy use of the elbow move of course. As for *Double Dragon's* influence? Well, Yoshihisa Kishimoto had his say on that too:

> "There are ten-thousand fighting games released every year, but they're all based on the mechanics I created. The systems and hardware have improved drastically, and I haven't kept up with all of them, but in terms of fundamental game mechanics, I still think I'm the best."

Well, that's a ballsy statement for sure... But it's also one that's pretty hard to argue against though. Yoshihisa Kishimoto did define a genre when he made *Double Dragon* and the mechanics he introduced are still widely used today too.

**66 OF THE MOST IMPORTANT VIDEO GAMES EVER!
(ACCORDING TO ME)**

METAL GEAR
**DEVELOPER: KONAMI
PUBLISHER: KONAMI
PLATFORM: MSX2
RELEASED: JULY, 1987**

There aren't too many games where you get to play as a character whose name basically translates to 'erect penis', but this is one of the very few... Or only. Often cited as the first-ever stealth game, and that's another thing that many gamers are wrong about. Okay, so let's get this cleared up first. By definition, a stealth game is one where you play as a character who, instead of going for an all-out blitzkrieg, you try to avoid the antagonists of the game to complete the game's objective. Yes, *Metal Gear* most certainly fits that definition, but it was far from the first. Just off the top of my head, the original two *Castle Wolfenstein* games were stealth games, the first released in 1981, beating *Metal Gear* to the market by six years. Also from 1981, Sega released *005* in the arcade, a parody of James Bond. In fact, *005* is listed in the Guinness World Records as being the first-ever stealth game... But it's not true.

Oh yeah, I've checked and double-checked. It was a very little known Japanese game called *Manbiki Shounen* (*Shoplifting Boy*), released in 1979 that was the first stealth video game. It was on the Commodore PET personal computer and developed by Hiroshi Suzuki. In it, you play as a young boy who had to shoplift (hence the title) while trying to avoid the shopkeeper. There was even a sequel in 1980, *Manbiki Shoujo* (*Shoplifting Girl*). I guess someone needs to update the Guinness World Records.

And so, back to *Metal Gear*. So it wasn't the first-ever stealth game, but it certainly was the one that popularised the genre. Directed and designed by the legendary Hideo Kojima, *Metal Gear* saw you playing as a member of the special forces group FOXHOUND called Solid Snake. Snake is a rookie, sent out on his first mission to learn what happened to Grey Fox, another member of FOXHOUND who went missing. Look, this is a Hideo Kojima game and trying to explain the plot would take up an entire book, so let's just skip. Snake manages to rescue Fox and he learns that there's a nuclear-equipped bipedal walking tank codenamed *Metal Gear*. Snake has to stop the behemoth and discovers plenty of secrets along the way.

So, here's an interesting titbit for you. *Metal Gear* was not originally a stealth game at all. In fact, it wasn't even originally a Hideo Kojima title either. *Metal Gear* began as a very different title indeed. The game was already being worked on before Kojima got involved however, its development was struggling and Kojima was brought on board to try to get the thing under control. The game that Kojima found himself working on was actually an all-out action game. Publisher, Konami had a pretty big hit with *Green Beret* (*Rush'n Attack*), a John Rambo-esque side-scrolling, shooty, stabby-stabby platformer in 1985, and they wanted to follow up on it. Now, the follow-up was never meant to be a full-on sequel, but an action game in the same vein as *Green Beret*. Konami just wanted another action-packed military-styled game.

But there was a problem, *Green Beret* was an arcade game. Homeports followed, but it was originally released in the arcade. Anyway, this new *Metal Gear* game would be released on the MSX 2 home computer which, was not only little known outside of Japan, but also vastly underpowered compared to arcade machines and even some of the other home computers. There was just no way it could handle a fast-paced, action game like *Green Beret*. In fact, it was the issues with the hardware that helped shape *Metal Gear* into what it would become. When the action got intense, the game would crash the MSX 2, and when I say 'intense', I mean more than two enemies on screen at the same time. So Hideo Kojima realised that they needed to cut back on the action. Taking inspiration from popular culture (something he would become famed for in the future), that being the movie *The Great Escape*, Kojima thought that instead of having to try and kill dozens of enemies... What if you just had to try and avoid fewer of them instead? Another influence for the game came from a childhood classic playground game, as Hideo Kojima recalls at a BAFTAs lecture:

"Of course, *Metal Gear* was based on the concept of hide & seek, and I wanted people to experience that tension that you experience when you're playing hide & seek."

66 OF THE MOST IMPORTANT VIDEO GAMES EVER! (ACCORDING TO ME)

Sneak around the enemy instead of trying to take them on, hide from the enemy and avoid direct combat. Yup, the technical limitations of the MSX 2 computer are what led to Hideo Kojima changing *Metal Gear* from an all-action *Green Beret* style game, to a much more slower paced and stealthy game. Kojima took his idea to the heads at Konami and they hated it. In fact, Hideo Kojima shared some images on his Twitter feed a few years back that showed early design documents with the big and very official red 'REJECTED' printed across them. Oh how Konami hated the idea, still, Hideo Kojima carried on regardless.

As great as Kojima's ideas were for *Metal Gear*, I think he was influenced by other games I've already covered. Namely, *The Legend of Zelda* and *Metroid*. Playing as Solid Snake, you start with nothing, yet as you progress, you find and use new weapons and items that make you more powerful and able to access new areas of the game, plus there is the cinematic nature of the game that certainly feels very *Metroid* too.

When it was released, *Metal Gear* sold pretty well, but it didn't exactly set the gaming world alight. Mainly due to the fact that the MSX 2 computer it was released for was just not known outside of Japan. It did have a very small following in Europe, where a really badly translated from Japanese version of the game hit the market. There was also a NES port later… And it's terrible. Hideo Kojima had nothing to do with the NES version and a lot of the content and his ideas were cut, including the titular *Metal Gear* itself. Yup, the NES version of *Metal Gear* didn't have *Metal Gear* in it. And Hideo Kojima had been very vocal on the poor quality of Nintendo's version for a few years now:

"It was just all-round bad. I wasn't involved with the Nintendo version at all, and yet it sold millions in America. And of course, I didn't really like what was going on, I'd never played the game because it kind of rubbed me the wrong way, but then one day I saw it in a bargain bin being practically given away for free so I bought it out of curiosity.

The MSX version, it started immediately while you were embarking on your stealth mission. But the Famicom version or the Nintendo version started a few steps ahead of that, before you embark on your mission. And you're trying to make your way to the building that you have to infiltrate, and these Dobermans come out. And honestly, no matter what I could do, I could not get past that stupid Doberman without being spotted.

I got frustrated with it and I never played it from that point on. I couldn't even get to the first stage without feeling frustrated, and that's just terrible. Although I didn't play the game all the way through to the end I have spoken to people who have, and I've heard that it's a *Metal Gear* game but there's actually no *Metal Gear* in the game. At the end there's a giant computer monitor, and when I heard that I just thought that's not right."

The Nintendo port 'not being right' is a massive understatement I think. It was fucking atrocious, a deep insult to Kojima's work and original vision. Looking back, it's truly amazing that *Metal Gear* became what it did. A hugely successful franchise with one of the deepest and most twisty-turny game stories ever. The original game had everything going against it, including the publishers themselves and that awful NES port too. Here's a little secret, I personally don't like *Metal Gear* as a game or franchise. Between you and me, it makes me feel asleep. 2004's *Metal Gear Solid 3: Snake Eater* is the only game in the series I actually enjoyed playing. Yet, the first game's importance can not be ignored and despite my lack of love for it, it most definitely deserves my respect, something Konami have not shown Hideo Kojima or the *MGS* franchise for a while now.

**66 OF THE MOST IMPORTANT VIDEO GAMES EVER!
(ACCORDING TO ME)**

THE KING OF CHICAGO
DEVELOPER: CINEMAWARE
PUBLISHER: CINEMAWARE
PLATFORM: AMIGA
RELEASED: DECEMBER, 1987

Metroid really hit a nerve amongst us gamers with its cinematic gameplay style and opened the doors to more thematic and even dramatic storytelling in video game form. And then there was developer/publisher Cinemaware (founded by Bob and Phyllis Jacob), a literal mushing together of the words 'cinema' and 'software'. Cinemaware wanted to create truly cinematic games... And they did just that. Their first couple of games, *Defender of the Crown* (an Errol Flynn/swashbuckling movie-inspired game) and *S.D.I.* (a Cold War-era space drama) really hit the mark too. They both had strong visuals and cut-scenes, coupled with impressive movie-like storytelling, all mixed with some rather innovative and interesting gameplay mechanics to boot. But it was their third game, which was designed by Doug Sharp, *The King of Chicago* when they would really nail that blending of cinema and software that the studio strived for. Studio co-founder Bob Jacob recalls his influences with Gamasutra:

"I was a hardcore gamer myself, but I developed certain concepts for what I liked about games and I wasn't seeing them in the games that I bought. I was a fanatic arcade gamer, and I realized that there were certain things about the fun in arcade games that I wanted to bring to the home marketplace. I also decided that movies would be a great and creative motif for doing games, people like movies, right? It gave us virtually an inexhaustible supply of ideas."

How best to sum up *The King of Chicago*? I guess you could call it an action-adventure, strategy-management game that uses classic Hollywood mobster movies of the thirties and forties for inspiration as its settling. You play as Pinky Callahan, a young gangster setting his sights on taking over Chicago after the notorious Al Capone is jailed for tax evasion in 1931. The game is really split into several mini-games with a little bit of micromanagement thrown in. You have to keep an eye on your budget, hire henchmen, pay bribes, etc to help take over Chicago one area at a time. The mini-games included bombing runs, assassinations, shoot-outs, car chases and more. Plus you have to maintain relationships, via multiple-choice conversations, with your girlfriend, the Mayor of the city, the press and other gangsters to try to keep them on your side, at the risk of having them turn against you. There really was a lot going on in the game and various gameplay styles that all worked together to create a very unique title at the time.

What made *The King of Chicago* really stand out was how varied and multifaceted the story told is unfolded. From branching paths, alternate endings and even alternate starts too. The game would randomly begin differently each time you played, though the main plot and aim of the game was always the same, how you achieved the goal of taking over Chicago really changed depending on how you played as the game featured a genuine branching system. Now, I don't mean like the faux branching we have today. Titles like the Telltale adventure games (*The Walking Dead*, *The Wolf Among Us*, etc) give you choices to make, yet they never actually affect the story in any meaningful way, you just get to see a slightly different cut-scene. Whether or not you chose to cut off Lee Everett's arm after being bitten by a zombie in *The Walking Dead* game, as an example, makes zero difference to the narrative of the game. He dies either way, so the cutting off (or not) of the arm is completely redundant despite having the choice to do so.

Some other modern games offer you a simple pick of two choices, usually a good or bad choice. These are often forced in and feel very irrelevant in the grand scheme. But in *The King of Chicago*, your actions could and would change the story of the game. There were no pointless decisions in the main story, as each decision you made had a deep impact on the plot and the characters. You didn't just see a slightly different cut-scene, you saw a different story. Character's attitudes would change depending on how you treated them. Nothing was ever static, it was always changing and each time you played, the game would be different. Just going back to the randomness of the start I previously touched upon. While the game would always start with Pinky (your character) trying to take over the northside HQ and trying to become the new boss of the gang, he would actually start at different

66 OF THE MOST IMPORTANT VIDEO GAMES EVER!
(ACCORDING TO ME)

times, places and points in the taking over of the HQ. Perhaps the gang would have a bombing planned for later, maybe they wouldn't. The old man, the gang's leader, could be in a strong position or he could be losing his grip, or even already dead. The rest of the gang could be thinking about looking for a replacement for their boss or they could be very much against anyone going up against him. How you handled each part, what path you chose to take affected the next part of the game. There were more factors that could change the way the game played too... And this was just the opening few minutes and the start of *The King of Chicago* remember. That randomness, those multiple branching paths, the alternate scenarios, scenes and set-ups carried over into the main game and right through to the finale. A finale that of course, would also change depending on how you played.

About those endings, there were loads of them. Not just a good or bad ending like we get today with our 'choices' that really don't mean anything. There were multiple different good endings, just as there were multiple different bad endings. Of course, your aim was to take over the whole city and become *The King of Chicago*. But more often than not, your game would end with the gang turning on you (because you treated them badly, didn't pay them enough, etc), your girlfriend running into the arms of a rival gang boss and becoming a spy against you, or even you being arrested. You could even end up in the electric chair, and even then, the choices still came as you could pick your final words before the switch is flipped and you were fried. Even though it made no difference to the game from that point on... Cos you'd be dead and all that, you could still choose what to say. It was amazing just how many choices you had in this game, relevant or not. You could go out like a bad-ass mobster boss, feeling like a real cinematic bad guy. It played like a video game version of those Choose Your Own Adventure books and it was awesome.

As mentioned, Cinemaware made games that felt very cinematic. Musical scores, proper scripts and each of their games was always inspired by the movies. *The King of Chicago* was obviously trying to recreate the look and feel of classic mobster movies. Even when you paused the game, the cinema feeling was there as you would be greeted with a little 'intermission' of various refreshments dancing their way to the lobby, just like those old cinema ads. But it wasn't just all the in-game shenanigans where Cinemaware plastered their love of films, even the disks the game was on were actually called 'reels', while the file you had to click on to start the game was called a 'projector'. Though the game was full of cinematic-like details, they really kind of made it up as they went along, as Bob Jacob remembers:

"This game was created by Doug Sharp, a school teacher in Minneapolis. When I put the first four Cinemaware titles in development, no one really knew what an interactive movie should be. We were all just guessing. We tried different things."

The King of Chicago wasn't Cinemaware's first foray into cinematic games, nor was it their last. My personal favourite was the monster B-movie inspired *It Came from the Desert*, complete with giant ants threatening a 1950s small town. But I feel it was this game that truly captured the cinematic feel the studio was pushing for. Plus, the sheer amount of choices and different scenarios the game offered was unmatched at the time too. I often scratch my head when playing modern games today and the pointless choices they offer us and wonder why, given the advancements in technology, why no one now is doing what Cinemaware was doing so damn well thirty-four years ago?

Now, the Amiga version was not the original release. *The King of Chicago* was on early Apple Macintosh computers, with their limited monochrome display and it featured some rather 'disturbing' digitised images of clay models for the graphics. Honestly, that original version of the game is truly haunting. But it was given a huge graphical overhaul and a visual and audible redesign for the Amiga port. It is the far superior Amiga version that most people remember and the one I first played. Just for the freedom and choices the game gave you, this is an important one. But then when you get into the whole blending of cinema and games, no one did it better than Cinemaware at the time and *The King of Chicago* is a wonderful example of this.

66 OF THE MOST IMPORTANT VIDEO GAMES EVER! (ACCORDING TO ME)

SUPER MARIO BROS. 3
DEVELOPER: NINTENDO
PUBLISHER: NINTENDO
PLATFORM(S): FAMICOM, NES
RELEASED: OCTOBER, 1988

Yup, it's that damn Italian-American ex-carpenter/ape abuser turned plumber/princes rescuer once more, and not for the last time either. The original *Super Mario Bros.* most certainly got the ball rolling when it came to platform games on home consoles and it really was the genesis of the entire Mario craze. But for me, it was with this sequel, *Super Mario Bros. 3,* where the evolution of Mario truly began. Of course, Shigeru Miyamoto is back as designer and director, back too was his sparring partner Takashi Tezuka. There was just something about when these two worked together that created pure Nintendo excellence. I think that one of the most interesting details about this game was that, early in development, Takashi Tezuka wanted to break the then Mario tradition and make a very different looking game, as he revealed in an interview with Nintendo.com:

"When we first began development, we wanted the game to have an overhead perspective, rather than a horizontal one."

Yup, *Mario 3* nearly became something very different during those original pitch ideas. From digging around and the info I've uncovered, the view was not going to be a fully overhead one, but more of an isometric one. A pseudo-3D, *Zaxxon* style thing. This new viewpoint was toyed around with early on, but Shigeru Miyamoto felt that it just didn't suit a traditional Mario game as this would be. He felt that you needed to see Mario's legs and feet to help with the platforming action that the series was famed for. Or as Miyamoto put it himself:

"He [Tezuka] said he wanted to look from a little above. But in *Super Mario Bros.* it is important whether Mario's feet hit the ground or not, even barely. With a diagonal view from slightly overhead, you lost your sense of distance to the ground. So I told him that development would be difficult."

Even though a more traditional view was used for the final game, there are still a few remnants of that isometric/3D idea in the game itself. The title screen with the chequered floor, the shading and shadows on some of the in-game platforms were there to highlight the pseudo-3D look the game originally almost had.

While the core gameplay of *Super Mario Bros. 3* remained pretty much unchanged, it did bring a lot of new ideas to the table too. Mario now has more actions than ever before, aside from his usual running and jumping, he can turn into a raccoon, use his tail as a weapon and even fly too. He can become a frog which helps with swimming and jumping when on dry land. There's the hammer suit that gives Mario the ability to throw hammers and even deflect certain attacks. Perhaps the most unusual power-up (and that's saying something) in the game is Kuribo's shoe, where Mario jumps in the shoe and this allows him to jump higher and stomp on tougher enemies. That is on top of all the usual powers and other items found in the game's levels. And about those levels too…

Mario 3 offers some of the most creative game worlds and levels in a platform game of the time, or even now. From starting out on very typical Mario-esque fare, to finding yourself in a world in the clouds, underwater, desert, ice and the ever foreboding final dark world where the main villain himself, Bowser resides. Oh don't worry, I'm not leaving out the giant world either where all platforms, blocks and enemies have been increased in size. One of the most visually pleasing and fondly remembered Mario moments ever. But it wasn't just the worlds/levels that made this game stand out, it was the way everything was brought together to create this huge and seemingly open world. The map screen where you got to chose your level on each world made everything feel much more alive than ever before in a Mario game. *Super Mario Bros. 3* really crammed a lot into the cartridge.

The whole game is one beautifully crafted piece of software. The mini-games, the power-ups, the levels themselves all felt like every possible detail had been polished to the point of perfection. Yet at its heart, the basic and much loved Mario gameplay was still there, not lost in all the new additions, but in fact, enhanced by them. Mario's multitude of skills via the power-ups really was amazing, don't forget, this was all on the two-button Famicom/NES controller. I've played modern games where

66 OF THE MOST IMPORTANT VIDEO GAMES EVER! (ACCORDING TO ME)

the protagonist doesn't have a control scheme that feels so 'right' with so many variables on a controller with a dozen or so buttons. Simply put, *Super Mario Bros. 3* perfected the controls for a platform game and very few games since have managed to follow.

Super Mario Bros. 3 was the last game that Shigeru Miyamoto had a designer credit on. For all of his games after *Mario 3*, he was credited as producer/director. For me, this is the most perfect 2D platformer.... Though if I'm being honest, I actually prefer *Super Mario World* on the SNES. However, it was right here with *Super Mario Bros. 3* where the greatness of the series and the sheer brilliance of the entire Mario franchise was truly born. Oh, and let's not forget Koji Kondo back as the composer for the game, who loved the fact that the advancements in the game cartridges meant he could be more creative with his music as he recalls:

> "Well, we had a lot of special sounds for the Famicom/NES, but we couldn't use them since they required a lot of memory. But by the time we developed *Super Mario Bros. 3*, we were able to use all those sounds because the cartridges had advanced and more memory became available. We could now use sounds like percussion and timpani, so the music became much richer compared to the original *Super Mario Bros.*"

Plus just to add to this title's importance, how many video games do you know that have had a Hollywood movie made for them. I don't mean a game to movie adaptation thing, I mean a movie made just to help promote the game itself?

Yes, I am going to cover 'that film' and yes, for that I am very, very sorry. In 1989, Universal Pictures released the family film, *The Wizard*. The film told the story of Jimmy Woods, a young kid who is suffering from PTSD after his twin sister died via drowning (you know, for kids!). Jimmy is committed to an institution by his mother and step-father (you know, for kids!). Jimmy's older brother, Corey, sneaks Jimmy out of the institution and takes him to 'Caliiiiifoooooorniaaaaa' (as Jimmy keeps annoyingly bitching about). When his parents learn Jimmy is gone, they hire a ruthless bounty hunter to force him back home (you know, for kids!).

Anyway, now in 'Caliiiiifoooooorniaaaaa', Corey enters Jimmy into 'Video Armageddon', a massive gaming contest... Well, a Nintendo specific contest, held in Universal Studios Hollywood. Long and very tedious story short, Jimmy takes part in various Nintendo game challenges, the biggest one being on the (at the time) unreleased in America, *Super Mario Bros. 3*. I'll not spoil the shitty ending, but let's just say that this was less an actual film and more an advertisement for both Universal Studios Hollywood and Nintendo, especially *Mario 3*. I'm not even going to get into the plot hole of how Jimmy knew about the secret warp in a game he'd never seen before. He suffers from some kind of disorder that may or may not be autism (it's not actually mentioned in the film), but being autistic doesn't make you some kind of future foreseer.

The Wizard is an awful, awful film, and ~~probably~~ the worst thing *Super Mario Bros. 3* has ever been associated with. Still, even with that very black mark against its name, the game is utterly brilliant and set a very high bar for platform games to be measured by for decades. One of the greatest games ever may have spawned one of the worst films ever, but I just can't hold that against it.

66 OF THE MOST IMPORTANT VIDEO GAMES EVER! (ACCORDING TO ME)

SIMCITY
DEVELOPER: MAXIS
PUBLISHER: MAXIS
PLATFORM(S): AMIGA & MACINTOSH
RELEASED: FEBRUARY, 1989

Who'd have thought that pretending to be a mayor in a game while planning/building a city and ensuring the roads were kept traffic free could be so damn interesting and fun?

Will Wright designed a game called *Raid on Bungeling Bay* for the Commodore 64 in 1984. The game was a top-down shooter type of thing where you control a helicopter, which has to bomb several war factories on numerous islands. What was quite remarkable about the game was that the longer the game went on, the factories on the islands would grow and develop. Interdependency would begin to show between islands. Supply boats would sail between them, as an example, as if they were trading between the islands. The longer this trading went on, the more advanced the islands would become. The factories would also evolve and they would develop more and more advanced weapons and defences, making your mission to destroy said factories harder and harder to achieve. It was a quite stunning piece of AI and an ever-evolving game world in a game that is often very much forgotten about these days.

Raid on Bungeling Bay also came with a built-in level editor, so you could create your own islands to destroy, which Will Wright said he enjoyed experimenting with more so than playing the game itself as he recalls in a Gamasutra interview:

"I was learning the Commodore [64]. Graphics were very important back then. I was trying to find things on the Commodore that you couldn't do on the Apple. I came up with the idea of this big scrolling window, and I'd always loved helicopters. So I just basically designed the end game around the technology, around what you could do on the Commodore that you could not do on the Apple. While I was making it I had to build other programs to help me build that program. I had to build a program that would realign character sets. Another one would let you scroll around the world and place these little tiles to build these islands and roads and such. I had more fun with that actually than flying the helicopter around."

This idea of creating your own islands in the game and the way the islands had a life of their own and ever-evolving, gave Wright an idea. A game where building and maintaining an island was the whole point. Will Wright had also been reading the short story, *The Seventh Sally or How Trurl's Own Perfection Led to No Good*, by Polish sci-fi writer, Stanisław Lem. The tale was about an engineer who creates a miniature city with AI citizens. With all of that going on in his head, Wright began developing his next game for the Commodore 64 in 1985 called, *Micropolis*, a game where you could design a city.

What was strange about this new game was that there was no goal. You couldn't necessarily win or lose at it. Brøderbund who had published the previously mentioned *Raid on Bungeling Bay* saw no point in the game at all and declined to publish it. Will Wright was sure he had something special with his new *Micropolis* game, and so he went to every major game publisher around at the time, none of them saw any merit in it and all turned it down flat. Will Wright had a great concept for a new game, but nobody was interested in backing it.

It was 1987 when Will Wright met Jeff Braun at a pizza party (whatever that is). Long story short, the two of them teamed up and co-founded a new software house, Maxis and they published their very first game in 1989. There was a bit of a legal issue though, Wright's city building game, *Micropolis*, was technically owned by Brøderbund because Wright used their computers while under contract with them, to make his new game, even if they didn't want to publish it, Brøderbund still had a legal claim to it. By the time all the legalities were worked out, the Amiga had become the dominant gaming machine while the Commodore 64, which the game was originally designed for, was dying out. So Will Wright took that *Micropolis* game idea, updated it, and even gave it a new name, *SimCity*, and it was finally given a proper release in 1989 for the Commodore Amiga and Apple Macintosh computers (though the original C64 version did eventually get released later). Will Wright remembers those early years:

66 OF THE MOST IMPORTANT VIDEO GAMES EVER!
(ACCORDING TO ME)

"I earned enough off of that game [*Raid on Bungeling Bay*] to live for several years, and that's when I was working on *SimCity*. I had my daughter around that time, took about a year off when she was born. That's around the time I met my future partner, Jeff Braun, and showed him *SimCity*. At that point he'd been running a small Amiga company making font-editing software, he wanted to get in the game business. He wanted to start a game publisher, and so together we started Maxis. *SimCity* was one of our first games."

As for the whole Brøderbund owning the game sticky wicket, they and Maxis actually had a great relationship according to Wright:

"When I started working on *SimCity*, I showed it to Brøderbund and they said, 'Sure, let's do it.' But they kept wanting to change it. I'd kind of programmed it to the point where I thought it was done, and they didn't think it was nearly done. They kept wanting a win/lose. They were expecting more of a traditional game out of it. But I always wanted it to be much more open-ended, more of a toy. So they never published it. They never gave me any money for it either, so I never got the advances. I wasn't in any real financial obligation. So it just sat on the shelf for several years.

You know, the Commodore version was all done; it was just never published. When Jeff and I started Maxis, we just went back to Brøderbund and said, 'Hey, we want the rights back,' and they said, 'Sure.' Then we invested our money into programming the newer versions of it. We were a very small publisher; we actually ended up working with Brøderbund as our distributor, so Brøderbund still got their slice of the pie. They were instrumental in launching Maxis; they were just really nice people, and they were showing us the ropes, and financially helping us, in terms of inventory management and all that stuff. We were like an affiliate publisher with Brøderbund for several years after that."

SimCity does exactly what it says on the tin. It's a simulation of running a city. You start with a piece of land, some money and away you go. While there is the objective of building a city, there are no real goals or even a game to 'win'. *SimCity* is completely open-ended, giving you the power to do whatever you want with your city, within the restrictions of the game's universe. Build residential areas for people to live in, those people will need jobs, so build industrial zones to provide employment in factories. Commercial zones are used for shops for your people to buy goods and provide jobs too. Place roads so your residents can get around the city, put down trains tracks for an improved transit system, if/when the traffic gets too much. Your city needs power, so build a power plant and power lines to provide electricity to your residents, and so much more.

But you can't just place buildings anywhere you like. Putting residential areas close to industrial is a bad idea as the pollution caused by all those factories will upset your people. And you really want to keep them happy as it's their taxes that keep you in money to help the city grow and evolve. Still, you don't want to place residential areas too far away from where the jobs are either, otherwise, they'll spend too much time commuting. Then, you'll need your people to relax and enjoy life, so build entertainment spots. Sports stadiums, parks to beautify and keep residents happy. Oh, but you need laws too, so build police stations and fire departments to keep crime down and control any fires. Build a port so you can trade with other cities, an airport to attract tourists. You just keep building your city, gain more money from taxes to build more of your city. Go from a tiny borough and grow to a sprawling metropolis.

While there was no goal to achieve in the standard play mode, *SimCity* did come with a scenario mode. Here, you would be given a goal and usually a time limit to achieve it too. Maybe you need to reduce traffic in Bern, Switzerland, 1965. Do something about the out of hand crime in Detroit, USA, 1972. Deal with mass fires in Hamburg, Germany, 1944. While there was no story to speak of, these scenarios were inspired by real-world events. Some of the events were pure fiction too. I mean, there was one where you have to sort out the (non-copyright infringing) Godzilla problem in Tokyo, Japan, 1961.

Godzilla was just one of several special events called 'disasters' and they were not just found in the scenario mode either. Your very own custom city could be affected by earthquakes, nuclear meltdowns, floods, fires, plane crashes... Even alien invasions! These disasters could occur completely at random, or the player could even trigger one themselves at

66 OF THE MOST IMPORTANT VIDEO GAMES EVER!
(ACCORDING TO ME)

will from the menu. Used for when you wanted to shake things up in your peaceful city and show your residents just how great of a Mayor you were as you fixed the problems these disasters caused.

SimCity was a huge hit and soon saw ports to pretty much everything. It also began Will Wright's career proper, and he would go on to create even more 'sim' games, including the mighty, *The Sims*. Praised for its openness and originality, *SimCity's* influence can still be felt today in games like *Cities: Skylines* and the *Tropico* franchise. *SimCity* birthed the urban planning genre of games... And yes, that's a genre that exists and it's still popular today too.

Here's an interesting titbit to finish with. The SNES version of the game featured a character called Dr. Wright (named after Will Wright) and Dr. Wright has appeared in other Nintendo games, including *Zelda* and the *Smash Bros.* franchises. Aside from creating a new genre, *SimCity* itself went on to spawn its own successful franchise with numerous ports and sequels. The most recent game being *SimCity: BuildIt* from 2014.

S. L. PERRIN

POPULOUS
DEVELOPER: BULLFROG PRODUCTIONS
PUBLISHER: ELECTRONIC ARTS
PLATFORM: AMIGA
RELEASED: JUNE, 1989

There have been a wide variety of gaming genres covered already, but now, something God-like. So, I'm about to look at a game from Peter Molyneux, one of the world's most detested game designers and published by Electronic Arts, one of the world's most hated game companies. But this was eighties Molyneux and EA, before all of that disgust and hatred even existed. In fact, this was Molyneux's first proper game... And what a game it was too.

So the basic idea behind *Populous* was relatively simple really. Grow your small gathering of people into a larger one. Have a larger population than the opposition on the map, then attack and destroy them to win. How you did this was via a raise/lower land mechanic. You would raise/lower land so your peeps could build homes, the flatter the land, the bigger the home and the bigger the home, the more people could populate it. The more and the bigger houses you had, the more your *Populous* would grow. But what gave this game its unique edge was that you didn't play as or control the little peeps directly yourself, you played as a God. It was your influence as said God that allowed you to manipulate the land, use Godly powers and other features to reach the goal of taking out the opposition. As simple as the game's premise was, its depth lay in its mechanics of being a deity. *Populous* was the first-ever God game and yet, it was all born from something so simple.

Bullfrog's artist, Glenn Corpes drew a basic landscape, in an isometric style after playing and being inspired by the games, *Spindizzy* and *Virus*. He had no idea what he was going to do with it, he just drew it. Peter Molyneux saw the drawing and came up with the idea to fill the land with little people ('peeps' as he called them) and built an early development demo. Between both Molyneux and Corpes, they began to play tennis with ideas, hitting concepts and suggestions back and forth between each other for the little peeps to have something to do. To help keep the frame rate up and to avoid major any slowdown, when there

66 OF THE MOST IMPORTANT VIDEO GAMES EVER! (ACCORDING TO ME)

were too many peeps on screen, the idea that the peeps would build houses was born. To partly help control the peeps from just walking around, the idea to raise/lower the land came about. Slowly but surely, a game began to emerge. Peter Molyneux famously used Lego to help describe how the land manipulation would work in the game, to help sell the idea to publishers. In fact, Les Edgar, co-founder of Bullfrog Productions, tried to sell the concept to Lego themselves, as he remembers in the interview from Edge magazine:

> "We couldn't sell it to anyone. I even rang up Lego, and tried to explain the idea to them. They didn't like the good versus evil idea for some strange reason, so they weren't interested, which is funny when you consider all the Lego sets with laser guns, cowboys and Indians, and so forth."

Anyway, though there was no interest from anyone to publish the game, Peter Molyneux and Glenn Corpes carried on regardless. While Copse handled the graphics and overall art (he created the book/HUD thing for the game, etc), Molyneux concentrated on the coding. Eventually, Les Edgar found a publisher with Electronic Arts and around the same time, Molyneux suffered a massive hard-drive failure and lost the source code for the game. There was no backup either, *Populous* as a game was gone. It took a great deal of pretty much of non-stop work, but Peter Molyneux re-wrote the entire game from scratch. Glenn Corpes remembers that the second build of the game was better than the first, so losing the initial source code was a good thing in the grand scheme.

It was this second build of the game where the idea to add God powers and more features came from, and the game began to really take shape as Molyneux recalls from the same Edge interview:

> "The first effect we put in was the volcano. We had this idea that a little power bar could grow when your people were inside their houses. That led to the introduction of earthquakes and swamps, but there was still one big problem. How could you finish a game more quickly? The last thing we added, and the solution, was the knight, the ability to combine the little people into one big soldier to go and fight."

S. L. PERRIN

All the time the game was being worked on, it never had a clear goal other than to defeat your opponent. The idea to use these powers made that goal far more interesting and added depth to the overall gameplay. When it was released, *Populous* was unlike anything else on the market. Even Peter Molyneux himself wasn't sure how people would react to it:

> "I can remember worrying, 'People are going to think this is completely weird.' We'd already seen that loads of publishers didn't get it and, as we had a comparatively bad deal with EA, we weren't really expecting any royalties. Without showing someone, or better still, letting them play *Populous*, we didn't really know how best to explain it."

The worries of royalties were short-lived though. Bullfrog's first payment was for £13,000. The one after that? £250,000, which the team at Bullfrog initially thought was a mistake. *Populous* was selling and selling well, as gamers lapped it up. It was something completely new and unique at the time and an entirely new gaming genre was born, the God game (gaming magazine ACE were the ones who came up with the God game moniker as a descriptive). But I think another interesting nugget is the fact that originally, *Populous* wasn't a single-player game. In fact, it was one of the very first examples, of what we would now call, a multi-player title as Molyneux recalls:

> "We linked up machines with a serial cable, which led to early multi-player games. Multi-player *Populous* came way before the single-player game. It was far more strategic and quicker than we thought it could be, flattening the landscape for your team. We even coined special terms for what we would do, like 'sprogging' and 'nippling'."

And no, I have no idea what 'sprogging' and 'nippling' are either. Back then, I was very much into arcade-style games, shooters, platformers and so on. Titles I could quickly pick up and play with ease. I used to watch my bother playing *Populous* on his Amiga and never got it, I found it boring. Then one day, I just decided to play it myself and once I learned its mechanics, I fell in love with it. *Populous* is the game that got me into games of depth, games that required some thought and games you had to learn to play. Even today, I have a major soft spot for these types of games and will quite happily sit there for hours playing them.

66 OF THE MOST IMPORTANT VIDEO GAMES EVER!
(ACCORDING TO ME)

PRINCE OF PERSIA
DEVELOPER: BRØDERBUND
PUBLISHER: BRØDERBUND
PLATFORM: APPLE II
RELEASED: OCTOBER, 1989

Platform games were becoming all the rage by the late-eighties, that Italian moustachioed plumber Mario, and his brother had already popularised the genre by then. As great as those Nintendo games were, they lacked 'something'. The gameplay was there, the characters were there and *Mario 3* really showed what could be done in terms of variety and creating a game world... But it still lacked 'something'. Rescuing princesses just needed a little more bite. Game designer, Jordan Mechner had already had some success with his first game, *Karateka* from 1984. A scrolling beat 'em up that had a touch of the cinematic about it. Mechner's second game was *Prince of Persia*, and what a belter of a game it was too.

Set in ancient Persia, you play as an unnamed protagonist, who over the years just became known as The Prince, and he has to rescue a princess. Evil vizier, Jaffar locks the Sultan's daughter away in a tower while the Sultan is away, forcing her to become his wife, so he can become ruler of Persia, she is given only sixty minutes to make a decision on the marriage or she dies. Meanwhile, the princess' true love, you The Prince, is taken prisoner by Jaffar and thrown into a dungeon. This is where the game starts proper with you having to navigate the trap-filled dungeons, taking out Jaffar's guards, as you make your way to the tower where your princess fair is being held captive. Kill the tyrannical Jaffar and reclaim your love. All before the sixty-minute time limit is up. Story-wise, *Prince of Persia* doesn't really do anything special, I mean, it is literally just another 'rescue the princess' thing going on. However, it was how the story and game itself was presented that made this stand out.

Prince of Persia is, looking at it as basically as we can, another action-platforming game. But it was more than just your typical 'running and jumping' title. From the moment *Prince of Persia* starts up, even before you get to actually play the game, as the introduction begins, you see the princess, she turns around as evil Jaffar walks in. You've not even seen the game playing yet and already the animation was unlike anything you had ever seen before. Jaffar magics up his sand-timer and that sixty-minute countdown begins before storming out, locking the princess up. Just that simple intro blew me away due to its super (at the time) realistic animations. As the box itself boasted, the game 'breaks new ground with animation so uncannily human it must be seen to be believed.'

For once, the box of a game wasn't lying either. Then, even after the intro, when the game itself starts and you get to control the in-game hero, and it hits you that the amazing animation was not just for the intro/story... It's part of the game itself. You run, walk, jump, climb, sword-fight and more. It all just looked so... Well, so uncannily human, as the box stated. As underpowered and ill-equipped as the Apple II computer was, in terms of playing games, *Prince of Persia* was stunning on it. The music on the other hand was awful.

Jordan Mechner actually began working on the game in 1985, after *Karateka* had been a hit. Drawing inspiration from classic action-adventure cinema, Mechner wanted to recreate some of that big-screen action on home computers. The super impressive animation was done via a technique called rotoscoping. Jordan Mechner had his younger brother dress in all white clothing and filmed him playing. Running, jumping, etc. He then took all the footage and traced (rotoscoped) it to be used for the movements in the game. For the sword fights, Mechner rotoscoped Errol Flynn and Basil Rathbone from the 1938 film *The Adventures of Robin Hood*. So yeah, that's Errol Flynn fighting in *Prince of Persia*. In an interview with Next Generation magazine, Jordan Mechner had this to say about the animation:

> "When we made that decision [rotoscoping] with *Prince of Persia*, I wasn't thinking about being cutting edge, we did it essentially because I'm not that good at drawing or animation, and it was the only way I could think of to get life-like movement."

Originally, the game was not meant to include combat of any kind, the hero was originally envisioned to be a pacifist. Early game testing (mostly by Tomi Pierce, a friend and college of Jordan Mechner) proved

66 OF THE MOST IMPORTANT VIDEO GAMES EVER! (ACCORDING TO ME)

to be a bit dull. The game had spike traps, falling platforms, pitfalls, guillotines to add to the excitement, but there were areas where a lot of nothing was going on. Pierce continually badgered Mechner to include something to break up the monotony. Sword fighting was chosen for a couple of reasons. Firstly, because of Jordan Mechner's love of classic 1930s action-adventure flicks, especially swashbuckling, Robin Hood movies. Secondly, he wanted to do something different from what was on the market at the time, no guns, no punching and kicking... Swords.

Prince of Persia really felt dramatic and cinematic and was full of great, memorable set pieces. Jumping through a mirror, for a darker and mischievous version of The Prince to emerge. Taking out one of the skeleton warriors with a sword really felt very Ray Harryhausen. The jumping over pits of spikes and avoiding the dungeon's many traps was almost Indiana Jones-like. Plus it was devilishly tricky to complete too, as that sixty-minute time limit ticked away, with every little mistake you would make costing you valuable seconds. It really was tense and exciting stuff. Jordan Mechner's love of films is very apparent in his games and if things had been a little bit different, we may never have even got *Prince of Persia* as Mechner mentions in this interview with VentureBeat:

"*Prince of Persia* was my next project after *Karateka*. By then I considered myself a veteran of the industry at age 21. Although most of the stuff I'd done hadn't been published. I was also kind of torn between thinking, 'Should I keep making games?' Because I also loved movies. I wanted to be a screenwriter. I wanted to do animation. If the Apple II hadn't come along when it did, or if I'd been born ten years earlier, I probably would have tried to be a comic book artist or a film director. That was my dream."

Prince of Persia was ported to pretty much any and every popular computer and console at the time (there have even been several unofficial fan ports very recently too). Many of those ports adding more to an already brilliant game. It also kick-started a new IP with *Prince of Persia* games made right up to 2018, not including the (now much delayed) upcoming *Prince of Persia: The Sands of Time* remake from 2021... if it ever happens. But if that is not enough, then the game even spawned a whole new and separate franchise. After the release and success of *Prince of Persia: The Sands of Time* in 2003, Ubisoft (who then owned the IP) wanted a new *Prince of Persia* game. The idea came about to make a title that would expand on the universe and introduce assassins called, *Prince of Persia: Assassins*. The title was in development for about a year, but when it became clear the game was focussing more on the assassin aspect over the titular Prince, the development took a slight turn and became something else, the first *Assassin's Creed* game from 2007. That's got to be pretty important right? If not, then *Prince of Persia* was a massive influence on *Tomb Raider*, another hugely popular gaming franchise. As well as being the impetus that kick-started the whole action-adventure, 3D platformer craze. *Ico*, *Uncharted*, *God of War* and others of that ilk all exist because Jordan Mechner filmed his little brother playing in a park and created *Prince of Persia*.

But, as for that 'something' that I alluded to before, which other platform games seemingly lacked? *Prince of Persia* began a new sub-genre, the cinematic platformer, games that added mood, style, drama and atmosphere to a pretty bog-standard bit of storytelling. Don't get me wrong (and I've not forgotten) *Metroid* really did add those features before, but they were unrealistic, fantasy-like. *Prince of Persia* felt more grounded and far more cinematic in its approach. Plus, the game and its rotoscoped animation concept began the journey to real-life/motion capture animation in games that we have today.

**66 OF THE MOST IMPORTANT VIDEO GAMES EVER!
(ACCORDING TO ME)**

STREET ROD
DEVELOPER: P.Z.KAREN CO. DEVELOPMENT GROUP
PUBLISHER: CALIFORNIA DREAMS
PLATFORM: AMIGA
RELEASED: DECEMBER, 1989

I do have a bit of a penchant for driving games, simulation or more arcadey titles, I'm good with either. It's that thrill of speeding around a track in an expensive car that I'll most probably never be able to afford in real-life attraction for me. The titles we have today are often very well-designed epics, games that allow you to tear around real-world tracks from all over the globe in realistic representations of stunning supercars. Titles in the *Forza* or *Grand Turismo* franchises don't just give you the opportunity to (digitally) be a racing driver, but also the chance to buy and upgrade your vehicles. There's this thing I always do with these types of games, where I buy the cheapest possible starting car, upgrade it as far as it can go to keep it as competitive as possible, for as long as possible. But here's the thing, that car upgrading idea is one that has been in games long before the *Forza* or *Grand Turismo* franchises hit the market. I mean, look at *Street Rod* from 1989 as an example.

Street Rod is set in Southern California, 1963, and the plot of the game is that there's this street racer who calls himself 'The King' who's doing the rounds. It's your job to dethrone him in the limited time frame of summer break. Being set in 1963 in the USA means you have access to some of the finest, early American Muscle Cars around. Manufactures such as Chevrolet, Dodge and Ford are represented. But if it told you that the racing in this racing game is probably the weakest part of it, you'll be questioning why it's in this book. The racing is pretty poor, to be honest, and it really amounts to nothing more than some basic drag racing. However, it is the game's customisation and car upgrading options that really sells this one.

So, you start off in your empty garage with only $750 and nothing else. There's a newspaper you can browse through for new and used cars. Given your initial tiny budget, used cars it will have to be. Your first car will most probably be something like a 1949 Chevrolet Styleline. A sure-fire classic by today, but a real aged piece of junk in 1963 when the game is set. When you finally had your first car, you could head to the local diner and wait for a challenger to turn up. Ask them for a race, for fun, money or even pink slips (ownership of the car). Keep making money and invest that cash into buying newer and better cars, until you have a set of wheels good enough to challenge and beat The King.

Still, you didn't necessarily have to buy another car, you could always upgrade your existing one. For this, you had to turn, once more, to that newspaper and look through the spare parts section. Buy new and used manifolds, gearboxes, carburettors, tyres and more. You can even buy whole new engines. Strip the bumpers, lower the suspension, chop the roof off, spay-paint your car, add decals. You can really go to work on your car and customise it in so many different ways. But it's not as simple as just buying new parts and hey-presto, upgraded car, like in today's driving games. In *Street Rod*, you actually had to remove each part physically yourself, undo bolts and screws, remove the part, add the new part, then tighten all those bolts and screws back up, in a kind of mini-game thing. You could even rebuild an entirely new engine from spare parts, plus you'd have to tune it the engine to keep it running smoothly. Then there was the fact that the individual parts of your car would suffer wear and tear too. If you didn't maintain those parts properly, or if you raced too aggressively, they could fail. Tyers could burst, engines would overheat and your gearbox could even fall out.

It was this level of detail and interaction to the customisation of the cars that really sold *Street Rod*. The racing itself may have been a bit below average, but just taking an old junker and turning into an awesome street racer was sublime. Each new part, new advancement got you a little bit closer to taking on (and beating) The King. Impress more and more racers at the diner, make more and more money, buy and sell cars as well as parts. There was an entire commodity kind of gameplay mechanic thing that lay under this rather plain racer. I used to love finding some cheap $400 junker of a car, strip it of its parts to sell, scourer the newspaper and buy better parts, fit them and then sell that vastly improved car on for a profit. In fact, you didn't even have to race in the game as you could make money from buying, customising and then selling the cars on, like some kind of car restoration expert.

66 OF THE MOST IMPORTANT VIDEO GAMES EVER! (ACCORDING TO ME)

There was this real sense of progression and genuine depth to the game, it felt great looking through the newspaper and finding a clapped-out heap to do it up and turn it into Greased Lightning. Continually looking at the better and more pricer cars on offer, the V-8 Chevrolet Roadster, a Dodge Polara, the Ford T-Bird. Or if you had enough cash, a dream car, the 1963 Chevrolet Corvette. I honestly don't think any driving game since has ever managed to recreate that feeling of ownership and love for the cars like *Street Rod* did... Except for the sequel, *Street Rod 2*. Even today, upgrading cars in modern racers feels very bland and pedestrian by comparison over *Street Rod's* much more tactile, physical removal and replacing of individual parts. A game mechanic that helped you fall in love with the vehicles that you were creating.

Street Rod has even gone on to create a rather strong cult following over the years too. There have been several fan remakes over the years. Someone even purchased the rights to the original game a few years ago and set up streetrodonline.com, offering updated versions of this classic game, there's even a *Street Rod* card game now.

But here is where it all really began, customising the vehicles and making the car the star over the racing. All these modern-day racers owe a lot to *Street Rod*. Aside from all of that, this was the game that got me into classic racing cars and that whole thing I still do today, by taking my first in-game car and taking it as far as I can with upgrades.

S. L. PERRIN

SWEET HOME
DEVELOPER: CAPCOM
PUBLISHER: CAPCOM
PLATFORM: FAMICOM
RELEASED: DECEMBER, 1989

I didn't plan this, but as I write this chapter, it's Saturday, October 31st, 2020. Halloween, and I'm covering one of the first survival horror games and one that was the grandfather of perhaps the most famous survival horror franchise ever.

Tokuro Fujiwara had already been behind some of the biggest arcade hits when working for Capcom in the eighties. *Ghosts 'n Goblins*, *Commando*, *Tiger Road* and *Strider* to name a few. Moving on to the home consoles with the Famicom, one of his earliest titles was this game, *Sweet Home*. But, before it was a game, it was a film. Directed by Kiyoshi Kurosawa and also released in 1989, Kurosawa worked on the game version as a supervisor too. Fujiwara got to see the script of the film and even took a tour of the studio where it was being filmed. Now, *Sweet Home* the game does not follow *Sweet Home* the film exactly, it's more a case of 'inspired by' then a directly 'based on' approach.

Anyway, the game follows a team of five people (though only three at a time are selectable to play as) who enter Lady Mamiya's mansion, which turns out to be a haunted house. The idea is to explore, investigate and record what is inside. The game is actually an RPG, but one full of blood, gore and horror. In fact, so gruesome *Sweet Home* was that it was never given an official release outside of Japan. You'll cross paths with living-dead rotting corpses, vomit-spewing zombies, rabid dogs, ghouls swinging axes and many more macabre monsters. The mansion is huge, almost maze-like and you'll need to use various skills to explore it fully, solve puzzles and more as the dark secrets of the haunted house and its residents are slowly revealed.

Featuring multiple endings, depending on how many of your party survive and each character having their own unique abilities. *Sweet Home* offers a lot of scary gameplay. The game was actually given a full English translation in 2000 from Gaijin Productions, then another

66 OF THE MOST IMPORTANT VIDEO GAMES EVER! (ACCORDING TO ME)

(improved) translation from The Siege in 2017. But *Sweet Home* is not in the book just because it was gory or due to the fact it took eleven years for it to get an English translation. See, this game had some cute little touches, like a first-person view of doors opening, doors that needed lock-picking and more. If you can't see where this is heading, then maybe this little snippet from the instruction manual will help: 'You must escape this house of residing evil'. A residing evil eh? Quick recap, a team of people trapped in a house full of horrors, first-person door openings, puzzles to solve and locks to be picked. If you still need some help, then *Sweet Home's* director Tokuro Fujiwara went on to produce another similar game, something called *Resident Evil*. In fact, it had been suggested that *Resident Evil* was a remake of this lesser-known Japanese RPG.

Yes, *Sweet Home* was the precursor to Capcom's mega-successful *Resident Evil* franchise. *Sweet Home* is often called the first-ever survival horror game… But is it? If you do an interwebs search, then yes it is. But as you've probably cottoned on by now from reading this far, I often dig up a little something that brings those 'first' claims into doubt. I mean, *Where Time Stood Still* from the ZX Spectrum in 1988 is certainly a survival game and some would even call it a horror game too. Sure, it's not classic haunted house, zombies and rabid dogs horror, it is more of a prehistoric, Sir Arthur Conan Doyle's *The Lost World*, kind of horror. But still, it is a survival horror game that came before *Sweet Home*.

Anyway, splitting hairs over which was probably the first survival horror game aside, there's no doubt that *Sweet Home* certainly put in place a lot of the standards which are still found in the genre today. Without it, *Resident Evil* would never have existed. *Sweet Home* is darkly moody, bloody gory and horrifically atmospheric. All of those big-name, modern survival horror games owe a little something to *Sweet Home*. Not just *Resident Evil*, but if the likes of *Silent Hill*, *Fatal Frame* et al were to take DNA tests, they would definitely find their parentage in *Sweet Home*.

S. L. PERRIN

MIDWINTER
DEVELOPER: MAELSTROM GAMES
PUBLISHER: MICROPLAY SOFTWARE
PLATFORM: MS-DOS, AMIGA & ATARI ST
RELEASED: JULY, 1990

I've already established that open-world games were not exactly a new thing and how they had existed long before the likes of *Grand Theft Auto* came along. While some of those early open-world titles are still held in high regard today (*Elite* as an example), many of them have sadly been long forgotten or in some cases, not even known to exist by a great many people. *Midwinter* is a game that falls into the latter of those two. Before I do get into this one, I just want to point out that *Midwinter* was originally released in 1989 and not 1990, first on MS-DOS and the Atari ST. But I'm going to be covering the (better) Amiga port here, which came out in 1990. Just checking the rules I set for myself in the introduction.... Yes, I put in a cheeky 'get out' clause in terms of ports. So it's all good.

Set in the future year of 2099 and the entire planet has been covered in snow and ice. Yup, we're in a post-apocalyptic world here. There was a novella included with the game that covered the whole back-story, something about a catastrophic meteorite that brought on an impact winter across the entire globe or something. The game takes place on a one-hundred and sixty-thousand square-mile island called *Midwinter*. The tyrannical General Masters is trying to take over the island by force. You play as Free Villages Peace Force (FVPF) Commander John Stark and have to help *Midwinter's* residents stand up to and defeat General Masters by creating a resistance before he takes over the island. That's yer plot, onto the gameplay.

You can actually play as multiple people in the game, not just Commander Stark. However, you have to find and recruit said people first. As *Midwinter* is set in a literal ice age, getting around the island can be a little tricky. You start the game with pretty much nothing other than a sniper rifle and a pair of skis. You'll be using those skis a lot to get around the snowy and very hilly environment. Seek out settlements, search for supplies and (hopefully) some citizens of *Midwinter* that may

66 OF THE MOST IMPORTANT VIDEO GAMES EVER!
(ACCORDING TO ME)

want to join your rebellion to defeat General Masters. Explore the map, collect resources find more settlements, more civilians. Slowly build your resistance. Take out General Masters' henchmen and his settlements to win.

That's the basic gist of how it works, but *Midwinter* actually has a lot going on that was much more complex than you first realise. For instance, those civilians you could recruit may not always be on your side, some were sided with General Masters. Each of the thirty-two islanders all had their own unique personalities, wants and needs too. Some would readily join you in your plight, others would be slightly wearier and only join if you had a certain person(s) in your party. Each of the characters had their own mini-bio found in the game's manual and you would need to read up on each of the characters to find out what (if anything) they needed to be recruited. Obviously, each one of them had their own skillset too and some of the more useful residents were the hardest to recruit. Need a medical expert or an explosives specialist? Well, those would be much harder to recruit than a standard resident with a lower skill set.

Once you had another person join you, the game took on a kind of turn-based style. You could play as each character for two hours of in-game time, once those two hours were up, you'd have to switch to someone else. Once you have played with all of the characters in your party, you could end your turn, then it was General Masters and his minions time to get in on the action. What made *Midwinter* so great was just how open it was. Just as with any great open-world game, you had a mission to achieve, but how you did it was really up to you.

As you explored the island on your skis, events were randomised. Maybe you'd stumble across an enemy vehicle that needed to be destroyed, maybe you'd find one of General Masters' settlements... And blow it up with explosives! Traversing the snowy landscape gave you amazing freedom, but at the cost of the health of your character. Skiing is very tiring, going downhill was easy, but skiing uphill would drain your stamina fast. Falling off your skis could cause damage like broken bones, which obviously would need medical attention and make travel a lot more difficult. All of these things would cost in-game time and so you'd have to plan your moves very carefully. But there was more than just sliding around on the snow on skis. Some settlements could house a garage and said garage could hold a snow-mobile, making traversing faster... But no less dangerous. You could still be attacked by the enemy and crash and yes, that would also give your character injuries. Then there were the larger Snow-Fox, Snow-Cat or Snow-Wolf vehicles. Faster, more robust and they offered you some decent protection from attacks... And crashes. They also came equipped with some weaponry, missiles to use against the enemy vehicles and help even the odds. *Midwinter* even featured cable cars. Find yourself at the bottom of a particularly steep hill or mountain? Just hop on the cable car and be taken to the top, really useful for a spot of recon and sniping. Then, if you want to get back down, sure you could get back in the cable car. Or you could hang-glide back down.

All of that exploration would tire your character though, so you'd need to find a friendly settlement to get some rest. Find something to eat, sleep, attend to any injuries and so on. *Midwinter* had a real survival element in the midst of all the action. In fact, the game was a great blending of several elements, open-world exploration, action, survival, strategy and more. You'd have to refuel any vehicles, resupply by finding or buying goods. All wrapped up in the massive (for the time) map. I think the best modern-day comparison would be to something like Ubisoft's *Far Cry* franchise. The big open map to explore, the taking over of settlements, the survival elements, etc. Only, *Midwinter* came out (originally) in 1989, fifteen years before the first *Far Cry* game and even then, the original *Far Cry* wasn't the big open-world game that the franchise eventually evolved into today. Then you can also look at modern games like *The Long Dark*, a survival game set in a cold, snowy environment. One where your character can sustain injuries, have to rest up, eat food, etc. *Midwinter* was doing all of that more than two decades earlier.

Midwinter was designed by the legend that was Mike Singleton. Sadly, Singleton died of cancer back in 2012. But he left a hell of a legacy behind, as he designed and worked on games for some huge companies over the years, including Melbourne House, MicroProse, Virgin Interactive, Psygnosis, LucasArts, Midway and Codemasters. Yet

66 OF THE MOST IMPORTANT VIDEO GAMES EVER! (ACCORDING TO ME)

despite all that work on so many other games, it was *Midwinter* that was his masterpiece, the one game Mike Singleton would become known for. His opus, which was way ahead of its time and the game that opened the door to other elemental based survival games and even open-world action titles too.

Midwinter was a huge game in scope. Yeah, I know *Elite* had galaxies to explore, but you were in space and everything looked the same really, especially with those basic (but still impressive, for the time) wire-frame visuals. *Midwinter* was presented in glorious, but chunky 3D polygons, hills and mountains, vehicles, and more all looked amazing, shaded 3D polygons that were like nothing we'd ever seen before. The island of *Midwinter* was a gargantuan game map for the time, full of things to do, places to explore and people to meet, with each of those people having their own unique personalises and traits. It was a genre-blending game, one that's actually still kind of difficult to define now. It's a FPS, adventure, strategy, open-world, RPG, turn-based, management, survival, action type thing. Just YouTube a playthrough of the game and see just how vast and open it was.

There was a sequel too. Released in 1991, *Midwinter II: Flames of Freedom* and offered more of the same, with many improvements. Shifting the setting to a much more temperate climate and also featuring multiple islands to liberate. Also designed by Mike Singleton, the sequel is even better, but it was the original game that really broke the ground for open-world survival games. If there is one game from this book that I would really love to see a full-on, proper respectful remake of, then that game is Bullfrog's *Syndicate* (coming up later). But if there were two games I'd love to see a remake of, then *Midwinter* would be the other one. Though I'd guess that people would call it a *Far Cry* rip-off if it was ever made.

S. L. PERRIN

STREET FIGHTER II: THE WORLD WARRIOR
DEVELOPER: CAPCOM
PUBLISHER: CAPCOM
PLATFORM: ARCADE
RELEASED: APRIL, 1991

How-do-Ken? Honestly, I thought Ryu was from Yorkshire asking his pal, Ken how he is for so many years. Even today, I'm surprised at how many people don't know that *Street Fighter II* is a sequel, I mean, the 'II' in the title is a dead give-away I've always thought. I think the fact that this game has colloquially become known simply as '*Street Fighter*' over the years doesn't really help the issue. Even back in the nineties, it was always 'let's go play some *Street Fighter*' or 'I'm the best at *Street Fighter*', etc. We just seem to have dropped the 'II' very early on and it just stuck. But yes, this was a sequel. Back in 1987, Capcom released the original *Street Fighter* into arcades.

Designed by Hiroshi Matsumoto, *Street Fighter* was a success too. Yeah, as already known by now, some versions of the arcade cabinet had those pressure pad buttons. The harder you hit them, the harder the character would hit in the game. But, it became clear that people were damaging the cabinets, due to hitting the buttons so damn hard (as well as occasionally damaging themselves too), so Capcom introduced a new six-button system, with each button representing a light, medium or hard punch and kick. *Street Fighter* was also the first beat 'em up to use special moves. Yup, those iconic Hadōkens, Shoryūkens and Tatsumaki Senpū Kyaku moves all started with the original game. Anyway, the first *Street Fighter* was a decent hit and Capcom wanted a sequel, it took a few years and original designer, Hiroshi Matsumoto, had left the company by then too. But the sequel arrived and made a huge noise when it did too.

Street Fighter II: The World Warrior (to give it its full title) was unleashed onto very unsuspecting arcade gamers in 1991. This time, designed by Akira Nishitani and Akira Yasuda as well as being produced by Yoshiki Okamoto. The idea was to make this sequel much bigger in scope than the first title. Right from the off, they wanted to

66 OF THE MOST IMPORTANT VIDEO GAMES EVER!
(ACCORDING TO ME)

bring back a handful of the characters from the first game, but also create all-new characters to add to the roster. The idea to make each character recognisable via their nationality came about, then the team gave each character a unique fighting style based on that nationality (excluding Ryu and Ken) that really made the concept stand out. The designers were given free rein to add their own ideas and flourishes to any of the characters they were put in charge of creating. Hence why Dhalsim with his stretchy limbs or man-beast Blanka and his electrocution skills exist. The development team were also given a list of special moves, but not told how to bring them to life and instructed to use their own imaginations. This really allowed the designers to create highly original and never before seen fighters. One of the main reasons *Street Fighter II* is so fondly loved today.

Improvements over the original game didn't just include a bigger selection of more versatile characters. Animations were vastly improved to give a smoother and faster feeling of gameplay. Backgrounds of the stages were given their own unique and very fitting animations, as well as having a parallax scrolling effect thrown in too. Characters were given a sense of weight to them too. Go and play the game now as someone like Zangief or E. Honda and compare how they move with Chun-Li as an example and you'll notice how different they feel. This was a first for a beat 'em up and helped to really give these characters a sense of existence beyond pixels on the screen. The special moves from the first game were also improved on, not just by giving the characters their own unique move sets, but making them easier to pull off. The time window to input the moves was far less strict in comparison to the first *Street Fighter*. This just made the game far more accessible and gave players a sense of 'power' by being able to use the impressive special moves with relative ease.

However, there was a slight downside when making the moves easier to do. It created a kind of bug of sorts. Game testers soon noticed that they could string together moves, one after another in quick succession. This was never the intention of the game at all. It was during the famed car smashing bonus stage where this was first noticed, someone managed to pull off two punches in a single attack. It was then tested in a fight…

And it worked. Capcom had just invented the combo system in beat 'em ups and completely by accident too. The system was tweaked and refined through various testing, and what was originally a mistake in the programming due to making the moves easier to do became a staple of not just this game, but the beat 'em up genre on the whole.

Now, I can't talk about *Street Fighter II* without mentioning Yoko Shimomura's amazing music compositions. From the immortal *Street Fighter II* intro music to each of the very memorable stages. Each piece of music in the game is engraved into my brain forever. All of the stages based on the various countries the game takes place in, all have their own flavour and style. I mean, you can hear that fighter select screen music right now can't you? How about Ken's stage music or the Chun-Li theme? Some of the most memorable music in any game ever can be found in *Street Fighter II*.

When *Street Fighter II* did hit the arcades, it was a smash hit. Though the game did struggle in Japan at first, as players mostly ignored its two-player feature, meaning it made less money. But it was over in the US where the whole one on one fighting action really took off. It did take a while, but Japan soon fell in love with the whole competitive angle of the game and *Street Fighter II* fever began to spread over the globe. *Street Fighter II* was far from being the first beat 'em up, but it kind of perfected it and became a worldwide phenomenon like no other before it. For years after its release, there was a slew of *Street Fighter II* clones. Pretty much every game developer on the planet wanted their very own *Street Fighter II* beater. Even Capcom themselves kind of got in on the act by releasing different versions of the same game into the arcades and on consoles with very slightly different tweaks and improvements. The spin-offs and sequels soon began to flow too. The impact of *Street Fighter II: The World Warrior* was and still is gargantuan. It is one of the most influential games ever made.

Oh, but was it really the first beat 'em up game to introduce combos as claimed? Go and play (or watch) Konami's Yie Ar Kung-Fu from 1985. When you hit your opponent, there's a slight pause where you can follow up with more hits... Or a combo if you will. Plus, take a look at *Shanghai Kid* by developer, Nihon Game also from 1985 for more combo action.

66 OF THE MOST IMPORTANT VIDEO GAMES EVER! (ACCORDING TO ME)

THE LEGEND OF ZELDA: A LINK TO THE PAST
DEVELOPER: NINTENDO
PUBLISHER: NINTENDO
PLATFORM(S): SUPER FAMICOM/SNES
RELEASED: NOVEMBER, 1991

It's only now, as I type this very chapter, that I realise just how Nintendo heavy this book has become over other developer/publishers, there's more Nintendo coming too. But let's be honest, there is a pretty damn good reason why... Cos the big N really did make some of the most important games ever. The *Zelda* series was still finding its feet in 1991. The first game was a definite, stone-cold, indisputable classic. Its sequel, *Zelda II: The Adventure of Link*, was very diversive and split opinions, mainly because it changed things up a tad over the first game. Don't get me wrong, it is now considered a great game, but back in 1987-88, it certainly had its haters, some still very vocal today. So, with a bit of a mixed bag in terms of the first two games, how would the third game in the series fair? The very short answer to that is, very well indeed. The longer answer? Well, that's what this chapter is all about.

The Legend of Zelda: A Link to the Past saw a couple of familiar names return, Shigeru Miyamoto and Takashi Tezuka as producer and director respectively. Seriously, these two were like the grand wizards at Nintendo, the video game equivalent of Lennon and McCartney. They produced some sublime games together over the years. Still, the original *Zelda* may have been a true innovator back in 1986, but a lot had changed, more and more games were copying its template as *Zelda* clones were popping up all over the place. Miyamoto remembers his initial concerns about making a new *Zelda* title in this interview with Famicom Tsuushin magazine, a few weeks before the game was released:

"Back when *The Legend of Zelda* was being made, having a world based on swords and magic was still a fresh idea, as was the concept of being able to save your game. A system that allowed you to buy items in-game was also new, not to mention solving dungeons. However, in the five years since the game's release, a lot of titles have appeared on the market that do the same sort of thing, so the sense of innovation has disappeared entirely. I thought hard about what we could do next that would entertain the players."

So, even before initial development on the game had started, Miyamoto was aware that the market was becoming a little stale, he knew he needed something special.

The first things that both Shigeru Miyamoto and his sparring partner, Takashi Tezuka, got to work on were the visuals and the controls. Coming from the previous generation and the NES console, the newer and more powerful SNES machine opened more than a few doors. Obviously, the 16-bit horsepower over the older 8-bit console meant that the visuals could be vastly improved upon. But it was the new and improved SNES controller where the ideas began to flow from. More buttons on the pad meant that the hero, Link, would be able to pull off more moves, add depth and more variety to the gameplay and more. Other ideas just seemed to fall into place.

The much-used spin attack found in *The Legend of Zelda: A Link to the Past* actually came from a controller limitation. In the first game, you could only move in the four basic directions. Up, down, left and right. But this new game allowed for diagonal movement. If you could move diagonally, of course, you'd want to be able to use the sword at the same time too. However, the development team just could not make it work in the game. So to get around the lack of a diagonal sword strike, the spin attack was added.

A lot of new ideas made their way into the game, but there were a few features both Shigeru Miyamoto and Takashi Tezuka wanted to include but had to cut out as Miyamoto recalls:

"There were a variety of ideas that didn't make it into the game. Using the lantern on a grassy area to cause an endlessly expanding fire, for example. And digging a ditch with the shovel or bombing the swamp breakwater to cause water to rush into the hole. Work on these was in progress. If we'd had another six months, we might have been able to make them a reality."

66 OF THE MOST IMPORTANT VIDEO GAMES EVER! (ACCORDING TO ME)

Mmmmmm, fire and water physics. Then there was the addition of the whole light and dark world mechanic. I still remember the first time I played *Zelda 3*. Conquered several dungeons, explored the over-world, interacted with a lot of NPCs, smashed many pots and collected hundreds of rupees. To then go up against the game's big-bad, Agahnim. Defeat the bad guy, rescue Princess Zelda and wait for the credits to roll... Only that's not what happened. Instead, Agahnim sends Zelda to the dark world and you with her. Then you find yourself in a whole new, explorable land, a dark mirror of the previous one. I was blown away, there I was thinking that I had finished the game, when the truth was that I had hardly scratched the surface. The whole light and dark world element of *The Legend of Zelda: A Link to the Past* is one of my all-time favourite mechanics from any game.

It's the explorable map (both of them), the memorable characters, that trademark *Zelda* style weapon and item progression system that made this game so damn special. Everything was just blended so perfectly and offered one of the finest action-adventure games to ever be made. Originally called *The Legend of Zelda: Triforce of the Gods* in Japan, it was given a title change shortly before release in the west to *The Legend of Zelda: A Link to the Past,* due to Nintendo of America's strict rules against religious images or references in their games at the time. Plus, the new title also made for a good pun.

The core structure of this game is what set the standards for pretty much all *Zelda* games from that point onward. Not just one of the best SNES games, but quite simply, one of the best games ever made. As Shigeru Miyamoto once said about *Zelda 3*:

> "In my opinion, a game isn't just the time spent playing it. It also includes moments when you're away from home and think 'I'm going to play when I get back'."

Well, I know I've certainly spent a lot of time thinking about *The Legend of Zelda: A Link* to the Past while not playing it. Even now, thirty years since its release, I still think about it. I think I might just go and play some right now.

S. L. PERRIN

MORTAL KOMBAT
DEVELOPER: MIDWAY GAMES
PUBLISHER: MIDWAY GAMES
PLATFORM: ARCADE
RELEASED: OCTOBER, 1992

MOR-TAL KOM-BAT! Bah-da, bah-da, bah-da. Buh-do, bah-do-da... And so on, as that rocking-techno tune plays in your head. But aside from that immortal theme tune, *Mortal Kombat* had one or two other things worth writing about too. *Street Fighter II* had already got the arcades packed back in 1991 and the beat 'em up genre was a hot commodity after that, with pretty much every gaming studio wanting to make their own. To be honest, the market got a little flooded with beat 'em ups for a while and they all pretty much began to merge into one and another, to form a huge and (mostly) forgettable blob of games. The '*Street Fighter* clone' era was very much upon us. So, for a new beat 'em up on the market to stand out, it needed to be bold, daring and... Well just not be a *Street Fighter* clone really.

Mortal Kombat was born from the minds of Ed Boon and John Tobias, with Boon being the main programmer while Tobias was the graphic artist. The pair were approached by Midway Games to make a new game from the ground up, and in less than a year too. The studio really wanted to ride the success wave that Capcom's *Street Fighter II* had kicked off the previous year. But it was a much earlier beat 'em up from where they drew their main inspiration from. Taken from an interview in the Deseret News, John Tobias said:

> "*Karate Champ* had really crude graphics, but it was the first that incorporated the whole martial arts theme."

Yup, the already covered in this book, *Karate Champ* was where *Mortal Kombat* really grew from. Boon and Tobias wanted to make a real martial arts style game, a game that would capture the art of martial arts as well as deliver a harder edged style of gameplay. Their first idea was to make a ninja-based game, that idea was quickly thrown out. For a good while, Midway wanted to make a game based on the science-fiction, action, martial arts flick, *Universal Solider*, starring Jean-Claude

66 OF THE MOST IMPORTANT VIDEO GAMES EVER! (ACCORDING TO ME)

Van Damme. 'The Muscles from Brussels' was fast becoming a huge action star in the early nineties, and a game starring the man himself could potentially shift a lot of copies and bring in plenty of coinage. There were a few talks, but Van Damme had already signed a deal to appear in another game from a different studio. So the idea to use JCVD was dropped. As a quick aside, that other game that Jean-Claude Van Damme signed up for never happened. Tobias talks about Van Damme in this chat with Polygon:

> "So the fiction behind *Mortal Kombat* was kind of already in development even prior to us chatting with Van Damme, and when he ended up not being involved, we just kind of marched ahead. So the idea of his involvement was he was either going to play himself in the game, in the fiction of the game, or he was going to play a character in the fiction of the game. His character is eventually what became Johnny Cage."

So, Boon and Tobias were pretty much back at square one. They had the idea to make an updated version of *Karate Champ* and a game to showcase real martial arts, but no real theme for the title to fit. That was when John Tobias pulled an idea from one of his previous gaming experiences. The first game Tobias ever worked on as an artist was the arcade shoot 'em up, *Smash TV*, he also worked on its sequel, *Total Carnage*, for Midway Games. Anyway, Tobias recalled the overtly violent and bloody nature of those two games and began to wonder if it would be possible to apply that level of violence to a beat 'em up. A *Karate Champ* style fighting game, but with the bloody gore of *Total Carnage*... It could work, I guess.

So, the germ of an idea was there. Those young gamers that grew up in the late seventies and through the eighties were just that, grown-up. Boon and Tobias believed that there was a gap in the market for a more 'adult' looking and stylised game, one those kids from the last couple of decades, now adults, could get a real kick out of. The infamous blood and gore of *Mortal Kombat* actually started out very tame. There was a little splash of blood here, a little squirt there, then it just kept on building as the game evolved. By the time they had pushed the blood as far as they thought they could, the idea of finishing moves came about.

S. L. PERRIN

Tobias believed that the violence in the game was so outrageously over the top that it would be seen as very comical, that it wouldn't be taken so seriously.

The characters themselves were specifically designed to tell a rudimentary story. Stories were something that arcade games didn't typically have back then, they were a case of pop your coins in and play. Early designs for the characters show that each of them fit a certain archetype to explain their behaviours and origins. Liu Kang was the hero and main protagonist of the game, Raiden was to be the mentor, Kano a henchman and so on. Right up to Johnny Cage as an arrogant movie star, inspired by... Yup, Jean-Claude Van Damme. A little residual from when *Mortal Kombat* almost became a *Universal Solider* game. Each of the characters was given a short bio that could be read during the arcade game's attract mode, along with a brief run-down of the overall plot of the game. All of which, gave you the player an actual story to follow. John Tobias remembers the fine-tuning of the story elements needed:

"We had to be careful of the setting, the theme, the high-level premise, each character's individual stories, and how, even when the player looks at them, just in their mind they're able to fill in the blanks. So it's almost like you're telling a story without telling exposition. It's just by the nature of who these guys are and how they look against each other, and how they fit into the larger world was an important part of our storytelling process in that first game."

When released in the arcades, *Mortal Kombat* really blew people away. The realistic-looking digitised graphics made passers-by stop, stare and want to play. Then there was the blood, the spurts of claret as the characters landed a powerful uppercut that always caught people's attention. And of course, there were those famed finishing fatality moves, when you saw a character have their spine pulled out with the skull still attached, you knew *Mortal Kombat* was different. *Street Fighter II* may have reinvigorated the tired beat 'em up genre the year before, but *Mortal Kombat* was the game that really got people's attention... Especially the mass media. There was outrage due to the game's use of violence and gore. *Mortal Kombat* was just one game (the other being *Night Trap*) that brought about the creation of the Entertainment Software Rating Board (ESRB) in America, established in 1994 to

66 OF THE MOST IMPORTANT VIDEO GAMES EVER! (ACCORDING TO ME)

specifically handle age ratings for video games. Europe eventually brought in a similar system in 2003 with the Pan European Game Information (PEGI). Even *Mortal Kombat* co-creator, Ed Boon agreed with and praised the new age rating system as mentioned in this interview with Eurogamer:

> "I always thought that they had a point you know. There was no ratings system when the first one came out, and to me it makes sense. I wouldn't want my 10-year-old kid playing a game like that. And our intention was not to make this game thinking 'oh, a 10-year-old's going to love this, ripping people's head off!'. The reality of games is that the average player is about 28, 29, the same guys who watch *Goodfellas*, *Scarface*, all these movies that have that kind of content, and that's what they were looking for in certain games."

This brings me nicely to my next point. It has often been said among gamers that *Mortal Kombat* was the first game to be given an age rating. As I have already covered in the *Dracula* text-adventure game earlier, that was the first video game to be given an age rating back in 1986 when publisher, CRL, actively sought an age rating just for the publicity from the BBFC. Also, as Ed Boon revealed in that quote above from the Eurogamer interview, the rating system didn't even exist when the first *Mortal Kombat* was released. Do you happen to know what the first game to be given an ESRB rating actually was? It's coming up later in this book. But anyway, *Mortal Kombat* may not have been the first game to receive an age rating, but it, along with *Night Trap* on the Sega CD, were the games to put the wheels in motion to get a dedicated rating system for games in place.

Aside from becoming a huge franchise with comic books, movies, sequels, spin-off games, and much more. *Mortal Kombat* did raise the bar in terms of adult content in games. So when you play a game these days, with all that blood and gore flying and so on, you can thank Ed Boon, John Tobias and *Mortal Kombat* for pushing the boundaries and creating 'adult' video games.

S. L. PERRIN

DUNE II: BATTLE FOR ARRAKIS
DEVELOPER: WESTWOOD STUDIOS
PUBLISHER: VIRGIN GAMES
PLATFORM: MS-DOS
RELEASED: DECEMBER, 1992

Dune, that 1984 David Lynch flick based on the science-fiction novel of the same name from Frank Herbert. A film that was ravaged by critics upon its release and has been put on numerous 'worst movie ever' lists. Still, despite its notable terribleness, *Dune* has become a huge cult classic and is now very much loved... By some. The film even had a pretty big merchandising campaign too, action figures, sticker books and of course, games. In 1992, Virgin Games released the Cryo Interactive developed *Dune*, an adventure-strategy, resource management type of thing. You know what? It was actually pretty damn good too.

An interesting little titbit, there were some issues with making the *Dune* game. In fact, that first title was very nearly cancelled when Virgin Games, who had paid for the *Dune* licence, felt the early development ideas just were not really going anywhere. Still, Cryo Interactive carried on regardless and the end result was pretty damn great. However, Virgin Games were unsure if that *Dune* game would ever be finished, so they hired another studio to work on another game using the same licence. Enter Westwood Studios, who got to work on a very different *Dune* title. Both games were being worked on at the same time with neither studio aware that the other was developing their own game. Anyway, when the development of both games finished (around the same time too), Virgin Games learned they had not one, but two great games based on the *Dune* licence. So what to do? They couldn't release both games and call them both *Dune*. So why not just release them both anyway, but call one *Dune* and the other *Dune II*, then just slap on a subtitle? So yeah, *Dune II: Battle for Arrakis* isn't a sequel, it's just another game based on the same licence and released at the same time by the same publisher.

The team at Westwood Studios had been playing several games when they were offered the chance to make a title based on the *Dune* licence. The 1989 game, *Military Madness* was a huge influence. This was a turn-based, sci-fi, hex grid strategy thing. Westwood loved *Military*

66 OF THE MOST IMPORTANT VIDEO GAMES EVER! (ACCORDING TO ME)

Madness, but felt it was a bit too restrictive, they wanted to give the player more freedom for their game. Then there was (the already covered in this book) *Populous* from Bullfrog. Having an entire land at your disposal, little people running around and you being in control. As Joe Bostic, lead programmer on *Dune II* recalls in an interview with Read-Only Memory:

"We knew the mouse was going to be important to *Dune II* because of *Populous*. It was an earlier real-time game where multiple units were also moving around a map and it showed us that mouse control was key to making that kind of game work simply and easily."

Plus, 1989's *Herzog Zwei* was also a major influence on the making of *Dune II*. This was a real-time combat simulation where you could train infantries and build tanks, etc. You then use your newly created army to take out the opposing enemy base. If you were to play *Herzog Zwei* and then *Dune II* directly after it, you can clearly see the similarities. Anyway, with their influences now in place, Westwood Studios began to put their game together.

There was a slight issue, the ideas that Westwood had for the game didn't really fit the narrative of the *Dune* novel or the film. They wanted to make this action-packed strategy title, not something bogged down with dialogue, character development and plot. They could've just dropped the licence, to be honest, and made their own game, creating a new IP along the way. But Westwood loved the universe *Dune* was set in, the endless seas of sand of the planet Arrakis, the awesome and deadly sandworms, the melange (spice) commodity and more. Westwood knew they wanted to make a *Dune* themed game, just not one that felt like a *Dune* themed game... If that makes any sense? A new angle was needed as Joe Bostic remembers:

"In order to give us the most freedom to take the IP into military ground combat realm, we decided to have *Dune II* take place thousands of years prior to the timeline of the book. This freed us from having to follow the plot of the book. We could create our own path since there wasn't any game like it at the time."

S. L. PERRIN

So yeah, this game called *Dune II: Battle for Arrakis* which, despite its title, is not a sequel, is in fact a prequel. So, lead programmer, Joe Bostic got cracking. Having their influences in place and now a setting for the game, Westwood decided to skip the customary concept stage and just jumped right into working on the game proper.

After some tinkering, play-testing and tightening up balancing issues. *Dune II* was ready for release and it was a hit, racking up high scores from pretty much every gaming magazine at the time. *Dune II* breathed new life into the RTS genre and created a blueprint for RTS games of the future. We gamers really wanted a sequel, but that would mean forking out money for the *Dune* IP again, which wasn't really that desirable. So instead, Westwood created their own IP using the same *Dune II* gameplay and mechanics (only tweaked and improved) with the awesome *Command & Conquer* series.

Still, more *Dune* games eventually did come later with *Dune 2000* and *Emperor: Battle for Dune*, both from Westwood Studios. But it all really began here with *Dune II: Battle for Arrakis*. That very specific blend of military micromanagement, resource-gathering, base-building, unit production and of course, a fog of war. Those fast became the staples of any RTS game from the point onward. *Dune II* may have had a few rough edges (like not being able to pick multiple units with a simple drag-select), but what it did have was pretty much perfect from the start.

66 OF THE MOST IMPORTANT VIDEO GAMES EVER! (ACCORDING TO ME)

SYNDICATE

**DEVELOPER: BULLFROG PRODUCTIONS
PUBLISHER: ELECTRONIC ARTS
PLATFORM: AMIGA
RELEASED: JUNE, 1993**

After the staggering success of *Populous*, Bullfrog and Peter Molyneux especially, were well and truly on the gaming map. Both gamers and the gaming press were keen to see what the studio had up their sleeves. They had already released a few titles after 1989 and through the early-nineties, *Flood* and *Powermonger* were perhaps their most notable games at the time. Then there was *Syndicate*. I'm really not sure how to define the game, to be honest, an action-shooter, strategic-business management, sci-fi, murder sim? I'm not convinced that *Syndicate* actually falls into any single gaming genre, it's more of a cocktail of several elements, and a cocktail with a hell of a kick too.

So, to summarise the plot. *Syndicate* is set in a dystopian future, governments around the world have been replaced with corporations. You are the head of one such corporation and are vying for world domination against other corporations to create a new world order. You do this by using cybernetic agents to complete missions, in order to take control of countries over the globe. The more countries you control, the more taxes you can claim, and that money can be put into research and development to help upgrade your cybernetic agents, which in turn, helps you to take over more and more countries.

I think the first thing I want to cover with *Syndicate* is just how dark, gritty and violent a game it is. Yet that element was largely ignored at the time. I mean, we are talking about a post-*Mortal Kombat* era now. The boundaries of violence in gaming had been pushed and even broken, to the point where specific age ratings for games had to be created. The stuffed shirts in power were looking at the impact violent games have on 'the kids', enforcing new rules and in some cases, trying to get violent games banned. Yet *Syndicate* was never swept up in any of that furore... And I don't know why.

S. L. PERRIN

I mean, let me just give you an insight into what you could do in this game. Taking control of your four cyber-enhanced agents, you can wander around a fairly open map filled with civilians, police and other agents from opposing corporations. Armed to the teeth with handguns, shotguns, uzis, even sniper rifles and mini-guns. Your agents are free to do whatever they like within the game world. Follow the mission objective if you like, maybe you'll be requested to kidnap a high ranking official. Maybe you need to assassinate a notable professor, blow up a rival's R&D department... Or even 'sterilise' (as the game calls it) an entire city. And what does this sterilisation entail? Murdering everyone on the map, police, rival agents, officials and yes, even innocent civilians. You can massacre dozens and dozens of people in this game, bodies line the streets like a carpet, there's pools of blood from dead people, twisted metal from destroyed cars, and more. You can mow innocent people down with a mini-gun or even set them ablaze with a flame-thrower. By the time you finish the game, you have been responsible for hundreds, nay thousands upon thousands of deaths... Yet this game never caught up in the whole video game violence controversy-thing of the early-nineties.

I honestly think that *Syndicate* is one of the most bloody and violent games I have ever played, at least at the time anyway. Yeah, I ripped a head or two off in *Mortal Kombat*, but I was murdering an entire population of a town in *Syndicate,* just because I could. In *Mortal Kombat*, you are taking part in an arranged and fully agreed to fighting tournament. In *Syndicate*, you're a huge corporation killing civilians for money, global power and control. I was surprised, yet entertained by *Mortal Kombat*... I was utterly shocked by *Syndicate*.

I still remember the first time I ever played the game on my brother's Amiga 500. Back then, I was a 17-year-old gamer who just wanted to play games. I didn't bother reading instructions or mission briefs. Just let me play the damn game. So I had no idea what was going on or what I was supposed to do. I just played, moved the mouse around, clicked on a few things and got my agents moving. I walked them over to a nearby road, a car was driving around and civilians walked the streets. I clicked the gun icon on the screen and my agents pulled out their weapons, the civilians panicked and ran away screaming. I shot them to shut them up.

66 OF THE MOST IMPORTANT VIDEO GAMES EVER! (ACCORDING TO ME)

The police arrived, I shot them and looted their corpses for weapons. I just walked around the map murdering any and everyone. That car was still driving around, so I shot it until it exploded, the bodies flew. I killed everything I possibly could on the map. Turns out that I wasn't supposed to, I was supposed to persuade a notable scientist to join my corporation. But the point was that I could and did kill everything instead.

Teenage me had never played a game like it before. Yeah, some games gave you a lot of freedom to explore before, but there was nothing like *Syndicate*, at the time, to give you such a power-rush with its freedom. I genuinely felt like a world-dominating corporation, it felt so damn great to be so damn bad. But it wasn't just the mega-violence in *Syndicate* that was amazing. The whole business management element outside of the action was fantastic too. Raise or lower the taxes of the countries you have taken over to make money. Pump that money into R&D and improve your technology. Buy more weapons and upgrades for your agents to keep yourself several steps ahead of your rivals. There was this balancing act between being able to massacre entire towns of people and maintaining an actual business that just worked.

Syndicate was designed by Sean Cooper and produced by Peter Molyneux at Bullfrog Productions, and it was a game that really opened my eyes in more ways than one. It got me into business sims, a genre I still enjoy today. It really did push violence in gaming even more so than the much more infamous *Mortal Kombat*. Not only that, it got me to watch one of the greatest sci-fi films ever made, Ridley Scott's *Blade Runner*. I had never seen the film up to that point in my life, and every gaming magazine made the comparison between the setting of *Syndicate* and the world of *Blade Runner*. So, after seeing the film continually mentioned in relation to the game I was playing so damn much back then, I got myself a copy of the director's cut of the film *Blade Runner* and it soon became a favourite of mine.

Still, how or why *Syndicate* never got caught up in the whole violent games backlash thing of the nineties, I really have no idea, it is seriously violent.

S. L. PERRIN

MYST
DEVELOPER: CYAN
PUBLISHER: BRØDERBUND
PLATFORM: MAC OS
RELEASED: SEPTEMBER, 1993

The CD-ROM format was still finding its feet in the early-nineties in terms of gaming. There had been a handful of CD format released games, *Fighting Street* (the PC Engine version of *Street Fighter*) from 1988 was the first... Just in case you were wondering. Though to be honest, those early CD-ROM games didn't really utilise the format that well, and pretty much all of them were just floppy disk games put on a CD to cut down on disk swapping. Enter the Miller brothers, Rand and Robyn, who together, co-created *Myst* and they really showed what the paring of CDs and gaming could do.

The Millers had already previously worked on a CD-ROM game, 1988's *The Manhole* (often wrongly cited as the first CD-ROM game). *The Manhole* was originally a floppy disk game, but it was one of those titles that I mentioned before which began life as floppy disk format, but given a CD release later in 1989. Anyway, *The Manhole* was a children-oriented adventure game, Robyn Miller remembers that early game in this article from Retro Gamer:

> "Rand had an idea for a children's book on a computer. A child would turn the page, click on items on each page, and those items would react in certain ways. Rand sent me a copy of HyperCard, which was like a predecessor to the web. The first drawing I did was of a manhole against a solid white background. But what became immediately obvious was that an entire world existed below that manhole, and I wanted to visit it. So I began to draw it and piece it together. The idea of the book altogether went out the window, or at least it quickly evolved into this idea of a more non-linear world. It was very exciting; I began moving my way through that world, making it all up as I went along."

After developing and releasing *The Manhole*, the Miller brothers wanted to do something a tad more grown-up and complex but still in the same vein. They wanted to create an adventure game where the player didn't

66 OF THE MOST IMPORTANT VIDEO GAMES EVER!
(ACCORDING TO ME)

have to follow a linear story, one where the protagonist had to make ethical choices and more. Plus they really wanted to push the CD format as far as is it could go and showcase a game that was as great to play as it was to look at. With their concept and ideas firmly in place, development on *Myst* began in 1991.

Drawing inspiration from a game already covered in this book, *Zork I*, as well as the literature of C. S. Lewis and Jules Verne, particularly the book *The Mysterious Island* by Verne, the Millers and a small team got to work creating a mythic universe involving portals to other worlds. An adventure game like no other on the market that would (hopefully) make us gamers gawp in awe. Robyn even drew ideas from his own childhood too:

> "There was no single thing we were inspired by. Looking back, I'm sure that some of the inspirations came from my own school years and childhood. For example, during high school, I used to paint these large scale canvases, I'd spend hours every day on them. They were surreal things, like glimpses into some bizarre universe. I'm sure my childhood fascination with these surrealistic visions influenced the visuals throughout the *Myst* world."

In *Myst*, you play as an unnamed protagonist simply known as 'The Stranger' who finds a book called *Myst*. Upon reading the book, you are whisked away to the world described in the book and are left to explore the island of *Myst*. The plot focuses on two brothers (played by Rand and Robyn Miller themselves) who are the main villains of the game. It gets a bit confusing as you try to track down books, within the book you are trapped in, in order to unravel the mysteries of *Myst*. You'll need to solve complex puzzles and make decisions that affect the game itself.

Perhaps one of the most interesting elements of *Myst* was the complete lack of any kind of violence. This was at a time when games were pushing violence boundaries further and further (see *Mortal Kombat* and *Syndicate*), when developers and publishers were striving to make more adult orientated games by cramming them with more grown-up content. *Myst* was still very much aimed at adults, yet, with none of that 'adult content' you'd expect to find. Some suggested the lack of violence in the game was due to the Miller brothers strict and deeply religious childhoods, they were sons of a Minster after all. But that theory is not too accurate so according to Robyn Miller:

> "It's not because Rand and I were on a campaign to stop violence in games. We were just out to make interesting, intriguing games. I think Rand would agree with me that violent imagery in art, film, games, or any other kind of story can be shocking in a way that can be considered good. Jarring, violent imagery is sometimes the only thing that kicks us in the ass and wakes us up to something we'd never otherwise consider. That's what art in general is supposed to do, show us a new way of looking at the world around us. But what doesn't make sense to me is when we turn that shocking sort of violence into fun, like shoot 'em up titles. They cause us to participate and sometimes even laugh at acts of violence. I can't agree with that. It seems as if we are ripping away some small piece of ourselves. It doesn't make sense to me."

A non-violent, adult-themed game? As strange as that sounds, it worked. *Myst's* point 'n click adventure style gameplay, FMV sections, truly amazing and wondrous graphics, all cemented together with those devilishly sublime puzzles that demanded your full attention was a true breakthrough in gaming. The CD format was still very much finding its feet back in 1993, many people didn't even own a CD drive for their computers at the time either (there had been a handful of early CD-based consoles though). Yet, *Myst* was the game that enticed gamers and other developers/publishers to really get on board with the format and *Myst* became the game that got PC owners buying CD drives.

Though originally released on the Macintosh operating system for Apple computers, it was when *Myst* saw a PC port, that was when it seriously blew up and became such a huge hit. *Myst* became the best-selling game on PCs for almost an entire decade, only beaten by sales of *The Sims* in 2002. *Myst* wasn't just the first CD-ROM game to use the CD format really damn well, it was also a title that enticed a lot of non-gamers to give it a try too. Anyone could play *Myst*, its accessibility was unmatched at the time. Though it was adult aimed, really anyone could play it from teens to pensioners. The game had a few naysayers when it was originally released and Robyn has a theory on why that most probably was:

66 OF THE MOST IMPORTANT VIDEO GAMES EVER! (ACCORDING TO ME)

"I think there was stuff that frustrated practised gamers. There were no command keys, there was only the mouse and one button, there was no avatar, the world was presented cinematically, and so on. Because of all this, *Myst* may have seemed almost too simple to gamers who were used to things that looked and felt like games. And yet this is partly what made *Myst* so popular with the majority of our audience, those who'd never played a game before. To them, *Myst* was approachable, it felt real."

Regardless of the initial backlash, *Myst* went on to become a staggering success. It changed adventure games forever and influenced the genre since its release, right up to today. *Myst* showed what could be done with the CD format and helped to make CDs the standard in gaming at the time.

S. L. PERRIN

DOOM
DEVELOPER: ID SOFTWARE
PUBLISHER: ID SOFTWARE
PLATFORM: MS-DOS
RELEASED: DECEMBER, 1993

Oh yeah, now this is one game that I've really wanted to cover since I came up with the idea for this book. *Doom* is, quite simply, one of the greatest games ever made and a title that should be on any gamers list of must-play games. But, it is why it's such a great game, its influence and impact, that's why it made it into this book. There really is so much going on behind the scenes of *Doom*, from its inception right up to the legacy it has created over the years that it could fill an entire book. Yup, a whole book crammed full of *Doom* history from start to end would be great…

But, I have a lot more games to cover here, so this will just have to be a massively truncated version of exactly what *Doom* is and why it's so important. For me, *Doom* was the first FPS game. Yeah, yeah I know that in actuality it wasn't, but just as how I'll argue why *Pong* was the first-ever video game (read the first chapter again), I'll use that same logic and reasoning to state that *Doom* was the first true FPS.

id Software were no strangers to the FPS genre, of course, they made the ground-breaking *Wolfenstein 3D*, a game many consider the grandfather of all FPS games. But even before William 'B.J.' Blazkowicz was shooting hundreds of Nazis in the face, id had already experimented with the idea of a shooting game viewed from a first-person perspective. *Hovertank 3D* and *Catacomb 3-D* were two id Software titles that both pre-dated *Wolfenstein 3D*, and there were even earlier examples too. 1980's *Battlezone* from Atari is often said to be the first FPS game. Though *Maze War* from 1973 should perhaps take that crown? Regardless of which game was the first FPS (debate among yourselves), it was with *Wolfenstein 3D* where the drive for id Software to push what the genre could do came from, as the company's co-founder and game programmer/developer supremo John Romero mentioned in an interview with N For Nerds:

66 OF THE MOST IMPORTANT VIDEO GAMES EVER! (ACCORDING TO ME)

"We made *Wolfenstein* and it turned out to be a game that set the standard in that genre of first-person shooters so when it came around to developing *Doom*, we knew what we were going to do that would be a lot better. We started working on it and in January 1993, we put out a press release telling everybody that it was going to be the best game in the world!"

But I digress, even with those earlier titles, *Doom* was where the FPS genre began proper in my eyes. The team at id were originally working on some new content for *Wolfenstein 3D*, a prequel in fact, called *Spear of Destiny*. It was while work on that game was underway when id Software co-founder and lead programmer, John Carmack, wanted to do something with a bit more bite, as he began work on an all-new game engine that would prove to be... Well, pure genius and a major leap forward in terms of 3D graphic engines.

The original idea was to make a new game in id's popular *Commander Keen* series of games. The issue was though, that the *Commander Keen* titles were platformers and that genre really didn't work with the 3D engine that John Carmack had created. They needed a new idea and two other co-founders of id, John Romero and lead artist, Adrian Carmack (no relation to John Carmack) wanted to make something with a much darker tone than those *Commander Keen* games. So, John Carmack got to thinking and he came up with something inspired by the movies *Evil Dead II* and *Aliens*. It was Carmack who thought up with a title too, *Doom*, which came from another movie, *The Color of Money*. The idea began to grow and a team of five, programmers John Carmack and John Romero, artists Adrian Carmack and Kevin Cloud, and designer Tom Hall got to work. It was Hall who came up with the 'Doom Bible', as he called it. This was a huge design document that detailed the game's plot, backstory and much more, a document that was streamlined as the game's development moved forward.

While *Doom* does feature a plot, it's not of the same depth that was in that original Doom Bible which Tom Hall had written. Some features and ideas had to be dropped due to hardware limitations, others were changed to make the game more fun overall. John Romero especially wanted to move away from the more boxy and maze-like levels of

Wolfenstein 3D and other similar FPS games, to offer something more abstract. Romero remembers the difficulty in creating those far more interesting level designs when he spoke to PC Gamer:

> "One of the biggest hurdles in developing *Doom* was the environments. Just before *Wolfenstein*, we made *Catacomb 3-D* and that was our first texture-mapped 3D game. Those environments were like dungeons. Just running through tunnels killing stuff. *Wolfenstein* had VGA graphics and it looked better, but it was still a maze game. And before *Doom*, every three-dimensional game was basically a maze game. Going back to 1974, everything that was 3D was a maze. If you played *Ultima*, *Wizardry*, or *Might & Magic*, or any game that had a 3D environment in it, you were always in a 90 degree walled maze. So we didn't have any example of how to do something different, and it was a lot of work trying to break out of that. Even the early *Doom* levels we made as examples when I was programming the *Doom* editor were still very *Wolfenstein*-looking, and they weren't fun to play in. They were basically boring. So I decided one day to solve the problem."

Tom Hall began to resent the fact that his Doom Bible was seemingly being pushed aside, he eventually ended up being fired by the others when he started to slack off and often not even bother to show up for work at all. Tom Hall was replaced by designer Sandy Petersen, just ten weeks before the game was due to launch. id Software also took on another programmer to help get the game finished, Dave Taylor.

John Romero and Sandy Petersen really clicked together and the two were designing more and more technically elaborate and far more interestingly complex levels. All powered by John Carmack's amazing and truly ground-breaking 3D game engine. Two multi-player modes were coded into the game that would allow people to play the game co-operatively via local area networking (LAN). Or they could play against each other in what John Romero lovingly termed 'deathmatch'. Online multi-player was even added later via the Dial-up Wide-Area Network Game Operation (DWANGO) service. Then, when the game was ready, they just had to release it.

id Software actually decided to self-publish. It was Jay Wilbur (who was the sole member of the business team) that came up with the idea to

66 OF THE MOST IMPORTANT VIDEO GAMES EVER!
(ACCORDING TO ME)

market and distribute *Doom* a little bit differently to other games at the time. He wanted to cut out the middle man and sell direct to customers, ignoring game shops as much as possible and use the shareware market instead. Though shops were still needed to get the ball rolling. Wilbur went to software retailers and offered the first episode of *Doom* for free, allowing them to charge the customer whatever they wanted for that first episode... But only if they would help plug the fact that the customer could then buy the rest of the game from id Software directly. It was a pretty clever tactic and kind of like how digital distribution works today.

Doom actually missed its initial release date as the guys at id kept coming up with new ideas that they wanted to include in the game. It was finally released proper and uploaded to the pre-internet, File Transfer Protocol (FTP) on the 10th of December 1993... After the team had worked thirty hours straight to get it finished. When the game (well first episode) was uploaded, over ten thousand people tried to download *Doom* at the same time, they managed to crash the University of Wisconsin–Madison network while doing so too, where *Doom* was originally uploaded to. And that was just the beginning. *Doom* had arrived and we gamers lapped it up.

Doom created the deathmatch multiplayer mode. In fact, the phrase 'deathmatch' was first coined by John Romero himself. The game also proved that developers didn't need publishers or even shops, paving the way for digital distribution. It put in place many staples of the FPS genre that are still used close to thirty years later. *Doom* is also responsible for the Esport competitions that we have today, as it was id Software that hosted the first-ever Deathmatch '95 professional tournament, a gaming contest that featured *Doom* as one of its games. Then there is *Doom's* open-source code that paved the way for the modding community, a concept that is not only still going with other games now, but one that is still strong within the *Doom* community itself. But aside from all that the game has given the industry over the years, most importantly, it is still bloody damn playable now, twenty-eight years after its original release. It is *Doom*... nuff said. Oh yeah, I almost forgot. Remember back in the *Mortal Kombat* chapter and I was trying to clear up which game was the first to be given an official ESRB rating? Well yup, it was *Doom*.

S. L. PERRIN

FINAL FANTASY VI (III)
DEVELOPER: SQUARE
PUBLISHER: SQUARE
PLATFORM(S): FAMICOM & SNES
RELEASED: APRIL, 1994

I've never been much of a *Final Fantasy* fan if I'm being honest. Yeah, yeah I know. Even that hugely popular *Final Fantasy VII* that everyone keeps going on about, the one that is currently in the midst of a multi-part remake as I write this, never liked it. I do enjoy a good RPG or even more specifically, a JRPG, but I just never personally found the *Final Fantasy* games to be good (J)RPGs. However, there was one game in the series that I quite honestly fell in love with, *Final Fantasy VI* (or III if outside of Japan). I'll not bore you with the stories of the differing numbered titles here. I'll bore you with some behind the scenes tales of the game instead.

Final Fantasy series creator, Hironobu Sakaguchi, could not be as involved with this game as he had been with others in the franchise before it. Sakaguchi was a little busy with several other projects after he became Vice President of Square. Hironobu Sakaguchi hand-picked both Yoshinori Kitase and Hiroyuki Ito to take charge and direct the game instead. Kitase would mostly handle the story and scenario of the latest *Final Fantasy* title, while Ito concentrated on the battle mechanics. Sakaguchi did serve as producer and oversaw the whole project though, to ensure it all came together and felt like a rightful *Final Fantasy* game.

I think that one of the great things about this one is that there is no singular, lead protagonist. Each of the main characters in *Final Fantasy VI* offers something. Each of the playable characters felt alive, as if each were actually driving the story and not just characters in a story. Yoshinori Kitase mentions as much in this interview with Edge magazine:

> "The idea was to transform the *Final Fantasy* characters of the time from mere cyphers for fighting into true characters with substance and backstories who could evoke more interesting or complex feelings in the player. Since the scale of each character's individual story was

66 OF THE MOST IMPORTANT VIDEO GAMES EVER!
(ACCORDING TO ME)

expanding, I began linking this to the concept of different dramas developing, according to the player's choice of character in the game."

It was *Final Fantasy VI's* concept of being able to play as multiple characters, and have each of them be actual characters, instead of just sprites on the screen, that really got the player invested into the narrative and their relationships. Each character not only had their own unique behaviours during the battles, but they also had their own deep backstories to uncover too.

For me, *Final Fantasy VI* was when RPGs really came to life and I don't think it has ever been bettered since either. From the opening in the town of Narshe, the wind blowing through the streets. To the grand finale when you finally got to bring an end to the main bad guy, Kefka… And his laugh. *Final Fantasy VI* is full of stand out moments, chocobos and opera house anyone? It's a truly epic game with a hell of a lot of heart and emotion running through it. The melding of battles and drama was and still is sublime, the multiple-choice scenarios and interweaving plotlines were fantastic. I'm sitting here writing this chapter and struggling to work out why the far less interesting *Final Fantasy VII* is getting the remake treatment, while this much superior title is being ignored? Even Yoshinori Kitase himself recognises the fact that *Final Fantasy VI* is the more popular title:

"In those days we didn't have the Internet and, as a more junior staff member, I wasn't given the opportunity to venture overseas, so I wasn't really aware of the reception the game received outside of Japan. However, in more recent years, I've regularly tagged along on PR tours to Europe and America and I have had a lot more opportunity to talk with foreign media and fans. I must say, whenever I go on these tours I'm taken aback by the number of westerners who ask me to sign their *Final Fantasy VI* cases. In Japan, that would apply more to the subsequent game, *Final Fantasy VII*, but I get the impression there's a large number of players in the West who prefer the earlier game."

Yes, *Final Fantasy VI* is the more popular (and even better) game over *FF VII*… So where is its remake? Get on it Square Enix and make the fans happy. Anyway, *Final Fantasy VI* had to have an English translation and Ted Woolsey was the man for the job, he was only given thirty days to complete that translation too. Considering the sheer amount of text in the game, that thirty days was very stringent, especially for one man to do alone. Plus, it wasn't as simple as just having to translate from Japanese to English, Ted Woolsey also had to deal with Nintendo of America's famed and very strict censorship at the time too, as Woolsey himself recalls:

"There's a certain level of playfulness and sexuality in Japanese games that just doesn't exist here [in the US], basically because of the rules and guidelines."

This all brings me nicely to the censorship of the game itself between the original Japanese version to the western release, from subtle little changes to the removal of some things entirely:

- Esper Siren's sprite had her clothes lengthened and shorts added for the Western release, as in the Japanese version, you could see her bottom cheeks.

- Esper Starlet's sprite, Critic/Alluring Rider spirit and The Goddess's sprite were also modified for the western version, much for the same reasons above to cover partial nudity. Some minor background details, statues, etc were also censored to cover cleavage and so on.

- In Kefka Tower, one of the characters is seen holding a pipe used for smoking. The smoke seen coming from the pipe was removed as to not depict anyone smoking in the game.

- Any of the locales and towns that you could visit in the game that showed a sign reading 'Pub' was changed to 'Café' to avoid any connection to alcohol.

- The in-game spells 'Holy', 'Jihad' and 'Hell's Rider' were renamed 'Pearl', 'Crusader' and 'Rider' respectively as to not bring anything related to religion into the game.

- In the same regard, the 'Death' and 'Death Gaze' spells were renamed 'Doom' and 'Doom Glaze' just to avoid the whole death connection.

66 OF THE MOST IMPORTANT VIDEO GAMES EVER! (ACCORDING TO ME)

Despite the rather over the top censorship of the game, *Final Fantasy VI* was brilliant. The pinnacle of JRPGs and the last main *Final Fantasy* title to be in full-on, glorious 2D as *Final Fantasy VII* jumped onto the 3D revolution that was going on at the time. But there was just something special about that 16-bit era of gaming when it came to RPGs, even Yoshinori Kitase agrees:

"It's maybe strange to say, but I miss the limitations of making games in those days. The cartridge capacity was so much smaller, of course, and therefore the challenges were that much greater. But nowadays, you can do almost anything in a game. It's a paradox, but this can be more creatively limiting than having hard technical limitations to work within. There is a certain freedom to be found in working within strict boundaries, one clearly evident in *Final Fantasy VI*."

Perhaps this is partly why I feel that *Final Fantasy VI* was the last, truly great JRPG game… because, in all honesty, it really was.

S. L. PERRIN

RISE OF THE ROBOTS
DEVELOPER: MIRAGE
PUBLISHER: TIME WARNER INTERACTIVE
PLATFORM: AMIGA
RELEASED: NOVEMBER, 1994

In 1988, Public Enemy released a song called, *Don't Believe The Hype*. And I really should've taken heed to their profound advice too. *Rise of the Robots* was one of the biggest and most anticipated games of the nineties. *Street Fighter II* and *Mortal Kombat* had popularised the bandwagon that so many wanted to jump on. The beat 'em up genre was taking over in both the arcades and on the home market, and you could find plenty of *Street Fighter II* and *Mortal Kombat* clones pretty much everywhere. I remember the December 1993 edition of the highly respected Edge magazine cover vividly. The image was of the main character from the game, the blue ECO32-2 Cyborg (catchy name) and the text boldly sprawled across the cover, which read: 'Graphics to die for'.

There was also a little blurb in the bottom corner of the magazine's cover, teasing a few more details of the game that proudly boasted:

"*Rise of the Robots* from Mirage - a graphically outstanding fast action beat 'em up. Each body part was modelled in 3D Studio and stored as individual sprites. The limbs are linked and animated to give life to each 3D mechanoid."

I mean, I hadn't even opened the magazine yet and it was already full-steam ahead on the hype train… Twelve months before the game would even be released. Nowadays, hyping a game a year or more before its release is pretty much normal. But back then as the mid-nineties crept upon us, you didn't tend to hear about a game until a few months before it came out. Well, to be completely fair, *Rise of the Robots* was originally planned to be released around January/February 1994, a month or so after that Edge magazine was published, but it was delayed until much later. Anyway, inside that Edge magazine itself was an eight-page feature, packed with behind the scenes info on the game's development. Even then, it was being hailed as a '*Street Fighter II*

66 OF THE MOST IMPORTANT VIDEO GAMES EVER! (ACCORDING TO ME)

beater'. Despite being a year away from release at the time, there were talks of toys, books, comics and even a big-budget movie too. Oh, and you just couldn't read or see anything related to *Rise of the Robots* without the constant mention of the fact that Brian May of Queen fame was doing the soundtrack too. One of the world's greatest guitarists from one of the world's greatest rock bands doing the music for one of the world's greatest video games? Yeah, I and many other gamers were sold and release day just could not come soon enough. We could not wait to get our hands on this great '*Street Fighter II* beater' that the gaming press had been hyping up.

Just looking at the images in the magazine, and *Rise of the Robots* looked simply amazing, Hollywood movie-esque graphics. *Terminator 2: Judgment Day* had hit cinema screens a few years before in 1991 and we were still marvelling at the impressive CGI used for the bad T-1000 liquid metal thing. Well, *RotR* had a very similar cinematic look... And on a 16-bit home computer too, marvellous!

As the weeks and months ticked by, the hype continued to build as more details of the game emerged. The enemies would feature ground-breaking AI, which would learn how you played and react accordingly. So, as an example, if you kept spamming one particular move to win, the AI would learn this and block that attack more and counter against it. This shit sounded truly revolutionary, quite literally game-changing. Then after almost a year of hype and delays, *Rise of the Robots* was released, originally just for the Amiga (where it came on a whopping thirteen 3.5" floppy disks... Thirteen disks! And yet, only seven of those were to actually play the game, the others were just for the intro movie), but other ports soon followed. *RotR* was released for DOS, SNES, Mega Drive, Game Gear, Philips CD-i, 3DO... There was even an arcade version developed too, though it was unreleased (YouTube it). A very rare example of the home versions spawning an arcade port. This game was gargantuan at the time, it was everywhere. It looked amazing, it sounded unbeatable (on paper) and it was poised to be the greatest beat 'em up ever made. But how it actually played was the big issue.

Well, reputable gaming magazines like CU Amiga Magazine and C&VG gave it high praise and scores of 80% and even 91% respectively

Other huge scores followed. This game was going to be awesome for sure… And then Amiga Power magazine gave their review and score, a 5%. Now, you may have noticed a slight discrepancy between scores there, one magazine give the game 91%, while another gave the game 5%, what? Well, let's just say that Amiga Power was well known for their honesty, while other magazines were perhaps a bit more inclined to give good scores to games for 'bonuses'. In fact, Stuart Campbell of Amiga Power wrote an open letter to the game industry as a whole. Dated December 1994 (Google 'Stuart's open letter to the games industry 1994', that's how I found it), it's a rant well worth reading and one that really questions gaming journalism in general. I'll just copy & paste my favourite bit of the rant here, but I do suggest that you seek out the letter and read the entire thing yourself though, it's amazing:

"And while we're here, how come this slimy turd from a dead dog's arse managed to score more than one 90% review? Didn't any of the reviewers notice either? Or has the single word 'exclusive' really come to represent the entire text of the reviewers' Holy Bible? How, in 1994, can a game score 3%, 5%, 19%, 20%, 33% and 35% in six reviews in very different magazines covering five different formats, and 90% and 92% in two other ones? 'Personal opinion' really doesn't cover it in this instance, does it? I won't name the reviewer who, when I quizzed him about the surprising nature of his high score, gave the response 'Arms were twisted... Let's leave it at that,' but perhaps the practice of reviewing games at the publisher's office with the entire PR department looking over the reviewer's shoulder is becoming a little, shall we say, unreliable? Or is it just paranoia on my part to think that there's maybe something a little sinister going on when the supposed release of the year isn't shown to any magazines before it hits the shelves, save for one or two 'arm-twisted' exclusives, coincidentally generating scores five to thirty times those of most other reliable reviews? Scared of something, are we?"

The 'didn't any of the reviewers notice either?' from the above quote relates to the absolutely terrible gameplay of *Rise of the Robots* specifically. I mean, do I really have to recount my disappointment here, have I not suffered enough already? Okay, just to drag up nightmarish memories again, here's why *RotR* was so bad:

66 OF THE MOST IMPORTANT VIDEO GAMES EVER! (ACCORDING TO ME)

- There's the fact that you can only play as one character in the game. Now, there are other characters, but you can only play as the ECO32-2 Cyborg. Well to be fair, that is applicable in the single-player mode only. In the two-player mode, the first player can still only play as ECO32-2, but the second player can select one of the other characters.

- You can't turn around and you have to face the same direction through the entire fight. Yes, a beat 'em up where you can't turn around, a feature that goes back through one on one beat 'em up for decades. As idiotic as that sounds, it didn't really matter much because you couldn't actually jump over your opponent for you to need to face the other way regardless.

- The much-lauded Brian May soundtrack was nothing more than a small snippet, a few seconds from one of his previously released songs, *The Dark*, which was taken from one of his previous albums. No really the killer soundtrack that was being advertised. Plus, those few seconds of May's music appeared on the menu screen only and not in the game during gameplay.

- That amazing new AI that would learn as you played? Well, it didn't even exist at all. You could actually finish the game in around ten minutes (including loading times and all that disk swapping) just using one move. The flying kick. Enemies would just stand there and take kicks to the face until they fell over, even the final boss.

- While the graphics were impressive for the time, the animation was terrible. The characters jerked around on the stages as if they only had a few frames of animation. Then the stages themselves were just soulless, static single-screens with minimal details and zero animation or interaction... even *Karate Champ* from 1984 had background animations.

Rise of the Robots is one of the absolute worst games ever made, and I don't mean that false, over the top, hyperbolic, *E.T. the Extra-Terrestrial* on the Atari 2600 'worst game ever' crap. I mean it really is one of the worst games ever made. So why is it in this book then? Well, this one game taught me two very important lessons in relation to the gaming world and I guess, the world in general. Rules that I have stuck to from November of 1994 right up to today. First, gaming journalists and well, journalists, on the whole, can't really be trusted and often write utter crap for certain favours. 'Integrity' is a word not known by many journos these days. Second, just as Public Enemy proclaimed:

"Don't believe the hype!"

But do you know what's even more incredible? There was a sequel, *Rise 2: Resurrection* from 1996. And yes, it too was a load of shit that met with terrible reviews.

Honestly, it really was annoying how this game was hyped up for such a poorly, underdeveloped title. The fact you could only play as one character, restricting the overall gameplay. The amazing new AI that learned from you, which didn't even exist. The '*Street Fighter II* beater' boasts. The plugging of Brain May doing the sound the soundtrack, for that to just be a few seconds from a pre-existing song. All just utter bullshit, marketing bollocks and misinformation to lure the buyer into the world of this terrible, shit-filled pants of a game.

I mean, that's like me boasting on the cover of this very tome that there are exclusive, never before seen interviews with massive industry pioneers, written just for this book... Only for me to just use small snippets from already available interviews and such. Misinformation being used to hype up a product that just doesn't deliver on that hype. Yes, I really did just make a very long-winded and slow-burning joke, just to annoy you, the reader, and highlight my ire toward this game from thirty years ago because they hyped it up so damn much, especially the Brian May soundtrack. That's how bitter I am about this game. A game that has turned me into such a cynical bastard.

66 OF THE MOST IMPORTANT VIDEO GAMES EVER! (ACCORDING TO ME)

SENSIBLE WORLD OF SOCCER
DEVELOPER: SENSIBLE SOFTWARE
PUBLISHER: RENEGADE
PLATFORM: AMIGA
RELEASED: DECEMBER, 1994

"You're a goal-scoring superstar hero.
You let your hair down and play to the fans.
You're a goal-scoring superstar hero.
And every goal, goal, goal says you're the best in the land."

One of the most memorable intro songs to any game ever! Football games have a long and very varied history through gaming. From a football-ish game that was on the Binatone TV Master MK IV console, simply titled *Football* (it was really just a *Pong* clone) in 1976 to the likes of *FIFA 21* and *PES 2021* of today, footie games have been around for almost as long as gaming has. Yet, none of those other footie games have ever been included in a list of the most important video games of all time... No, I don't mean this book.

If you have read my previous gaming book, *MicroBrits: A Tapestry Of The British Gaming Industry* (available from Amazon, buy it now!) then you already know what's coming. Anyway, back in 2007, Henry Lowood, curator of the History of Science and Technology Collections at Stanford University, compiled a list of the ten most important video games ever. Lowood, along with notable game designers Warren Spector and Steve Meretzky, academic researcher Matteo Bittanti and respected game journalist Christopher Grant, all worked together to make their list. One of the ten games on that list was *Sensible World of Soccer*, the only European developed game, only sports game and also the most recent game on the list too.

The *Sensible Soccer* franchise actually began in 1992, but it was with this particular version of the game where it all (pun fully intended) kicked off. Taking what was so fantastic about the original game and adding several layers, making an already amazing football game even more amazing. From the tiny, but full of character graphics, to the plethora of gameplay options and variables. *Sensible World of Soccer* really offered a world of soccer. Sensible Software co-founder Jon Hare, along with Chris Chapman, were the main brains behind the game. Hare was a die-hard football fan, as a kid, he used to make his own football teams by cutting out player's faces from magazines and newspapers, he'd then stick them to toy figures, grab a ping-pong ball and recreate some of his favourite matches and goals. This was pre-video games and Hare had to make his own football entertainment.

Sensi or *SWOS* (as the game is called by fans) was a real labour of love for both Hare and Chapman. They wanted to create the ultimate football game, pushing as many ideas into the title as they could. They never set out to make a 'realistic' game, but more of a very fun to play one. Even after the release of the original game in 1992, they wanted to add more and more features, as Jon Hare recalls in this Retro Gamer interview:

"After *Sensible Soccer* came out in 1992, we didn't stop working on it. Our programmer, Chris Chapman, ensured the development process was never broken. So as he carried on working, we were able to inject more features and work on a game that really would become the ultimate football game, in our eyes at least. That's how *Sensible World Of Soccer* came into being."

The original *Sensible Soccer* was based on and mostly inspired by domestic football. As great as it was, the game itself was still pretty limiting. Both Jon Hare and Chris Chapman wanted to expand from that domestic game and make it more international. They added more than twenty-seven thousand players, spread over one thousand, five hundred teams. And all because of that classic table-top game, *Subbuteo*:

"We were very thorough, and that is because of the roots which go back to *Subbuteo*. That game was international and it had different kits. You had all the different international teams and I think *SWOS* was an ideal way of just turning our game into a modern *Subbuteo* on a computer, not in the sense of flicking players around but playing football as realistically as possible, given the constraints. I think that that was probably part of it. Personally, I'm quite attracted to things that are about the world and different countries, and how that works, and it was nice to map the football world out of the game."

66 OF THE MOST IMPORTANT VIDEO GAMES EVER!
(ACCORDING TO ME)

The other thing about the original *Sensi Soccer* game was that it was just that, a game of soccer, a damn fine one, but still just football on a very basic level. Really, all Sensible Software had to do was update it with new teams and they could've had a great game, but they wanted more. The idea to add a player/management element with a career most lasting twenty years, which was perhaps the biggest addition. Jon Hare loved the idea, but he didn't want the game to be manager focused or heavy, a very careful balance between the fast and frantic football *Sensi* was known for and management was implemented. That's one of the things I adore about *SWOS*, the management angle was perfect. It never feels overly intrusive, you can buy and sell players, tinker with the team's strategy, formations and so much more. Yet it never felt like micro-management, it never got in the way of the main action on the pitch.

The size of the game was just unmatched, even today. You could play as any team from any league, from any country in the world. Manage a little known team like Cape Coast from Africa and take them to the top of the league. Perform well, and maybe you could get the job as manager for the international team, to then go on to win the World Cup. Each and every single one of the twenty-seven thousand players had their own individual stats too. The attention to and level of detail in *SWOS* was truly encyclopaedic, its sheer size and scope was unrivalled. A football game of its magnitude just could not exist today, it's truly amazing it existed in 1994 to be honest, as Jon Hare recalls:

> "If you imagine the scale of *SWOS* and imagine doing that on modern consoles with modern players, that's a big job. Imagine the whole scope of the work, the 3D models of the stadiums, the detail that would be needed. We did that on the technology we had available to us at the time in our own way and it worked so well."

I have said it before and will continue to say it. *Sensible World of Soccer* is the greatest football game ever made. The modern *FIFAs* and *PES* titles of today may be more 'realistic' sure… But *SWOS* is infinitely much more fun and exciting to play. Plus, as I covered earlier, the game now has genuine academic acclaim thanks to History of Science and Technology Collections at Stanford University curator, Henry Lowood and his team of experts.

S. L. PERRIN

RESIDENT EVIL
DEVELOPER: CAPCOM
PUBLISHER: CAPCOM
PLATFORM: PLAYSTATION
RELEASED: MARCH, 1996

I actually got to play the original Japanese release of *Resident Evil* (*Biohazard*) before I played the English version. I couldn't read Japanese at all, had no idea what I was supposed to be doing. But via some (a lot) of trial and error, I did manage to get to grips with the game and even progressed to the end. That introduction to the game with the S.T.A.R.S. team being attacked and the 'I got a shotgun' music was awesome. Then later, I got hold of the English version and found the intro had been heavily edited to remove the blood and gore even the 'I got a shotgun' tune was gone. That censoring never made sense to me either, I mean, the intro is in black & white, so you don't really see any blood anyway, just black goo. This was 1996, not 1966 and still, we were having our entertainment edited for us.

Directing *Resident Evil* was Shinji Mikami, who was approached by Capcom to make a game set in a haunted house. He originally envisioned the game as being in a first-person view, an idea taken from the battle sections of the previously covered *Sweet Home*. The original *Resident Evil* concept was going to be a much more action-focused, horror first-person shooter too. A prototype was even made and shown to the heads at Capcom, and they really didn't think much of the game. Apparently, it was too generic for them and they didn't feel that it would stand out from any of the other endless FPS games that were flooding the market at the time, that the game didn't feel very horror game-like either. Mikami remembers those early issues when he spoke with Variety:

> "They were saying, 'It's a horror game. Why are you having the main character hold a gun in a horror game? Isn't it bad to have the main character actually defeat the scary creature in the game?' They were against that idea. And I didn't have a logical answer to that, and so I had to just keep telling people whatever I could to make the development continue and push forward."

66 OF THE MOST IMPORTANT VIDEO GAMES EVER! (ACCORDING TO ME)

Plus, the PlayStation hardware didn't really cut it to make the full-on 3D polygon FPS that Shinji Mikami was aiming for, or at least, he wasn't quite familiar enough with the hardware to make the game work how he wanted. From all accounts, that early version of *Resident Evil* was basically nothing more than a bog-standard *Doom* clone with fancy 3D graphics instead of pixel-sprites, but featuring a more supernatural, psychological Japanese style horror instead of hellspawn demons.

So, the idea to make a Japanese horror influenced game was dropped along with the FPS idea. Instead, American cinema would be the main well to draw from, particularly the work of George A. Romero. Zombies soon became the main monster of choice instead of traditional Japanese ghosts. Shinji Mikami has also said that the Lucio Fulci flick, *Zombie* (or *Zombie 2* depending on where you are from in the world) was a major (negative) influence in this interview with GamePro magazine:

"My main inspiration was *Zombie*, a famous Italian horror movie. When I saw the movie, I was dissatisfied with some of the plot twists and action sequences. I thought, 'If I was making this movie, I'd do this or that differently'."

Anyway, as mentioned back in the *Sweet Home* chapter, *Resident Evil* is often considered an unofficial remake of that Japanese only horror RPG game. In fact, *Sweet Home's* director, Tokuro Fujiwara was even a producer on *Resident Evil* too. Using *Sweet Home* as the main inspiration, Mikami used several of that game's ideas for his now, zombie game. The limited inventory, emphasis on puzzles, notes found in-game to fill in the backstory, survival elements, the first-person view of doors opening and more, including the obvious setting in a mansion, all of that came directly from *Sweet Home*. Another game also helped with that troubling FPS angle that just didn't work, 1992's *Alone in the Dark*. The fixed camera angles of *Alone in the Dark* were what led to Shinji Mikami ultimately dropping the FPS idea in favour of the now very familiar style of *Resident Evil*. With his new zombie-based game idea in place, Mikami set about developing it proper.

What is pretty impressive is that for the first six months or so of development, Shinji Mikami worked completely alone. He designed the characters, the mansion (inspired by the Overlook Hotel from *The Shining*) and even wrote a forty-page script too, all by himself. One early feature that never made it into the final game was a co-op mode. The idea was to have the two main characters, Chris Redfield and Jill Valentine, having to work together to make their way through the mansion. It's not clear if it was going to be a two-player experience, or a one-player mode with you controlling both characters, akin to the feature used in *Resident Evil 0*. Maybe it could have been either? Regardless, it never made it into the final game, but early beta footage of *Resident Evil* with the co-op feature can be found on YouTube. Also, fan-favourite and classic stilted dialogue deliverer, Barry Burton was never part of the original concept. In fact, early in development, *Resident Evil* had a big sci-fi element in the shape of a character called Gelzer. This character was a huge, muscular Arnie/T-800 inspired cyborg, complete with a very Terminator-like ocular implant. Gelzer was also the one that would rush in to save Jill from becoming 'a Jill Sandwich' in the room with the descending ceiling/shotgun-trap (which makes a lot more sense). Ultimately, Gelzer was swapped out for the more human Barry Burton.

When released, *Resident Evil* was a huge hit with critics and gamers alike. Two updates followed in the shape of *Resident Evil: Director's Cut* (1997), which added new content and gameplay modes. Then *Resident Evil: Director's Cut DualShock Ver* (1998) was the same game as above, but now with added support for the then-new PlayStation controller, the DualShock and a few other bells and whistles.

Of course, *Resident Evil* went on to be a huge franchise, with sequels and spin-offs games that are still being made today, even if Shinji Mikami himself didn't think it would be, as he recalled with Fandom:

> "During the time when we were making it, my personal feeling was that *Resident Evil* was not a game that should be made into a series. This is because horror tends to have strong patterns that are easy to get used to, meaning they're easy to get tired of. I never thought that the game would become such a huge hit."

Yet, a huge hit it was. *Resident Evil* not only spawned a game franchise, but a live-action movie series too. A collection of novels, starting with *Resident Evil: The Umbrella Conspiracy*. Plus so much more besides.

66 OF THE MOST IMPORTANT VIDEO GAMES EVER! (ACCORDING TO ME)

But perhaps the biggest thing the game can be credited with (outside of creating the phrase 'survival horror game') is that it breathed new life into an undead classic movie monster, the zombie. Zombies were most definitely out of favour in the early-nineties after being so damn popular through the seventies and eighties, largely thanks to George A. Romero. Alex Garland, writer of the flick *28 Days Later* and Simon Pegg of *Shaun of the Dead* fame have both said that *Resident Evil* was a primary influence on their films. But if that's still not good enough for you, then the grandfather of the modern zombie, the late, great George A. Romero himself said in an interview with The Telegraph newspaper about zombies that:

"I do think the popularity of the creature has come from video games, not film."

And the game that started the zombie craze that is still massively popular today (for better or worse) was Capcom's *Resident Evil*. When the man credited with creating the modern zombie is crediting video games with keeping the creature alive, you know that's pretty damn major.

S. L. PERRIN

SUPER MARIO 64
DEVELOPER: NINTENDO
PUBLISHER: NINTENDO
PLATFORM: NINTENDO 64
RELEASED: JUNE, 1996

Oh yeah, I've got more Mario for your eyes (I did pre-warn you) and perhaps the single most important Mario game since *Donkey Kong*. The Nintendo 64 was the first console I ever bought with my own, hard-earned money and the fact it came bundled with one of the greatest and most important games ever was just a bonus.

The mid-nineties were certainly a very confusing era for gaming. The 16-bit machines with their glorious 2D sprites were on the way out as the next generation of home consoles began. The rise of 3D graphics came with the advent of the 32 and 64-bit era. The previously conquering Mega Drive from Sega and SNES from Nintendo gave way to the Saturn and Nintendo 64 respectively. Oh, and some new guys called Sony threw their hat into the ring when they came up with something called a PlayStation or something like that. Anyway, there was this almost awkward transitional period where graphics had evolved, yet the games themselves perhaps had not yet caught up. Many, many strangely cumbersome and even flat out incompetent games were released, especially in terms of the platform genre. Titles like *Jumping Flash!* and *Bubsy 3D* were certainly 'ambitious'. With *Jumping Flash!* being cited as the first-ever true 3D platformer and *Bubsy 3D* being known as one of the most awful games to ever be made.

For me, I never really got on with the 3D platformer genre generally speaking. I don't know, there's just something about platforming games that work perfectly well in 2D in my opinion. Just quickly going back to the *Super Mario Bros. 3* chapter for a second, Shigeru Miyamoto himself pointed that very thing out when that game almost became an isometric one instead of the more traditional 2D platformer the series was known for at the time. Well, Miyamoto-san must've had quite a change of heart when it came to making *Super Mario 64*. Mario was no longer a 2D sprite in a 2D world, he was now in full-on 3D.

66 OF THE MOST IMPORTANT VIDEO GAMES EVER!
(ACCORDING TO ME)

Super Mario 64 had around fifteen people working on it, headed up by Shigeru Miyamoto who served as both director and producer. The game actually started out as nothing more than a cube moving around an open 3D space. Eventually, that cube evolved into an animated Mario and those open 3D spaces became early level prototypes. Miyamoto would just sit there, moving this new 3D Mario around those early level designs coming up with ideas. Items were added for Mario to grab and throw, obstacles for him to navigate and avoid. A small rabbit was added called MIPS, which was the name of the N64's CPU (MIPS R4300i). Miyamoto became obsessed with trying to catch the rabbit, which led to refining Mario's controls within a 3D environment, something that was all very new to the man who created Mario fifteen years earlier.

Shigeru Miyamoto wanted Mario to feel 'real', he wanted to include actual universal laws of physics in Mario's movements to help add to the 'real' feeling. Mass, momentum, inertia and more. Speed was important too, depending on how much or little you pushed the N64's analogue stick, Mario would walk, run and sprint, which in turn, would affect his jumping. Yet some basic physics laws were broken to add to the fun, such as being able to control Mario in mid-air. Miyamoto talks about how Mario's physics worked in a *Mario 64* strategy guide:

> "The area around his hips is a big 'joint' that controls which way his body moves. We created all his movements from that point of origin. When he accelerates and inclines forward, when he turns and leans left or right, etc. So Mario sort of runs like Arale-chan (a popular anime character in Japan), with the correct sense of weight in the body."

As soon as you picked up the controller to play *Super Mario 64*, it just instantly felt right. The game didn't just offer 3D environments and graphics. It gave us gamers actual 3D movement and 3D controls. You were able to move Mario around with ease and the leap from 2D to 3D had been cracked. Nintendo succeeded where so many other developers had previously failed. The game just felt like such a joy to play... A joy, not a battle as with some other 3D platformers of the day.

The thing about the previous Mario titles and them being in 2D meant linearity, as great as they were, you are still basically running from left to right to get to the end of a level. A few instances aside, there was little to explore in the levels of those games, just get to the end. *Super Mario 64* was much more open by comparison and encouraged you to explore each of the levels. I mean, there was the main star collecting mechanic. Play and replay the same levels, but each star you had to nab entailed a different set of rules and goals to get, which would take you to different parts of a level to test different skills. And yet, it all still felt very Mario-esque despite the game breaking so many of the franchise's established rules. Usually, when a game franchise changes its direction like this, it often falls flat, but *Super Mario 64* defined the 3D platform genre. Some of the high praise the game gets can be credited to several small children, including his own, as Shigeru Miyamoto explains:

"Truth be told, we did something with *Mario 64* that we don't usually do, we had children play-test it. We had a row of about ten middle schoolers and had them play around on the King Bob-omb's stage for half a day, while we observed from behind. My child was one of them, actually...

But seeing him try dozens of times, over and over, to get up this unclimbable hill, as a parent I couldn't help but think, 'Geez, does this kid have any brains?'

Afterwards, we asked the children what they thought of the game, and they said it was fun, and that they wanted to play it again. Up to now, I think there's been this image with games that if you can't beat it, it's not a fun or good game, right? That's a philosophy we've stuck to at Nintendo, too, but I figured that if a game was this fun to play even if you weren't getting anywhere, well, it must be alright. Until this game, I was very sceptical about something like this being fun."

I still remember the very first time I ever played *Super Mario 64*. Finding myself in the grounds of Princess Peach's castle, which was where the main game takes place. I spend hours just running around that opening area, climbing up trees, experimenting with this new 3D Mario to see what he could do, jumping into the water and going for a swim, triple-jumping, backflipping, sliding, etc. I didn't even start the game proper for a good while as I was just so damn impressed and enthralled with how Mario moved and felt. The controls were perfect... Perfect. Those grounds in front of the castle are not exactly huge either, it's not as if they were packed with hours and hours of explorable content. But, I

66 OF THE MOST IMPORTANT VIDEO GAMES EVER! (ACCORDING TO ME)

still spend plenty of time doing a lot of nothing, just because playing as Mario felt so right, because those controls nailed 3D movement like no other game had managed to do before it. It was understanding the difference between 2D and 3D that made *Mario 64* so damn amazing, something Miyamoto was very much aware of when making the game:

> "In the Mario games up to now, we've carefully crafted every stage and level down to the individual pixel. Take jumping, for example. Implementing jumping in 3D is really difficult. In earlier Mario games, we were able to measure the number of pixels Mario could jump and know exactly what was possible. But this time, we had to design the levels so that as long as your jump was close enough, you'd make it, it was too hard for the player to judge. This was a design change we made in the middle of the development, when the game was far already very complete. There was a lot of booing from the staff. But that's the decisive difference between 2D and 3D. At the same time, it's what accounts for the dynamism players enjoy in a 3D game. The essence of what makes a 2D game 'fun' is entirely different."

For me, it is that playfulness and the fun factor that really sells this game. Playfulness and fun which actually begins before the game even starts. Yup, it's one of the most iconic start screens ever in a game, it's 3D Mario face time. Pulling Mario's cheeks, distorting his nose and brow, yanking on his ears and more. You could really create some terrifying abominations of a Mario. Then, it could all just bounce back into place for you to create more Mario monstrosities. The game hadn't even started and the fun was there right at the title screen. Completely unnecessary? Definitely, but no less important or fun.

As for Yoshi and Luigi and why they were not in the game proper. There have been quite a lot of fan theories about that, but Shigeru Miyamoto already explained their absence:

> "There was originally an event with Yoshi. We weren't satisfied with how it came out, though, so we removed it. But since it would be a waste not to use the model we had made, we included him there at the end.

> He [Luigi] was in the game. Ultimately, due to memory issues, we had to take him out. Then we were going to include him in a *Mario Bros.* style mini-game, but because most users probably only have that one controller when they first buy their N64, for that reason, we decided not to."

Super Mario 64 went on to influence the 3D platforming genre for years, even today. Its 3D architecture was just perfect. For me, I don't think future Mario games have got it as right as this title did. *Super Mario Sunshine*, *Super Mario Galaxy* (and its sequel) and *Super Mario Odyssey* were all certainly fantastic games. But they just didn't capture that lighting the same way that *Super Mario 64* did. There's also something to be said about playing the game with the original N64 controller too. I have played some of the various ports of *Super Mario 64*, yet, none of them 'feel' right without that iconic N64 pad in my hand. The controls are just not as fluid or as responsive as they were on the N64. *Super Mario 64,* on the N64, is the epitome of 3D platformers and one (for me) that has never been bettered.

66 OF THE MOST IMPORTANT VIDEO GAMES EVER!
(ACCORDING TO ME)

TOMB RAIDER
DEVELOPER: CORE DESIGN
PUBLISHER: EIDOS INTERACTIVE
PLATFORM: SEGA SATURN
RELEASED: OCTOBER, 1996

It's funny, but in my mind, I always remember the original *Tomb Raider* game as being a massive PlayStation exclusive, I think that a great many other gamers do too. But not only was it not a PlayStation exclusive, it wasn't even originally released on the PlayStation either. *Tomb Raider* was first released on the Sega's Saturn console in October of 1996, before it was unleashed onto Sony's PlayStation in November of the same year. Regardless, *Tomb Raider* became a phenomenon after release and etched its protagonist, Lara Croft, into gaming history forever.

It was artist and animator, Toby Gard, who first came up with the original concept of what would become *Tomb Raider* and its iconic lead character. It has been said that Gard suggested that they make an Indiana Jones inspired action-platformer type of a game, and it was also Toby Gard who created Lara Croft. Details on just how Lara came to exist seem to be a bit 'sketchy' to say the least, as there are several conflicting reports on her origins. Some ex-Core Design employees say that Lara was based on Frances Gard, Toby Gard's sister and that the character was always going to be female. Others say the original idea was for the protagonist to be male and a blatant Indiana Jones rip-off, but he was later changed to female to avoid any potential messy lawsuits from George Lucas. Whichever is true, early concept art shows that at some point in development, Lara Croft was originally called Laura Cruz. Oh and apparently, Lara Croft's name was picked out from a telephone directory in Derby. Glitzy!

Toby Gard teamed up with programmer, Paul Douglas and the two worked at fleshing out the early concept into a full-blown game. The FPS genre was still very much in favour, thanks to *Doom*. However, Core Design wanted something different to stand out, and the advent of 3D gaming made that possible. The idea of a third-person game over a first-person was chosen, to not only to show that not everything had to be a FPS, but also to show off the main character model... For reasons that will soon become apparent. Early test levels were created and Gard got to demonstrate his creation for the first time. Seeing a fully animated character on screen, that was what really impressed other Core Design employees at the time. The *Tomb Raider* dev team began to grow just based on that early test alone, adding more programmers and designers to get the game really underway.

It has never really been established just why Lara was designed the way she was. Hyper-sexualised is one way to describe her, I guess. The thin waistline, rather large (and very, very pointy) breasts, the fact gamers would be viewing Lara from behind for the most part. I don't think it would be too much of a stretch to assume that Tony Gard knew exactly the kind of gamer he wanted to attract with his creation. Young heterosexual males, who really were the main demographic for games back in the mid-nineties in the midst of all the 'lad culture' that was going on. Still, Lara wasn't just all about sexuality at all, she also had a personality... And a ballsy one at that too. She was strong of mind, intelligent and no-nonsense. Not the first female protagonist at all, but one that caught the attention of both sexes, just for very different reasons. Then there's that rumour of just how Lara got such big, polygonic melons in the first place. Programmer, Gavin Rummery weighs in on that rumour in this interview from Eurogamer:

"Toby was obviously trying to make her [Lara] sexy, because that was meant to be part of her character. He always claims he slipped on the mouse and made the breasts bigger than he meant to, but how true that is, I don't know. She was just meant to be curvy and attractive. Toby said, if you're going to be following behind her, she might as well be appealing to look at. It worked for both men and women on that basis, because women liked they were playing as a female character in the first place."

Publisher, Eidos Interactive really just left the development team to do what they were doing, with little to no interference. Trusting the team to deliver a fantastic product in the end. The only major stipulation was that the game had to be finished and released by Christmas, 1996. From what I've managed to discover, the development cycle was a pretty brutal one with many long hours. The team would often work late at night and even over the weekends. Some programmers would often

66 OF THE MOST IMPORTANT VIDEO GAMES EVER! (ACCORDING TO ME)

finish working at the office, just to carry on working from home, putting a strain on their home life and personal relationships. Level designer, Heather Stevens (née Gibson) remembers the hectic and heavy workload:

"I felt I had to get home, even if it was just to be in the same room as my partner. Granted, he might not have got much of a conversation out of me, but just to keep our relationship, there was no way I could afford to spend hours and hours in the evening at Core."

Oh yeah, 'crunch time', that phrase that's being thrown around a lot right now, was very much a thing back then too. The shit really hit the fan though when the head of Core Design made an exclusive deal for *Tomb Raider* to be released on the Sega Saturn first, before the originally planned PlayStation release in November of 96. The team had already been working their collective nuts off to get the game ready for Christmas… Then they found out it needed to be ready before then. There were heated discussions and arguments between the development team, the publisher and Core Design co-founder, Jeremy Heath-Smith. Still, the deal for the Saturn version had already been made, the team HAD to make it work. Around six weeks or so was removed from the development cycle due to that exclusive Saturn deal and the team had to get down to some serious crunch time, on top of the crunching they were already doing. They just did it as Gavin Rummery said:

"We were all in our mid-twenties and kinda coped with it then. It was before we had kids to worry about. We all worked like nutters for a burst. It wasn't much fun, but we all got it done. We weren't exactly forced at gunpoint to do it. We just realised we needed to work, and we started working later to try and get things done, and then later and later, trying to get everything in. We didn't have producers breathing down our neck or anything like that. We just got on with it."

Publisher Eidos knew that they could use Lara Croft to sell the game even though this was the first *Tomb Raider* title and no one actually knew who she was. For a while, alternate titles for the game included *Lara Croft: Tomb Raider* and *Lara Croft's Adventures*, they just really wanted to push the whole Lara Croft thing from the start. They knew they wanted her name in the title somewhere. Eventually, they settled on sticking with the original title of *Tomb Raider*, however, Eidos insisted on adding 'featuring Lara Croft' on the bottom of the box art... Oh, and a design that was pretty much all Lara too. But it didn't end with the box art, real-world models were hired to play Lara at conventions. One such model being Katie Price from when she used to be damn attractive and before the whole Jordan, stupid fake titties crap. Billboards and the sides of buses proudly displayed the in-game Lara as a model herself. Again you have to remember that no one knew who this Lara girl was at the time, and yet, all the advertising surrounded her more so than the actual game itself.

Anyway, Eidos' marketing worked and the team got the game finished in time too. *Tomb Raider* was released on the Saturn in October of 1996. It did well, but it was when it hit the PlayStation a few weeks later when the impact of the game really became clear. It was a match made in heaven, Sony's new console was being marketed directly toward slightly older gamers, those twenty-somethings with plenty of disposable income. The exact same demographic that Eidos wanted *Tomb Raider* to attract and a franchise was born.

Lara Croft became a pop culture phenomenon, not just in the games. She was advertising SEAT cars, Lucozade energy drinks, Visa credit cards. She was plastered on the covers of and the insides of the 'lad mags' of the nineties, featured in a U2 live gig and music video (for a song from the first *Tomb Rider* flick) and much more besides. Lara Croft was everywhere, even if you didn't know the games, you knew who Lara was. That's pretty much why *Tomb Raider* made it into this book, due to how a game character became such a huge cultural icon. I mean, yes there certainly had been famed gaming icons before. *Pac-Man* was the first, Mario is definitely one of the most famous. But Lara Croft was a whole new level for a gaming character, she had a successful 'career' outside of the games... And I'm not sure if that has ever happened before or since. Oh, and the fact that *Tomb Raider* was an amazing action-adventure-platformer to boot, that's another reason why it's in this book.

66 OF THE MOST IMPORTANT VIDEO GAMES EVER! (ACCORDING TO ME)

GOLDENEYE 007
DEVELOPER: RAREWARE
PUBLISHER: NINTENDO
PLATFORM: NINTENDO 64
RELEASED: AUGUST, 1997

James Bond has had quite a lengthy life in gaming. From his first digital outing in the 1982 text-adventure, *Shaken but Not Stirred*, to the very recently announced, as I type this very sentence right now, at this very second, *Project 007* (working title, date to be confirmed). However, Bond games have always been a little 'uneven' shall we say. With nearly thirty games covering almost four decades of gaming, there just aren't too many truly great James Bond video games. There have been some okay Bond games, some downright terrible ones. But there has only ever been one James Bond game that gamers tend to universally look back on with fondness and great respect, this one, *GoldenEye 007*.

Developed by Rareware for Nintendo, *GoldenEye 007* was directed and produced by Martin Hollis with David Doak as writer and designer. I think what is most impressive about the game is that it was developed by a relativity small, eleven-person team of mostly first-timers with little to no game development experience at all (only one of the team had previous game development experience). The fact it was also released two years after the film was made, had the gaming press think that the game would be a big flop. A small team of inexperienced devs, making a game based on a two-year-old James Bond film when the new film was just about to be released? Quite honestly, *GoldenEye 007* really had very little going for it on paper. As for just why it was released two years after the film?

Normally, a movie tie-in game is released around the same time as the film it is based on is out in cinemas. This is so the (hopefully) popularity of the film would (hopefully) help boost sales of the game. In fact, this game almost did come out in time for the movie release. Well, that should read 'a *GoldenEye*' game almost came out in time for the movie release. The idea to make a game based on the then up and coming Bond film first came about in late 1994. Nintendo and Rare had been talking about the possibility of making a James Bond game when Martin Hollis approached Rare co-founder, Tim Stamper, expressing interest in heading up the project. At first, the game was conceived as being a 2D platformer-shooter on the SNES. Using the same technology behind Rare's smash hit and graphically ground-breaking, *Donkey Kong Country*. The 2D platformer idea was on the table for a while, until Hollis suggested that they make a 3D shooter for the then, still being developed, new Nintendo console, the Nintendo 64 (codenamed the Ultra 64). Martin Hollis sat down and began writing his proposal of idea for the game and tried to include as many Bond tropes as he could.

The development team were given access to the movie's production and got to visit the famed 007 Stage at Pinewood Studios too. They saw an early version of the script so they could make the game follow the plot closely, took photos of the sets and locations for reference and more. Karl Hilton, lead environment artist on the game recalls the set visits with MEL Magazine:

> "The early concepting for *GoldenEye* involved myself, Martin Hollis and Bea Jones going down to the film set for several days to take photos of everything we could find, from props and costumes to all of the actual film sets and even models and miniatures. I took hundreds of photos on 35mm film, we used them as reference for all of the in-game art."

Eon Productions and MGM, who own the James Bond film rights, allowed Rare to use some creative licence, so they could add their own flair to the game as long as they stayed faithful to the movie and Bond lore. While the film's production team were happy to share their secrets, Nintendo were no quite so forthcoming. The big N's new console was being kept very much under wraps and as Martin Hollis and his small team at Rare got started on their *GoldenEye* game, they didn't know a great deal about the platform it would be made for, which was due to be released in the summer of 1996. The final Nintendo 64 specifications and development kits were not made available to Rare either. So, they had to do a lot of guesswork when production of the game began proper in the January of 1995.

While Rare were confident that the new console could handle 3D graphics, it was the controller that was the major issue. The team didn't

66 OF THE MOST IMPORTANT VIDEO GAMES EVER!
(ACCORDING TO ME)

know anything about the N64 pad, how many buttons it would have, whether it would be digital or analogue, etc. So to play it safe, they decided to work on the game as an on-rails FPS, with Sega's *Virtua Cop* being a major influence. They even had to use a slightly modified Sega Saturn controller for early playtesting as David Doak remembers:

"The N64 controller wasn't finalized when we started, so we used some kind of hacked Sega Saturn controller cobbled together. It was very much, 'Put some stuff together, see how it feels, is it capturing the story and do we need extra stuff added in?' Then I'd go back to Mark Edmonds [gameplay and engine programmer] and say, 'If we could do this, it'd be better.' And Mark would fiddle about and say, 'Well, there aren't tools for doing that, so try to go and build it from scratch.'"

Mark Edmonds also recalls the game when it evolved from an on-rails shooter:

"The hit-test and detection-work probably came about as we originally started making the game in the style of the arcade games *Virtua Cop* and *Time Crisis*, where aiming and hitting the right thing was a crucial part of the gameplay. Martin Hollis wrote the code for hit-testing, then I took it and kind of bodged it so it could be used for shooting tests as well. Then I added on some simple cuboid hitbox testing on the character limbs and other props, like crates, so you could actually shoot and destroy stuff."

But when Rare did finally get N64 development kits and controllers, that was when they realised just what they could do with the hardware. The game was changed from a restrictive on-rails shooter, to a much more open and interesting FPS.

Programmer, Steve Ellies was brought onto the team and he worked on several elements of the game, including the famous cheats. Ellies was also the main person who implemented *GoldenEye 007's* most fondly remembered feature, the multiplayer mode. One of the best things to ever been included in any N64 title, and yes, using Odd Job is cheating. Something interesting that I dug up was that Nintendo and Shigeru Miyamoto especially was not too happy with all the violence. In fact,

Miyamoto even suggested a rather strange way to get around the shooting and killing of bad guys in the game, as Martin Hollis told The Guardian:

> "One point was that there was too much close-up killing, he [Shigeru Miyamoto] found it a bit too horrible. I don't think I did anything with that input. The second point was, he felt the game was too tragic, with all the killing. He suggested that it might be nice if, at the end of the game, you got to shake hands with all your enemies in the hospital."

Yes, James Bond going to a hospital to shake hands with everyone he had previously 'killed' was suggested by the man who created Mario. Instead, Hollis came up with the idea of adding a credit sequence featuring the 'actors' to keep Shigeru Miyamoto happy:

> "It was very filmic, and the key thing was, it underlined that this was artifice. The sequence told people that this was not real killing."

GoldenEye 007 hit the shop shelves in August of 1997. Long after the film that it was based on had been released. In fact, the next Bond film (*Tomorrow Never Dies*) had already finished filming and was in post-production, ready to be released a few months later. *GoldenEye 007's* release certainly wasn't very timely at all. Not that it really mattered that much because the game was a huge hit regardless. The FPS genre was everywhere on PCs due to *Doom*, yet the genre didn't really translate to consoles all that well. It was this game that changed all of that. *GoldenEye 007* proved that yes, a top-notch FPS could be achieved on a console, and it really opened the doors for the future.

There were a few features that were considered, but not included. One was the likenesses of all the previous Bond actors. Rare mistakenly thought that them having the licence to the movie *GoldenEye* meant they could use any previous James Bond assets... They couldn't. The feature was in the game, but disabled. Not removed, just disabled. Yes, the 'all Bonds mode', as it became known, is still in *GoldenEye 007*, you just can't access it... Unless you cheat. Fan-site, The Rare Witch Project even discovered that the graphics for the other Bonds are still on the game cartridge and they can be mapped onto other multi-player characters to be used, it just takes a lot of tinkering to get it to work.

66 OF THE MOST IMPORTANT VIDEO GAMES EVER!
(ACCORDING TO ME)

Another dropped feature was the ability to reload the in-game guns by pulling out and re-inserting the N64's Rumble Pak. This too was in the game for a while, but it was Nintendo themselves who requested the feature be pulled (no pun) for unknown reasons. There were even ten other games hidden on the released cartridge too. The development team at Rare rather cheekily programmed a fully functional ZX Spectrum emulator into *GoldenEye 007*, packed with ten games from Ultimate Play the Game. Ultimate, being the company Rare founders, the Stamper brothers, ran before Rare. Anyway, said ZX Spectrum emulator and games were just put in as a bit of fun for the developers of the game, with the intention to remove it for the commercial release of *GoldenEye 007*. Of course, it was disabled from the final build of the game. Not removed, just disabled. And yes, it too can be accessed if you know how.

Anyway, *GoldenEye 007* was universally praised upon release. The very low expectations of a game from a small team of inexperienced unknowns, based on a two-year-old film were soon forgotten about when you finally played it. *GoldenEye 007* was the third best selling game on the Nintendo 64, and is still looked on now as a true pioneer of the FPS genre, especially on consoles. Or as David Doak put it when talking to MEL Magazine:

> "Its recognition and enduring legacy, a lot of that is luck, the kind of perfect storm of some things that came together. It was significant because it was a great four-player split-screen game on N64, there was no console FPS that had such a compelling single-player game at that stage, especially given 3D was totally new."

For me, *GoldenEye 007* is one of the most important FPS games ever made, it's right up there with id Software's *Doom*. Not as good as *Doom* gameplay-wise, but equally as important in terms of its legacy and influence.

S. L. PERRIN

GRAND THEFT AUTO
DEVELOPER: DMA DESIGN
PUBLISHER: BMG INTERACTIVE
PLATFORM: MS-DOS
RELEASED: OCTOBER, 1997

Who'd have thought that when a quartet of friends founded the development studio, DMA Design in Dundee in 1987, that they would go on to create a title which would change the industry forever? I'll not bore you with the founding of DMA Design, so let's just skip right to the main course that is *Grand Theft Auto*. Having already had some pretty big hits with the likes of the classic puzzle game *Lemmings* and hard as nails shooter *Walker*, DMA co-founder and programmer, Mike Dailly came up with the concept for a new game. On the 22nd of March 1995, a design document for this new game called *Race'n'Chase*, was presented. Taken from that design document (uploaded to flickr.com by Mike Dailly himself), *Race'n'Chase* was said to be:

"A fun, addictive, and fast multi-player car racing and crashing game which uses a novel graphics method."

The document also laid out some of the game's basic details:

"Players will be able to drive cars and possibly other vehicles such as boats, helicopters or lorries. Cars can be stolen, raced, collided, crashed (ram raiding?) and have to be navigated about a large map. It will also be possible for players to get out of their car and steal another one. This will mean controlling a vulnerable pedestrian for a short time. Trying to steal a car may result in an alarm being set off which will, of course, attract the police."

Originally, *Race'n'Chase* was set to have four different, playable game modes. 'Cannonball Run' would be a straight-up race across the city the game would be set in, inspired by the film of the same name. 'Demolition Derby' was to be a classic 'smash into and cause as much damage to other players as possible' style mode. The 'Bank Robbery' mode would have you playing as the bad guy driving a getaway car and trying to escape the chasing police, all while trying to commit as much

66 OF THE MOST IMPORTANT VIDEO GAMES EVER! (ACCORDING TO ME)

chaos as possible without getting caught. Then finally, 'Bank Robbery-Cop' where you controlled the police, chasing after the getaway car in a reverse of the previous mode. These game modes were thought to have been themed around the title's original intention of being a multiplayer title. Set to be played across a network on PC, or with two people at the same console. Rather boldly, the design document pencilled in a release date of the 1st of July 1996. Bearing in mind that the design document was dated March of 1995. That's only a little over a year of development. In reality, the game took a bit longer.

Of course, things changed as the development of *Race'n'Chase* continued. The multiplayer angle was dropped to make it a single-player game. The idea of having four specific game modes was also changed, and the game became much more open with multiple, varied missions. Oh yeah, it also had a title change to *Grand Theft Auto*. The game's producer, David Jones, said that *Pac-Man* was a big influence on *GTA*. The idea of being chased by police came from those colourful, cartoony ghostly apparitions. The maze-like cites of *GTA* also came from *Pac-Man*. There was another game that was a huge influence on the development of *Grand Theft Auto* too. Gary Penn, creative director of DMA Design, explained in this article from Gamasutra while *GTA* was still in development:

> "The game as it stands now is basically *Elite* in a city, but without quite the same sense of taking on the jobs. You take on the jobs in a slightly different way, but incredibly similar structurally. It's just a much more acceptable real-world setting."

Yup, going right back to that space trading and influential game from 1984. *Elite*, pretty much the origin of the open-world genre, was one of the biggest influences for *GTA*. You know, as I type this right now, *Pac-Man* meets *Elite* kind of works as the perfect way to describe the original *Grand Theft Auto*.

Development on the game was not exactly smooth sailing though. The 3D detailed polygons era of gaming was very much taking over by the mid-nineties, and yet, here was this top-down, 2D sprite-based game. *GTA* seemed positivity dated by comparison to most other games hitting the market then. The structure of the game was so open and non-linear that quite a few of the higher-ups just didn't 'get it'. Deadlines kept getting pushed back as DMA wanted to add more and more features. It was obvious that the proposed July 1996 release date clearly would not be met. Conference calls to the publisher, BMG Interactive, often got more than a little 'heated'. The publisher just wanted the game to be done, but DMA kept asking for more time to make the title better and better. More than once, *Grand Theft Auto* was almost cancelled. Head of PR for DMA, Brian Baglow recalls in this interview with PCGamesN:

> "It was under constant threat of cancellation. At least three-quarters of the game's development we had no idea what was going to appear at the end. In fact, I'll go further, it was probably about six-sevenths of the game's life, it could've been a horrible disaster. The publishers were nervous about it and really weren't sure if it was going too big and if they should continue to support it and if it was actually going to produce something of any value at the end."

Can you honestly imagine a gaming world where *Grand Theft Auto* never existed? Take-Two would never have purchased BMG Interactive, the Houser brothers would never have co-founded Rockstar North/Games and the entire Rockstar Games empire would never have existed. But exist it did and when *Grand Theft Auto* was released, it kicked up a huge fuss. The crime-based gameplay and penchant for bloody violence of *GTA* really got the backs up of a lot of press and politicians. At one point, *GTA* was even discussed in parliament. Brian Baglow looks back on all the infamous controversy of the game:

> "In all honesty it was hilarious. We hadn't set out to build the world's most controversial game or even a slightly controversial game. All we were looking for was something fun. All we were looking for was something that worked and we thought was worth playing. We knew from the outset that there was something there, it took an awfully long time to drill down and figure out exactly what the hell it was, but we certainly didn't set out to shock and offend and upset humanity.

> When we were starting to get denounced in the houses of Commons and Lords, when the press were up in arms, we were amused by it. Sorry, I should say bemused by it. We were like, really? You think this is bad?

66 OF THE MOST IMPORTANT VIDEO GAMES EVER! (ACCORDING TO ME)

Because it's all top-down, there was no actual real cut scenes or animation or anything and everything was implied. At every point, it was just text that served to tell you the kind of things that were happening, the kind of things that were going on. It was absolutely not a game where we set out to try and be provocative."

One of the original *Grand Theft Auto's* standout elements, that wasn't violence or controversy related, came from audio director Colin Anderson. It was Anderson who came up with the idea of having radio stations in the game. He wanted the music of the game to come from the vehicles themselves. When the player got out of a car, the music would stop, when they got into a car, it would start again. 'Interactive audio' is what Anderson called it, then when the radio station idea was worked out, everything else just fell into place. DJs, news reports, even different music depending on what car you were in at the time. As an example, the poor handling, low-speed pick-up truck would belt out country and western music. This radio stations style music isn't just something that had been worked into every *GTA* title from the original game onwards, it's been worked into pretty much every open-world game ever made since. And in a genius bit of publicity, the publishers of the game BMG Interactive, were originally a music media and publishing company, BMG standing for Bertelsmann Music Group. So, the music division of the company actually got the word out that the bands and artists and music in the game were from real-world musical artists and that they were licensed exclusively for *GTA*. But the truth is that all the music was created in-house at DMA Design and the bands and artists were completely fictional. But the word on the street was that this new game got all these up and coming artists exclusively working on this new game, which added an element of 'coolness' about it.

It wasn't too long after the release and massive success of *Grand Theft Auto* that BMG decided to pull out of the games industry completely. They just helped create one of the biggest, most important and most influential games ever and then just stopped.

Grand Theft Auto is often (wrongly) credited with creating the open-world genre. We already know it didn't, there are plenty of examples of the genre already in this book alone. But, *GTA* did, at the very least, evolve the genre and make it more popular than ever. Then there was the attention to detail and sheer passion behind getting the game made from such humble beginnings. I honestly don't think the open-world genre of games would be as big or as popular today if not for the original *Grand Theft Auto,* a small game made by a small team from Scotland who changed the face of gaming forever.

Oh, and just to finish, I want to quickly clear a little something up. *Grand Theft Auto* has always been remembered as being and known as a 2D game, I'm even guilty of calling it just that in this both my previous gaming book, *MicroBrits* (still available from Amazon) and even in this very chapter. But here's the thing, *GTA* was actually 3D. Don't believe me? Just go and play it right now, or look up a video on YouTube. Pay attention to the buildings and scenery graphics, they are 3D models. In fact, Brian Baglow had this to say about the original *GTA* when he spoke to PCGamesN:

> "It was entirely new, nothing else like this had been done, but at the same time it didn't look ground-breaking, it looked like this silly wee top-down game that was only two-dimensional, despite the fact you had X, Y and Z-axis. I nearly punched more than one person that said it wasn't 3D. "

Grand Theft Auto may have been a top-down view, but it was still 3D with 3D graphics in a 3D world. As Baglow said, it even had X, Y and Z-axis too. So from now on, don't go around saying that *GTA* was 2D, otherwise, Brian Baglow is very likely to punch you in the face.

66 OF THE MOST IMPORTANT VIDEO GAMES EVER!
(ACCORDING TO ME)

GRAN TURISMO
DEVELOPER: POLYPHONY DIGITAL
PUBLISHER: SONY COMPUTER ENTERTAINMENT
PLATFORM: PLAYSTATION
RELEASED: DECEMBER, 1997

I do love a good driving game and there was no shortage of them in the nineties either. I recall playing titles such as *Daytona USA*, *Ridge Racer* and *Cruis'n USA*, among others, in the arcade. Those brash, audacious and awesome games in even more awesome arcade cabinets. Anyone remember the *Ridge Racer* full-scale arcade cabinet? It had an actual, full-size Mazda MX-5 that you sat in, in front of a ten-foot-high, triple-wide screen. The car's real controls worked to play the game itself, including turning the ignition key to start the game. Fans hidden in the car's dashboard would blow air into your face as you played and more. It was amazing. Still, while arcades were offering a semi-realistic racing environment, the games themselves were very much... Well, arcadey.

Driving simulations had been a thing for a while up to that point, but they were mainly focused on sports like Formula 1. Real road cars, as in those you could drive every day, they were not really that much of a focus or draw for driving games back then. Racing games were more about fantasy, the joy of tearing through the sun-kissed environments of *OutRun* in a blood-red Ferrari Testarossa, the thrill of sliding around muddy tracks in *Sega Rally Championship* in a Lancia Stratos HF were great fun, but still very much full of fairyland dreams for your average gamer. Then along came *Gran Turismo* from Polyphony Digital, giving you the chance to drive everyday cars like a Honda Accord Sedan, the kind of car a middle management stationery shop worker type would use.

Well okay, to be fair, *Gran Turismo* did offer you cars that were a bit more 'special' than just the sort that Susan from HR would most probably favour. The likes of the Chevrolet Corvette Stingray, Honda NSX-R GT1 Turbo, TVR Cerbera LM Edition and many other proper race cars were available too. But the thing about *Gran Turismo* was how 'real' it all felt. I mean, it was dubbed as 'The Real Driving Simulator' right on the box.

It was producer and designer, Kazunori Yamauchi, who brought *Gran Turismo* to the PlayStation. Yamauchi had a bit of experience when it came to racing games on the PlayStation, being the man behind *Motor Toon Grand Prix*. Not exactly the 'real driving simulator' that *GT* was boasting about, the game was a very cartoon-like karting game. But it was making *Motor Toon Grand Prix* that landed Kazunori Yamauchi the job of bringing *Gran Turismo* to life. In fact, the idea of a racing sim on the PlayStation came before his cutesy karting game. The suits at Sony didn't see the appeal of a realistic racing game, so Yamauchi came up with a plan, as he remembers in this interview with PlayStation.com:

> "What I did was to start a project in the racing game genre that was easier to understand for the executives. We secured the budget for creating *Motor Toon Grand Prix* and we pushed the project forward, but in the background, we'd actually already started the development of *Gran Turismo*."

His plan worked too as *Motor Toon Grand Prix* was a hit, it even got a sequel. Those suits at Sony loved the game, and that was when Kazunori Yamauchi tried pitching his realistic driving sim game idea to them once more. This time, and due to his work on that cartoony kart game, they trusted his judgement… Which was just as well because Yamauchi had already started work on the game. *Gran Turismo* may have been released in 1997, but it actually began production in 1992.

Right from the start, Kazunori Yamauchi strived for authenticity, the car physics had to be spot on, the vehicles had to react as they would in real life when cornering and more. Adding new components to your car, such as spoilers, brakes, turbo kits and so on would also affect how the cars drove and felt. The team gathered actual car data from the manufacturers to ensure the digital versions were as close to the real thing as possible. Yamauchi even learned to drive real race cars, just so he could make the game as close to the real thing as it could be.

Gran Turismo captured racing like no other game had done before it, a genuine showcase of real motorsport. The cars featured were as close to their real-world counterparts as the PlayStation could make them, all one hundred and forty of them. That was an absurd amount of drivable cars in a game. We were used to a couple of cars to choose from, maybe half

66 OF THE MOST IMPORTANT VIDEO GAMES EVER! (ACCORDING TO ME)

a dozen at a push and even then, they were never what you would call 'manufacturer accurate'. Then we suddenly had *Gran Turismo* with well over a century of different cars from multiple real-world manufacturers. Plus, each of those cars could be customised and upgraded too. It really put me in mind of that other customisable racing game, *Street Rod* from 1989... Only more 'real'. Kazunori Yamauchi looked back on the original GT game with Eurogamer:

> "What I aimed for in *Gran Turismo* was very simple. It was really to make a real driving simulator, and to have real-life cars appear in the game. I didn't know if it was possible with that hardware back then to achieve what we wanted to do. The first *Gran Turismo*, it was one of the first 3D racing games, and one of the first, if not the first to introduce physics simulations. There was no definite future for either one of those subjects, so we were very much in the dark."

I remember seeing *Gran Turismo* for the first time. That cinematic and awesome looking introduction. Cars screeching around tracks, smoke pouring from the tyres. The breathtaking scenery and reflections in the windows of the cars. Then there were the cars themselves, stunning looking 3D models that were really damn close to the real thing. But, pretty much all PlayStation games had those flashy CG intros back then thanks to the use of the CD format. Then you'd press start and the game would look nothing like that mini-film you had just watched. *Gran Turismo* was different because that visually stunning intro was made using in-game graphics and the racing in the game looked just as impressive as the stunning introduction.

The thing about *Gran Turismo's* famed 'simulation' was that although it was certainly authentic in many ways, It never was a full simulation. *Gran Turismo* still had the right amount of arcade-like gameplay mixed with all of the simulation stuff to make a driving game that was as fun as it was as real. It paved the way for future real-world driving sims and even managed to make driving more grounded cars like a Toyota Corolla Levin exciting.

S. L. PERRIN

HALF-LIFE
DEVELOPER: VALVE
PUBLISHER: SIERRA STUDIOS
PLATFORM: WINDOWS
RELEASED: NOVEMBER, 1998

Former Microsoft employees, Mike Harrington and Gabe Newell founded Valve in 1996 (Newell actually set up the company and signed the papers on his wedding day) and the duo quite quickly settled on the idea of making a FPS game as their first title. They knew from the off they wanted to make a scary shooter and their biggest influence was, of course, *Doom*. Another influence was Stephen King's novella, *The Mist*. In fact, the working title for *Half-Life* was *Quiver*, which was taken from the Arrowhead military base from King's story.

It wasn't just *Doom* as a game that gave Valve a step in the right direction, id Software themselves were a huge help. First, id allowed Valve to use their *Quake* source code to help create their game. Secondly, they also gave Valve a couple of names that could help to get the game off the ground. Steve Bond and John Guthrie, who had started up a massively popular *Quake* fan site called Quake Command, and they had made several custom maps and mods for id's shooter. At the time, both Bond and Guthrie were college students, delivering pizzas to make a bit of extra cash on the side, while running the fan site. One day they received an e-mail, as John Guthrie recalls in a Gamespot article:

> "We got this e-mail from a guy named Gabe Newell. He told us he wanted to talk to us and left his phone number. Steve eventually called him. That day, Gabe bought Steve a plane ticket, a rental car, and a hotel room."

Gabe Newell flew Steve Bond out from Florida where he was in college, to Kirkland, Washington, East of Seattle, where Valve had set up their HQ. After a chat, Newell offered Bond a job as a designer/developer on their new game. He snapped up the offer, dropped out of college to work at Valve full-time, John Guthrie joined him a week later. The team was added to and when they felt ready, Valve began work on the concept of their very first game.

66 OF THE MOST IMPORTANT VIDEO GAMES EVER!
(ACCORDING TO ME)

The technology was there, thanks to id Software, the team was (mostly) in place and they had settled on the genre of game they wanted to make. Next, they needed a publisher to actually get the game onto shop shelves... Which was easier said than done. They tried several big-name publishers, and all of them turned Valve down flat. Why? Mainly due to the fact that the studio was new, they didn't have an actual game to show, just a concept. Despite the continual knock-backs, Gabe Newell believed in their game idea, so he sent off an e-mail to (Seattle based) Sierra On-Line. Ken Williams, who co-founded Sierra, got that e-mail as he remembers:

> "I had been looking aggressively for some product in the *Quake* genre. I was looking at licensing one of the 3D shooter engines and was negotiating with id and some others."

It was as if the stars had aligned, Williams was looking for a *Quake*-esque 3D shooter and really wanted to work with id Software. Then along came this new studio who had got permission to use the Quake engine from id themselves, as well as recommending a couple of guys experienced with making *Quake* maps and mods that they could use. It was as close to working with id Software without actually working with them as you could get. A meeting was quickly arranged and a few of the team at Valve got to talk to Ken Williams at Sierra On-Line's HQ. Gabe Newell took in a deep breath and began his pitch for this new game, he only managed to get a few minutes into his spiel when Williams stopped him before he had even really started. He just didn't want to hear any more, he didn't need to, Williams was in.

Interesting titbit for you. In the early-nineties when id Software was just starting as a game studio, Sierra almost bought them out. This was before *Doom*, and the talks broke down over a matter of money (what else?). Then when *Doom* was released, id became so huge in the industry they didn't need Sierra or anyone else to give them a leg up.

Anyway, not long after that very positive meeting, Ken Williams left Sierra On-Line before a signed deal between Valve and the publisher could be made. Things looked a little bleak for a while as Valve were back at square one without a publisher once more. Scott Lynch took over at Sierra On-Line and was not too sure if Valve were the right guys to work with, he initially had reservations over the whole thing, as Lynch recalls:

> "I think the big question with Valve right from the beginning was, 'OK, you've got the Quake engine, but is this just going to be new *Quake* levels?'. What we all wanted to see was Valve take the technology as a foundation and add something new. When they started talking about telling a story and creating a persistent world, it was pretty obvious they weren't going to do a mission pack with the *Quake* engine."

Scott Lynch took a chance and gave Valve a one-game deal, as well as changing the name of the company from Sierra On-Line to Sierra Studios. Valve wasted no time in getting to work on their FPS game, which was then called, *Quiver*. Over time, *Quiver* became *Half-Life* as the game evolved through development. Goals and ideas were put in place for *Half-Life*, action was one such goal of course… Lots of action. But both Mike Harrington and Gabe Newell wanted their first game to stand out against other games in the same genre. Puzzles were added just break up the action a little and offer a bit of a breather. Then, of course, there was the plot. FPS rarely had a story, or at least, they hardly ever had much of one. Still, not everyone was on board with the idea of a FPS game having a story as Newell explains:

> "For a long time 3D action games seemed to keep treading down the same path, an increasing focus on a narrow definition of gameplay and a focus on the rendering [graphics] instead of the gameplay. We'd occasionally get people who would say things like: 'Stories? Who needs them? I just want a rocket launcher that fires faster'. It's pretty scary to be spending a big chunk of your own money and be going in a direction that's different than the norm."

Still, ignoring the naysayers, the plot was going to be paramount for *Half-Life*. Valve even hired award-winning science fiction and horror writer, Marc Laidlaw to pen the story. Everything began to meld together through a lot of hard work. Originally aiming for a November 1997 release date, *Half-Life* even had its first public viewing at E3 97… Kind of. That E3 showing was really an animation demo more so than a game trailer, or even a decent representation of the game that Valve

66 OF THE MOST IMPORTANT VIDEO GAMES EVER! (ACCORDING TO ME)

wanted to make. It was around the summer of 1997 when it became painfully clear that *Half-Life* was just not going to be ready for November. A delay was inevitable and that didn't do a lot of good for the working relationship between newcomers Valve and seasoned industry experts, Sierra Studios. The publisher was not at all happy that the game, which they had been backing for a big Christmas release, wasn't going to be ready for Christmas. Promotion and PR for *Half-Life* had already begun too, which all costs money and publishers don't like to waste money.

Yet, that delay was not just inevitable, in retrospect, it was the best thing that could've happened to the game. The guys at Valve quickly realised that work on a lot of the levels and that pretty much all of the AI had to be scrapped and completely reworked from the ground up. All the while, Valve co-founders Mike Harrington's and Gabe Newell's pockets were only so deep and getting emptier and emptier as the days and weeks ticked by. They made it to E3 1998, and once more, the game was shown. Only this time, it wasn't a basic animation demo, it was a proper showing of just what *Half-Life* would be like… And it looked 'effing amazing too, like no other FPS on the market at the time.

The reaction from that E3 showing was a huge boost to the team, all they had to do was finish it. Everyone at Valve pushed to get the game ready for release, and they did too. It suffered a few delays along the way sure, but *Half-Life* made it and was released in November of 1998. Not just another FPS, *Half-Life* blew us gamers away. Yeah, it was another shooty-shooty game, but it had a depth that we had never seen before. Characters that talked… Except for the very silent Gordon Freeman who you play as. That long intro of Freeman arriving at the Black Mesa Research Facility where he worked was amazing. For a while, *Half-Life* was the best-selling FPS game of all time. Only to be beaten by *Counter-Strike: Global Offensive*… Which actually began life as a mod for *Half-Life*.

Just waiting on *Half-Life 3* now Valve, whenever you're ready…

S. L. PERRIN

THE NEW SUPERMAN ADVENTURES
DEVELOPER: TITUS INTERACTIVE
PUBLISHER: TITUS INTERACTIVE
PLATFORM: NINTENDO 64
RELEASED: MAY, 1999

Now, you are probably thinking, 'what Superman game on the Nintendo 64? I can only think of one and it was called *Superman 64*... the utter pile of shit-bollocks that it was!'. Well yes, this is the one you are thinking of, as its proper name is *Superman: The New Superman Adventures*. It just got colloquially known as *Superman 64* due to various publishers insistence of putting '64' at the end of a lot of their titles. So now that is cleared up, you're probably now thinking, 'why the hell is this crap in your book?'. A couple of reasons really. Firstly, back in the *E.T.* for the Atari 2600 chapter, I said how that game is far from being 'the worst game ever', despite the infamy the title has. There's a reason why I said that too, because *Superman 64* exists. As for the other reason why I have chosen to include this steaming turd in this book? Well, just keep reading.

Look, *Superman 64* was bad... Really, really bad. I know it, you know it and I'm pretty sure even people who've never played a video game before in their lives know it too. I'm not sure if I would label it 'the worst game ever', but it certainly has to be close. Bringing up how bad the game is, is a tad pointless. So this chapter covers something else.

Eric Caen was one of two brothers who co-founded Titus Interactive in the eighties. Anyway, Caen came up with the idea to get the license for Superman from Warner Bros., who at the time, was producing the *Superman: The Animated Series*. A deal was made in 1997 for Titus to make games based on that animated show... And yes, I did mean to write 'games', plural up there. Oh yeah, *Superman 64* was not an only child. In fact, the first Titus *Superman* game was released on the Game Boy, only a few months after that Superman deal had been made, later in 1997. Quick review, it's really not very good and served as a warning sign of what was to come. The N64 version though, well that's a slightly longer and much more interesting story, as it didn't take a few months to develop, it took around two years and many, many different changes.

66 OF THE MOST IMPORTANT VIDEO GAMES EVER! (ACCORDING TO ME)

Eric Caen's initial concept for his *Superman 64* game was for it to be a *Tomb Raider* inspired, 3D action-adventure kind of game. Superman would have full use of his powers to make the player feel like you really were playing as The Man of Steel. Caen gives a glimpse into the game before its release in this interview with IGN:

> "We wanted to create the first 'superhero' based video game where players really behave as a superhero. So of course you control Superman's movement in full 3D, jump, fight, but you can also fly very fast, use X-ray vision to see through certain walls, heat vision to burn some objects or enemies, and you can lift big objects and throw these objects at bad guys. The character/objects/background interactions system is so complex that you can throw a car that will collide with another car that will push a third object that will kill an enemy next to it!"

It actually sounded pretty damn good (for a late-nineties game), but if you have ever played *Superman 64*, then you already know that the game felt and played nothing like what Eric Caen described there. But why? Well, not too long after the deal was made between Titus and Warner Bros. to make games based on Superman, there was a change in the management team for licensing at WB. The new team didn't much like Caen or his ideas (according to him). He claims they felt his concept for the game wouldn't work and that another studio (namely Electronic Arts) should be the ones handling the Superman licence. This was when the licensor's interface began proper and when they would cause as much trouble for Eric Caen and his team as they could.

First, the WB licensing department told Eric Caen that he must change the entire genre of the game. Moving from that 3D action-adventure game that he envisioned, to a *Sim City* style management one instead. In this new game, Superman would be the 'mayor' of Metropolis (no joke) and responsible for its building and upkeep. You know, just like Superman doesn't do in the comics and films. So the genuine feeling of being a superhero, and more specifically Superman, was going to be pushed aside so Kal-El could try to keep Metropolis' traffic moving, provide citizens with safe energy and ensure there were enough jobs to go around... SUP-ER-MAN!

Caen and his development team basically told the WB licensing guys, 'no'. Which of course, they didn't like that one bit, and so WB began to make things very difficult for Titus. Warner Bros. began to micro-manage Titus and even harass the development team (according to Eric Caen), block pretty much any and all ideas they ever had as they continued to push their 3D action-adventure *Superman 64* game. Warner Bros. became purposefully obtuse to try and cause Titus to give up. Eric Caen recalls some of the issues in this interview with Playboy:

> "It took us months to get every single character approved. I think they were trying to stall us, and we have heard recently that WB even planned to pay a huge litigation settlement, because they forced us to kill the PlayStation version. But, we never ended up suing them. They argued against any decision we made in the game, under the pretext that 'Superman would never do that'. We had to prove Superman could go underwater, because they had doubts it would be acceptable in terms of 'legacy'. We had tons of documentation, and had to go through it in order to tell them something like, 'In the October 1957 comic book on Page XX, you can see Superman was 'flying' underwater'. We also developed the 3D world to have significant destructible portions such as doors, walls, and floors, which could tear away when struck. But DC was totally against that, arguing that Superman could not 'act as a bad person'."

Cos Superman has never broken a door or acted bad in any way through his entire history has he (*Superman III* anyone)? You could just go and watch an episode of the animated show that the game was based on, Superman certainly does everything that DC were claiming he would never do in it, even in the intro alone. DC and WB tried to stop Titus from making the game how they wanted to make it, forcing them to strip the rather decent sounding ideas for the game to pretty much nothing. In fact, it had been said that only around 10% of the original ideas that the dev team worked on made it into the released game. For those bad at maths, that's 90% of *Superman 64* that had been cut because of interference from the suits... 90%!

See, this is why you spend most of the time flying through rings in the game. Titus didn't want that at all, outside of a tutorial in the opening just to get you used to the flying mechanic. But all the encroaching from

66 OF THE MOST IMPORTANT VIDEO GAMES EVER! (ACCORDING TO ME)

WB and even DC forced Titus to make a game they really didn't want to make, so many features and ideas were removed at the behest of both Warner Bros. and DC themselves. That is why Superman doesn't really do any Superman-like stuff in the game, why he (hardly) battles bad guys, why he doesn't really use his powers. Warner Brothers. and DC Comics just cut Last Son of Krypton's balls off, pretty much out of spite.

Now, you are probably saying to yourself, 'the controls, why are the controls so bad then?'. Yeah, I guess you can't really blame the fucking awful controls on the fact that the licence holders restrained the developers and cut 90% of the original game. From a gameplay point of view, they still could've made it 'playable' despite the lack of content, at the very least. But let me attempt to explain it like this. What if someone told me that I could write this book, only using 10% of the English language? Yeah, I probably still could manage it, but I certainly wouldn't give it my all and the end result would be a mess... Or less of a mess. Just why should the guys at Titus work their nuts off to create a good game when their hands are being tied so tightly?

It's learning of the backstory to the whole thing why I'm just not that angry at *Superman 64* as a game like so many others are. This is not like *Rise of the Robots* where the developer/publisher blatantly lied while (over) hyping the game, to then go on and deliver a very poor final product. Titus were getting fucked behind the scenes and couldn't do right for doing wrong. They were being heavily controlled by both Warner Bros. and DC Comics, it was that control that made the game bad, not Titus or Eric Caen and his development team.

Here are a few nice little bits to end on. The original prototype (pre-studio interference) for the game was dumped onto the interwebs a few years ago and it can be played... Or even seen if you search YouTube. You know what? Yeah, it's rough, it is an unfinished prototype after all. Even so, the prototype shows a very different game. A completely different plot, more enemies, Superman has many more moves and he's not having to fly through rings. In fact, in the first level of the prototype version, it has Superman saving the civilians of Metropolis and being Superman. It really is worth looking into so you can see for yourself just how much the WB and DC messed things up for Titus.

S. L. PERRIN

Then there's the cancelled PlayStation version. Yup, there was a PS version. The story goes that Titus were hard at work overseeing this version (they outsourced the development to BlueSky Software), but all the delays caused (purposely) by Warner Bros. and DC Comics with the N64 game meant that the Superman licence expired, and after all the mistreatment, Titus really didn't want to renew it and work with WB and DC ever again. But the PlayStation game was said to be around 90% finished before the plug was pulled. And yes, a quick interwebs search and you can find this version too. All in all, it looked pretty good, much more like Eric Caen's original *Tomb Raider*-like Superman concept, with Superman actually being a superhero, stopping the bad guys and saving people... And NOT flying through rings.

It's kind of interesting when the two unfinished Superman games look far superior to the retail release of *Superman 64*. And that my friends, is why I chose to put this game in this book. I think that *Superman: The New Superman Adventures* (to use its proper title) is important as it's perhaps the perfect example of just how studio and outside interference can ruin a potentially good or even great game. It just goes to show that sometimes (most times), game developers actually know what they're doing. It goes to show how the suits higher up should stick to sucking each other off in the boardroom and let the talent do their job of making the games. The thing is, this crap still goes on today too, with the clueless suits messing around the development team and forcing out an unfinished and inferior product. Do I dare quickly mention CD Projekt and the disastrous *Cyberpunk 2077* launch? Yes, yes I do.

Yes, *Superman 64* is one of the worst and most hated games ever made and that will never change either. But it's not bad due to the developers not caring, they very clearly did care judging by the two prototypes, they wanted to make a worthy game from the Superman IP. It's bad due to idiots who knew nothing about game design forcing the developers into making a shit game they really didn't want to make. I mean, *Sim City* with Superman as the mayor? Actually, I'd quite like to play that now.

Also, DC Comics. Is it just me or does that not sound right? I mean, the DC stands for Detective Comics... so the company known as DC Comics is actually called Detective Comics Comics?

66 OF THE MOST IMPORTANT VIDEO GAMES EVER! (ACCORDING TO ME)

SHENMUE
DEVELOPER: SEGA
PUBLISHER: SEGA
PLATFORM: DREAMCAST
RELEASED: DECEMBER, 1999

This is a big one eh? One of the most beloved and respected games ever made. You know what? I don't like *Shenmue*. Didn't like it back when it was first released, I bought it a while back when it was re-released in 2018 and still didn't like it. I think it's a horrible game. But that doesn't mean that I don't feel that it's important.

By the late-nineties, Sega supremo, Yu Suzuki was already established as a man who could design, produce, direct and even program a game or seven. *Hang-On*, *Space Harrier*, *OutRun*, *After Burner*, *Virtua Fighter*, *Daytona USA*, *Virtua Cop*... The list goes on and on. Suzuki was the main man behind many of Sega's biggest and most popular hits. But there was a bit of an issue, those games, as great as they were, they were, well they were arcade games. Nowt wrong with that at all, but arcade games were not exactly known for their depth. They were designed for quick-fire play and more importantly, to get kids to empty their pockets of change into the machines as fast as possible. By the early to mid-nineties, Yu Suzuki wanted to create a game with a bit more meat on the bones, a game you just wouldn't find in the arcades.

Suzuki got to work, with the famed Sega AM2 R&D team, on a prototype for the Sega Saturn console called *The Old Man and the Peach Tree*. It was an RPG-adventure game with martial arts as its main theme and driving force. The game was to be set in the 1950s and feature a main character called Taro, who was in search of a kung-fu grandmaster called Ryu. Sega liked the prototype and encouraged Yu Suzuki to keep working on it, the game evolved into one with the working title of *Guppy*. In 1996, Suzuki took a trip to China and began to research martial arts, as well as to take in the scenery. That was when his idea began to grow and grow. The game slowly evolved into an RPG spin-off of one of Suzuki's other projects, *Virtua Fighter*. The main character from the prototype became Akira from the 3D fighting game and other *Virtua Fighter* assets were used too (of which, screen-shots exist on the interwebs). Originally set to be released for the Saturn, the development eventually shifted over to Sega's newest console, the Dreamcast.

With the added power of a new console came fresh opportunities to push that early RPG prototype into new directions, now re-titled, *Virtua Fighter RPG: Akira's Story*. Sticking with that martial arts RPG-adventure game concept, Yu Suzuki and his team began to make their game a much grander and more of a cinematic experience. A story was fleshed out and Suzuki constructed it in a specific way, as to give the plot four separate and distinctive acts and themes. Act/theme one would deal with 'sadness', as Akira's father is murdered. Two was centred on 'fight' and this was where the hero decides to seek out whoever was responsible for killing his father. The third act/theme covered 'departure', when Akira leaves his home town in search of clues. Then finally, there was act/theme four, which was 'starting afresh', where the protagonist would meet someone new and rebuild their life. Or, as Yu Suzuki himself said when talking to Redbull.com:

> "It is the story of a boy who travels to China on his quest to avenge his father's death, but it is also a story of love and friendship, and the bonds he shares with the people he meets as he matures to manhood through his martial arts training."

As development continued through 1997 and 98, Sega felt they wanted to give their new Dreamcast console a bit of a boost, so they suggested the idea to create an all-new IP. The *Virtua Fighter RPG* game was changed once more and most of the *VF* assets dropped too. The game's development continued and evolved into what would eventually officially become titled, *Shenmue: Chapter 1: Yokosuka,* in 1998. Yes, the idea was to split the previously mentioned four acts/themes into four separate chapters of games, of one much bigger and cinematic game for the Dreamcast. To keep the whole cinematic feeling alive, Yu Suzuki hired a screenwriter, a playwright, and a few film directors to help him shape his plot into something that would feel like playing a kung-fu movie. So new was the idea of the game, that Sega felt they had to come up with an entirely new game genre to describe what *Shenmue* was. In 1998, they came up with F.R.E.E. But what did the acronym stand for?

66 OF THE MOST IMPORTANT VIDEO GAMES EVER! (ACCORDING TO ME)

Well, according to Sega (mainly Yu Suzuki) themselves, it actually stood for 'Full Reactive Eyes Entertainment'... Whatever the hell that meant? The project continued to grow and evolve to a massive level. Suzuki himself did try to explain what the new game genre F.R.E.E really meant:

"The genre that is the closest to describing *Shenmue* is what nowadays is called an open-world game. The concept of *Shenmue* was to maximize the level of gameplay freedom by offering the highest potential number of different ways one could enjoy the game."

That's all well and good Suzuki-san, but the open-world genre already existed long before *Shenmue*, so I'm not really sure the whole F.R.E.E thing needed to exist really. Anyway, so big was the game that, to keep it the open-world title that Yu Suzuki strived for and with all the things he wanted to include, it was suggested that the game would have to be released on a crazy fifty to sixty CD-ROMs to contain all the data... Just imagine the size of the box! Something had to give some ideas had to be held back or even scrapped. The team got to work on special data compression algorithms to help fit the game onto fewer CDs. Any and everything was tried to try to make this gargantuan game exist.

Eventually, some ideas had to be dropped, but most of Suzuki's original concepts still made it in (thanks to that data compression). Actual Interior decorators were hired to create the insides of buildings in the game. NPCs were given daily routines to follow, going to work, eating, going home... Even if you never actually saw it in the game yourself, the NPCs were 'living' their lives. Weather was included that actually mapped with the real-world weather of the game's setting, that being Yokosuka, Japan in 1986. The level of detail in *Shenmue* was insane.

Real-world branding was added. Coca-Cola vending machines (in the Japanese version), Timex watches and more. There was even some in-house branding with the addition of playable Sega arcade games in the in-game arcade, all Yu Suzuki titles of course. *Shenmue* was huge in both scale and scope, like nothing else on the market back then. A true evolution of the open-world genre. Going back to the plan of splitting up and releasing the game in four parts (another necessity to cut down on the number of CDs used). Well, that's exactly what happened... It just took a lot longer than expected. The original *Shenmue* was released in 1999 and *Shenmue II* in 2001. While *Shenmue III* was stuck in development hell for years and only saw the light of day in 2019, after a very successful Kickstarter campaign. As for *Shenmue IV* and if it will ever happen? Well, Yu Suzuki has said it's likely he'll do it eventually, as he mentioned in this IGN Japan interview:

> "With *Shenmue III*, I created a game for the fans, but if I have the opportunity to make *Shenmue IV*, and I think I will, I know how to satisfy casual users, so I want to make a game that everyone can be satisfied with."

As I said at the start of this chapter, I don't like *Shenmue*. I really, really don't. I found it slow, clunky, repetitive and cumbersome. Walking around a town asking where I can meet some sailors just didn't appeal to me, then having to wait for specific times of the day for specific events to happen was more than slightly annoying. I never even bothered to finish it when it was first released as it just bored me so much. Instead, I just played *OutRun* in the in-game arcade, much more fun. However, I did force myself to play through it when it was re-released a few years ago and I still didn't like it. But saying all of that, I certainly do respect *Shenmue* a whole hell of a lot.

It wasn't the first open-world game, it didn't create the QTE mechanic as many like to claim (see the previously covered *Dragon's Lair*), I'm not sure you could even call it the first kung-fu-RPG-adventure game either (*Fist II: The Legend Continues* anyone?). But what *Shenmue* did do, its attention to detail, its level of immersion, its feeling of a living world and more was truly outstanding. Even now, twenty-two years after the original release, *Shenmue* has concepts in it that many open-world games lack. It still has the power to impress, despite its clunkiness. When I did force myself to play through the re-release in 2018, I was stunned by just how much interaction and freedom you had and that is why it is in this book. I may not personally like *Shenmue*, but I do have a lot of respect for the game and can't help but admire how it helped to evolve the open-world genre. Sorry... F.R.E.E genre.

66 OF THE MOST IMPORTANT VIDEO GAMES EVER! (ACCORDING TO ME)

THE LEGEND OF ZELDA: MAJORA'S MASK
DEVELOPER: NINTENDO
PUBLISHER: NINTENDO
PLATFORM: NINTENDO 64
RELEASED: APRIL, 2000

This one was a bit of a tough call to include. For a while, I did have *The Legend of Zelda: Ocarina of Time* on my list of games, but I swapped it out for this because... Well, I'll get to that later. Anyway, *The Legend of Zelda: Majora's Mask* is another game in the *Zelda* franchise. And yes, I am fully aware of the amount of Nintendo/*Mario*/*Zelda* games in my book. But as I said before, there's a damn good reason why, because Nintendo made some of the most important games ever. This one is no exception.

The Legend of Zelda: Ocarina of Time was a massive game, and I don't mean in terms of the map size, I mean how it was received by critics and fans alike. It sold over one million units in the first week of release alone, and then went on to shift more than 2.5 million units by the end of the year. Bearing in mind that *Ocarina of Time* was released toward the end of November in 1998 too, that's a lot of sales in around thirty-nine days or so. Suffice it to say, *Zelda: Ocarina of Time* was a big hit, so understandably, Nintendo wanted another one and fast. But there was an issue or two. First, the previous game took four years to develop from start to finish. Second, most of the team were busy working on other projects. Nintendo just didn't have the time or spare bodies to make a proper *Ocarina of Time* sequel, but Nintendo, and Shigeru Miyamoto specifically, wanted a new *Zelda* title in just twelve months. *Majora's Mask* director, Eiji Aonuma, remembers the challenge of creating a new game and just how he made it work in this interview with Shacknews:

"This was an idea that came from Mr. Miyamoto. The challenge he gave to me, to try and make a sequel to *Ocarina of Time* in just one year. *Ocarina of Time* was the first 3D *Zelda* game. When you make a 3D game, you have all these 3D models. But in a 2D game, you're drawing all these 2D images. Even if you wanted to make another game right away, if the background is different, you actually end up having to redraw everything. But in a 3D game, you can put those 3D models in different backgrounds and animate them. So Mr. Miyamoto thought 'well, actually shouldn't this make it easier for us to make a sequel?'"

Ocarina of Time was a game that, due to it being the first-ever 3D *Zelda*, had to be built from the ground up… This new one didn't. That was the answer, to re-use assets from the last game to help cut down on the workload. Another idea was to limit the openness of the previous title to create a small and more confined game, which would also cut down on production time. While the game was to be 'smaller', Shigeru Miyamoto insisted that it still have deep gameplay. That was when the 1998 movie, *Run Lola Run* and its themes of chaos theory's butterfly effect and a looping timeline became a huge inspiration. Shigeru Miyamoto and Yoshiaki Koizumi came up with the story of *Majora's Mask* between them as well as setting the game in a three-day system as Aonuma recalls in an Iwata Asks interview from Nintendo.com:

> "The three-day system, the idea of a compact world to be played over and over again, came down from Miyamoto-san and one other director, Koizumi-san. We added that to the mix, and then, finally, we saw the full substance of a *The Legend of Zelda* game we could make in one year."

The game began development at around the same time as another *Zelda* game (one of the reasons why there were not enough free staff). Yes, there were two *Zelda* games being developed, one was tentatively called, *Ura Zelda*. This title was later released as, *The Legend of Zelda: Ocarina of Time Master Quest*. Now, this particular *Zelda* game was a remake/update of the original *Ocarina of Time* and set for release on the Nintendo 64DD add-on. As the device was a flop, this new *Ocarina of Time* remake never saw a release on the device, but it did eventually emerge on the GameCube instead. And I'm going off on a bit of a pointless tangent here.

Anyway, *Zelda: Gaiden* was the name of that other *Zelda* game, as revealed by Nintendo themselves in June of 1998. With a playable demo shown at the Nintendo Space World Exhibition in August of 1999. The big N also announced a 'Holiday 2000' release date for *Zelda: Gaiden*.

66 OF THE MOST IMPORTANT VIDEO GAMES EVER! (ACCORDING TO ME)

Then in the Spring of 2000, the game was officially re-titled, *The Legend of Zelda: Majora's Mask.*

Majora's Mask needed to use the N64's 4MB Expansion Pak to play. One of only three games that actually used the peripheral, the other two were *Donkey Kong 64* and *Perfect Dark*. Though other games would have extra features when played with the Expansion Pak, only those three had to use it to play properly. But why did this game need to use the Expansion Pak if it was a smaller game compared to *Ocarina of Time* which didn't use it? Well, even though the two games used the same game engine and reused a lot of the same assets too, there were still various improvements in *Majora's Mask*. There was a greater draw-distance, improved dynamic lighting, more detailed textures, smoother animation, more characters on screen and other additions that mean that the Expansion Pak was required.

I remember really disliking *The Legend of Zelda: Majora's Mask* when I first played it. I was expecting *Ocarina of Time II* and the fact the game was so different to the *Zelda* games that came before it, that it didn't play in the action-adventure style I was expecting really pissed me off. It took me a few years to 'get' what the game was doing, but when I did 'get' it, it just suddenly clicked. Its departure from the series is why it is so damn good, the fact *Majora's Mask* dared to throw a spanner in the works and take a major left turn may have been what initially pissed me off. But it's also what eventually made me realise just how brilliant the game is. Besides, that moon was 'effing scary.

Plus, this only took a year to create... A year! I've played games that have had a much longer development cycle and still don't offer deep gameplay ideas and mechanics as rich and textured, involving and as rewarding as *The Legend of Zelda: Majora's Mask* does. It just goes to show how a dedicated team can still put out a truly fantastic title within the time constraints given and with a strong studio backing it.

S. L. PERRIN

THE SIMS
DEVELOPER: MAXIS
PUBLISHER: ELECTRONIC ARTS
PLATFORM: MICROSOFT WINDOWS
RELEASED: FEBRUARY, 2000

Will Wright had already impressed me, and the gaming world on the whole, massively with *SimCity* back in 1989. He continued to impress with other games featuring the Sim prefix too, *SimAnt* was awesome. In fact, it was after finishing work on *SimAnt* in 1991, when Wright first came up with the idea that would lead to his opus, *The Sims*. In *SimAnt*, you control a colony of ants, with the goal of taking over the garden and house in which the game is set in, while battling a rival ant colony. *SimAnt* also featured a human that would randomly walk around, causing problems for your eusocial insects. The human in *SimAnt* had some very basic programming behind it and almost non-existent AI, it would just walk around stepping on the ants with no clear definition or direction. Wright realised that the ants in *SimAnt* were far more intelligent than the human, that was when he came up with the idea to try to make a more accurate in-game human that could be as clever and robust as the ants.

One of the main inspirations for *The Sims* came from the rather dull-sounding 1977 book, *A Pattern Language: Towns, Buildings, Construction* written by Christopher Alexander, Sara Ishikawa and Murray Silverstein. The basis of *A Pattern Language* looks at functionality in architecture and examines design principles that focuses on structural usability over aesthetic values... Yeah, not exactly riveting video game material eh? Wright wanted to create a game that was the equivalent of that book, tied with his intelligent human idea born from *SimAnt*. A game that explored the structure and functionality of human behavioural patterns via the creating and constructing of buildings.

With *SimCity* still fresh in his mind back then, Will Wright began to think of a game where actually designing and creating the buildings themselves could be more interesting over just placing them, pre-built on the map, à la *SimCity*. In fact, Wright originally saw his new title as a more architectural take on his massively popular city building game.

66 OF THE MOST IMPORTANT VIDEO GAMES EVER!
(ACCORDING TO ME)

After pitching his idea for his new game, Will Wright was met with a less than enthusiastic response. He really struggled to get anyone at Maxis interested in helping to get his idea off the ground. He knew his concept needed a bit more of an angle, something players could really get their teeth into. He began to wonder why those buildings needed to exist in the first place. Wright came up with the idea of having little people live in those player-created structures. These little people could interact with the buildings in various ways while they lived their lives. It got to a point where Wright's initial idea of a game which focused on, basically being an architect/builder, soon shifted over to those little people, as Wright says in this article from Retro Gamer:

> "It turned out that controlling the little people was actually more interesting. It was still fun designing houses for them, but controlling their lives actually turned out to be far more compelling, so the whole project took a turn towards the people. I kept the architecture tools in there, but then I just really started focusing more on the people and objects and their behaviours and relationships, all that sort of stuff."

After some tweaking of and building on his ideas, Will Wright pitched it to Maxis once more, and once more, it really didn't go down too well at all. He was trying to convey this new idea for a game where you would basically be playing a simulation of real-life, and Wright's co-workers just did not get it at all. All the team at Maxis could see was a game where you had to clean the bathroom, go to work, pay the bills and so on, it all just sounded rather mundane and un-game like, an idea that lacked excitement. Maxis even held a focus group where four new games were pitched to the group for feedback, Will Wright's building/life simulation idea bombed with no one liking it. Dismayed, Wright moved onto making the sequel, *SimCity 2000* (released in 1993, hence the title?) and his architecture/human behaviour concept game was pretty much forgotten about... For a while. It was around 1996 when Will Wright managed to score a very small team from Maxis, in secret, and he began exploring and building on his concept which he codenamed, *Project X*.

Early development continued as Wright and his small team began to flesh everything out. The little people were to become caricatures and have a more comedic, humorous tone over accurate representations of real-world people. This helped add to the fun and entertainment of the game. Those little people were meant to be grounded in their in-game lives, yet still enjoyable to play with nonetheless, but without going into the absurd... Mostly. I guess the word 'verisimilitude' would be the best one to choose. Wright knew the game had to be fun and just a little bit silly, but still with one foot firmly in real life. Even the language the people would speak, eventually called 'Simlish', was carefully crafted to sound like an actual language, but also gibberishy enough to allow interpretation by the player to do some of the work, as Will Wright explains:

> "One of the key decisions was the fact that they wouldn't actually be speaking English, that we would actually have them speak their own language. This is one of those situations where the computer is pretty good at simulating certain things and really bad at simulating other things. We could have had them speaking pre-recorded lines or something like that, but it would have destroyed the illusion of reality pretty quickly just because we couldn't provide that level of AI. By having them speak this kind of gibberish, your human imagination actually fills in the blanks and will imagine the conversation. That's really an example of us offloading a portion of the simulation to the human imagination, the portion that the computer is very bad at."

So anyway, *Project X* was slowly coming together and it had evolved into a kind of interactive dolls house, a high-tech, fully animated and cleverly programmed dolls house that existed in a computer. Will Wright himself even called the game *Dolls House* for a while, before finally settling on *The Sims* as a title. A human simulation of life with a good dose of humour and plenty of freedom to play. It really is quite impressive just how open *The Sims* was back then. From its creation tools of both the sims themselves, to the options for constructing and designing your home for the sims to live in. Then there was controlling those little sims directly, take care of their basic needs such as hunger, sleep, social interaction, washing and of course, going to the toilet. But then you could get them a job and work at getting promotions, earn some cash and rebuild and remodel your home. Build up friendships, blossom into love, get married and have children, discover alien life... Or just sit around watching the TV in your undercrackers. It was a

66 OF THE MOST IMPORTANT VIDEO GAMES EVER! (ACCORDING TO ME)

fictional real-life for you to live however you wanted. There were no endgame goals to achieve, no missions to complete. You really could create your own custom life in the game with almost endless possibilities. Be as bold or as boring as you wanted to be. *The Sims* is really very much like directing and acting out your very own soap opera on your computer, one where you could forge your own unique and endless stories. Or as Will Wright put it when he spoke to Rock Paper Shotgun:

> "It really drove home the point that the players in their minds were almost seeing this as an interactive movie, and they were making this epic story as they were playing the game and we wanted the game to have a deeper recognition of the story that was in the player's imagination."

Indeed, Mr Wright, I don't think I could've summed up what *The Sims* is better myself... So I won't.

S. L. PERRIN

THE ELDER SCROLLS III: MORROWIND
DEVELOPER: BETHESDA GAME STUDIOS
PUBLISHER: BETHESDA SOFTWORKS
PLATFORM: MICROSOFT WINDOWS
RELEASED: MAY, 2002

The RPG genre of games is almost as old as gaming itself. Decades-old with a huge and very differing selection of titles from all over the globe. But when it comes to RPGs, you'd be hard pushed to find a franchise that is as epic in scale and scope, as richly textured as *The Elder Scrolls*. The sequels, *The Elder Scrolls IV: Oblivion* and *The Elder Scrolls V: Skyrim* are probably more famous now. In fact, *Oblivion* was the first *TES* game I ever played. And while there were other titles in the franchise before it, *Morrowind* was where the franchise grew and put the standards in place for not only *The Elder Scrolls* itself, but also great many RPG games from 2002 onwards.

Directed by Todd Howard and designed by Ken Rolston, *The Elder Scrolls III: Morrowind* was the most grandest RPG made to date at the time. Or as Howard described it when talking to IGN before its release:

> "*Morrowind* is the third instalment of *The Elder Scrolls*, following *Arena* and *Daggerfall*. It's huge, open-ended, pure RPG goodness. The classic *TES* game is single-player, first-person, has some elements of action; you get to run around and swing the sword yourself. The goal of every *TES* game is to create something that resembles a pen and paper RPG on the computer. Our main goal has always been to make the world as real as possible and let the player do what they want, when they want. There is a main quest, but you really don't have to follow it. The whole point of the game is to role-play the character you want, and do the things you want."

Pre-production on the game actually began before the release of the previous game, *The Elder Scrolls II: Daggerfall* from 1996. However, it soon became clear that the ideas for the game were too grand for the technology at the time. What Bethesda Game Studios could've done was strip back *Morrowind*, make it smaller and crack on with it. But no, they

66 OF THE MOST IMPORTANT VIDEO GAMES EVER! (ACCORDING TO ME)

decided to just wait it out for the tech to improve and catch up with their ideas. But not wanting to leave the fans waiting, they developed the spin-offs, *An Elder Scrolls Legend: Battlespire* and *The Elder Scrolls Adventures: Redguard.* In the meantime. *Morrowind* just sat on the back burner, simmering away, waiting to be fully cooked and served.

When the team felt they could continue with the game, they did. When quizzed by IGN on what they wanted to improve on over the last game, Todd Howard has this to say before *Morrowind's* release:

"Bugs. Zero bugs. We're sick of it. It's too bad *Daggerfall* had so many on release. We did seven patches. We had a patch team! We knew we screwed up. We put in the time to fix it, but many people weren't able to enjoy the game because of them. We're taking a great many steps to make *Morrowind* as clean as possible. We have to be way, way better than the average game on this one."

A Bethesda RPG released with zero bugs? Around two decades since Todd Howard's claim... Yeah, moving swiftly on. Even though the team waited it out for the technology to catch up with their ideas for the game, *Morrowind* still had to be stripped back somewhat. Yet, despite this reduction in scale and ideas, *Morrowind* was still a massive title. Bethesda has said that the game took around a hundred man-years to create. Give or take a hundred man-years, that about how long it took me to write this book. In order to get *Morrowind* made, Bethesda had to triple the size of the team over the previous games. A year was spent just making, what they called, 'The Elder Scrolls Construction Set'. A powerful tool that allowed the team to modify, fine-tune and balance the game as development continued. A tool that has been updated over the years and served as the backbone for all *TES* games since.

Morrowind had its first public viewing at E3 in 2001, it was only an early beta build but even so, it looked great, despite its roughness. There was even a surprise announcement thrown in too. All the previous *TES* games had been released on PC exclusively, and of course, *The Elder Scrolls III: Morrowind* would also see a release on PC. But it was also going to be released on the then-new Microsoft console, the Xbox. A console, which at the time, was still very much being kept top secret.

The game was even given a release date too. November 2001... Which was suggested to be set back to March of 2002 instead, as GameSpot reported on at the time:

"Bethesda Softworks' ambitious upcoming role-playing game *The Elder Scrolls III: Morrowind* most likely won't arrive in stores this holiday season. Online retailer EBGames has updated its release date for the game to March 2002 from its previous release date this November."

They were right too as that rumour of a delay was finally confirmed by Bethesda as GameSpot also reported on shortly after:

"Bethesda Softworks has officially announced a new release date for its upcoming role-playing game, *The Elder Scrolls III: Morrowind*, confirming our previous report from earlier this month that the game had been delayed. The game had been scheduled for release this holiday season, but its release has been postponed until spring 2002. The new release date affects both the PC and Microsoft Xbox versions of the game."

The delay was attributed to the fact that the dev team wanted more time to fine-tune and work on some balancing issues... And possibly work on that 'zero bugs' thing that Todd Howard was so adamant to do... *cough*. By April of 2002, the game had gone gold, but only on the PC. The Xbox version was to be delayed a little longer. Then on the 1st of May 2002, *Morrowind* made it on to PCs while Xbox players had to wait until June.

The Elder Scrolls III: Morrowind was a massive success on both PC and Xbox. Critics and gamers alike lauded it for its scope and depth. And about Todd Howard's 'zero bugs' ideology, did it happen? Well, it was a Bethesda RPG, what do you think? Of course, there were bugs, but nothing that ruined the game and ones that were easily patched out later. Even today, fans often cite *Morrowind* as the best *TES* game made to date and if not at the top of their list, then it's a very close second behind *Oblivion*. But with Bethesda announcing *The Elder Scrolls VI* a couple of years back, we'll have to wait and see just how well or even if *Morrowind* will still be fondly remembered. Bah, of course it will be, it's 'effin amazing and one of the most important RPG games ever made.

**66 OF THE MOST IMPORTANT VIDEO GAMES EVER!
(ACCORDING TO ME)**

GRAND THEFT AUTO III
DEVELOPER: DMA DESIGN
PUBLISHER: ROCKSTAR GAMES
PLATFORM: PLAYSTATION 2
RELEASED: OCTOBER, 2001

The original *Grand Theft Auto* game most certainly left its mark on the gaming world. A couple of add-ons and a sequel kept the franchise alive and very much in demand for us gamers too. As great as those initial *GTA* titles were, it was here with *Grand Theft Auto III* where the franchise was really 'born'. The small team at DMA Design in Edinburgh were still relatively small-ish in the year 2000 when work really began proper on the next *GTA* title, following 1999's *Grand Theft Auto 2*. Around twenty-three or so people worked on the game, headed up by producer, Leslie Benzies.

Even back when the first game was released in 97, as great as it was, those top-down, 2D (actually 3D, sorry Brian Baglow don't punch me) graphics felt a little dated. They felt even more ancient when *GTA 2* was released in 1999. The 3D graphics revolution was pretty much going full-tilt by then, so it was painfully clear the next *GTA* game had to make the jump into the third dimension properly, sooner rather than later. Using the RenderWare game engine from Criterion Games, DMA got to work on their new, 3D *GTA* title. Plus, they had the added power of the PlayStation 2 to really push what a *GTA* game could be. The fact the PS2 used DVDs over the previous console's CD format meant more data could be stored. This really opened the doors for DMA as they could now cram their game with so much more, better graphics, smoother animations, vastly improved sounds, bigger maps, more detailed environments and of course, more open-world gameplay.

Right from the start, Leslie Benzies wanted to create a 'living' city, one that felt as real as possible. He wanted traffic, pedestrians, weather effects and so on. Originally, the plan was to make the in-game city based on a real-world city, to help add to the realistic tone the game was initially going for. It didn't take too long before the idea of creating a hybrid city, one that was more so inspired by the real world than being based on it, came about. This decision gave the development team a lot more freedom as, if the city was based on a real-world locale, then there would be certain expectations people would want from it. But if they created their own unique city, they could do anything they wanted. So, they went back to the first game and chose to use Liberty City from *Grand Theft Auto*. To give the city some unique character, it was going to be inspired by... But not 'based' on New York. Dan Houser, executive producer on the game, has said that Liberty City actually draws inspiration from multiple different cites, not just New York as he mentioned in an interview with Entertainment Weekly:

> "Liberty City was not particularly meant to be New York. That was meant to be a hybrid of a generic American city: Chicago, Pittsburgh, Detroit, New York, Philly. An old, post-industrial American city."

So yeah, Liberty City in *Grand Theft Auto III* is really meant to represent America as a whole, and not just New York itself. The hybrid city and parallel realism of *Grand Theft Auto III* really allowed the team to delve deep into social commentary and take a good satirical stab at America and its culture, bearing in mind that this all came from a fairly small to an average-sized team from Scotland. It was Dan Houser who was the main guy behind the story and setting of *GTA III*. Citing films and TV shows such as *Goodfellas*, *Heat* and *The Sopranos* as major influences throughout development. It has also been said that games like *The Legend of Zelda* and *Super Mario 64* (of course) helped the direction *GTA III* went in as the game evolved, it became a gangster movie/TV show mixed with an action-adventure game. It was also that awe-inspiring 3D camera and real 3D movement from *Super Mario 64* which gave the game its third-person view.

After around ten months of development, *Grand Theft Auto III* really began to take shape. The city itself was pretty much done, a big chunk of the weapons and vehicles had been designed... And that was when a major problem became very clear. The previous *GTA* games didn't really have a story, a plot for the characters to follow. There was some mild direction, but generally, the other games were just you going on various unconnected missions to earn enough points (money) to advance to the next city in the game. Dan Houser had a story written and ready to go, he just had no idea how to make it work in a game as open as *GTA*

66 OF THE MOST IMPORTANT VIDEO GAMES EVER!
(ACCORDING TO ME)

III was. This was an issue the team struggled with for a while as Houser recalls in this Gamespot interview:

> "One of the things that *GTA 2* had become bogged down with was this idea of non-linearity. There was no story. With *GTA III*, we came to terms with the idea that what non-linearity meant was choice. The skill was combining the strengths of freedom of choice with the strengths of narrative. On some levels, they're diametrically opposed, so the skill was trying to figure out a structure to everything that would allow you to reconcile as best you could some element of narrative while still giving the players constant choice."

The key was to have one main story going on that was revealed as the player progressed through the game, but tie the main story with the individual missions. The team at DMA Design crafted each mission to be its own little story, a series of mini-stories that served as the framework that the main story would be told through. It was a clever little bit of storytelling structure that you don't even realise is happening. As an example, a mission may have had you going to deliver a package to someone and that package really had nothing to do with the main plot at all, but the person who gave you that mission, or the person the package was for would've been important to the main plot and used to continue the plot. It was those little spikes that kept everything connected, while still giving the player the freedom to explore and play the game their way. Maintain the non-linearity that the previous games were known for and yet still be structured, ensuring the player got the point of the story being told.

Grand Theft Auto III was first shown to the public at E3 in 2001. It's funny looking back on it now, but no one really cared or was even remotely interested in the game at the time and the E3 show was a bit of a blow-out for Rockstar. It was actually another title that was getting all the buzz and praise, as Dan Houser remembers:

> "There was enormous excitement around a few other games coming that fall. We went to E3 and everyone was obsessed by *State of Emergency*, and no one gave a crap really about *GTA III*. *State of Emergency*, we thought, was interesting, but not without its flaws. Some of which never

got resolved. But *GTA III* was already running, and we thought, 'This is amazing!' But E3, I think, isn't the best place to show a game anyway, and that's definitely become solidified in our thinking since then."

State of Emergency... Does anyone even remember that game now? It was another Rockstar Game published title, but one people really don't seem to recall much of, or even at all. Also, have you ever noticed that Rockstar Games don't really bother with attending E3 anymore? Well, this is the reason why, after E3 in 2001, they just didn't see the point.

Still, when *Grand Theft Auto III* was released in October of 2001 (originally given a September 2001 release date. But the 9/11 terrorist attacks led to a delay of a few weeks), it really did change the gaming industry. *GTA III* wasn't the first open-world game, not even the first 3D open-world game either. Yet, it set the standards and raised the bar of what a 3D, open-world game could and should be. A game whose influence is still felt two decades later and a template is often copied, but very rarely bettered. Or as Dan Houser once put it when talking about *Grand Theft Auto III's* legacy:

"When it turned up on PS2, it created something that felt very radically new. It was this combination of an environment that was full of content that you accessed through geography as much as timeline. And now what seems incredibly obvious but at the time was incredibly progressive, but seamlessness between mechanics or modes. You were driving because you got into a car, not because you entered the driving mode. You were shooting because you pulled out a gun, not because you entered the shooting bit. You can do anything, anywhere, within reason, reason based on logic rather than mechanical limitations, if that makes sense. That's been its biggest legacy. Games, as a medium, show off space very well. Better than a film can, better than a book can. So we used that as a strength rather than a weakness. That's definitely been a legacy of *GTA III*. It made a genre, whether it's called this or called that doesn't really matter, that's one of the most vibrant genres today."

The open-world genre has thrived since the release of *Grand Theft Auto III* twenty years ago now. Despite not being the first in the genre, you just can't imagine a gaming world without *GTA III*, can you?

66 OF THE MOST IMPORTANT VIDEO GAMES EVER!
(ACCORDING TO ME)

WORLD OF WARCRAFT
DEVELOPER: BLIZZARD ENTERTAINMENT
PUBLISHER: BLIZZARD ENTERTAINMENT
PLATFORM: MICROSOFT WINDOWS
RELEASED: NOVEMBER, 2004

I have made a few confessions in this book so far. From not liking massively popular and critically acclaimed games, to defending some of the worst games ever made. So here's another... I had never played *World of Warcraft* before writing this book. I certainly have known of it, just never played it. The truth is, I just don't like MMO games at all, they don't appeal to me. But for this book and only for this book, I set up a free trial account and jumped into Azeroth for the first time ever. Conclusion? I still don't like MMOs.

Developer/publisher, Blizzard doesn't tend to release the numbers themselves. Yet, as I write this chapter at the end of 2020 and by using various statistical sites, it has been said that *World of Warcraft* currently has just under four million players daily. A total of a hundred and nine million subscribers and it is the number one ranked MMO game in the world... And it was released back in 2004 too. For a video game this old, that's really quite amazing.

It all started back in 2001 when Vice President of Blizzard, Bill Roper, attended the ECTS trade show in London. That was when *WoW* was first announced and seen via a cinematic trailer. Well okay, so it really started a little bit before then. The *Warcraft* franchise actually dates back to 1994 with *Warcraft: Orcs & Humans*. Back then, the games were RTS titles that were heavily influenced by *Dune II*. A few sequels, expansions and spin-offs later, and *World of Warcraft* went into active development in late 1999 or early 2000. A big departure from the previous and very much loved RTS titles, *WoW* was going to be a massively multiplayer role-playing game. Giving the player the freedom to explore the *World of Warcraft* as their own uniquely created characters. There was some trepidation due to changing the franchise's genre so radically. I mean, Blizzard Entertainment were masters of the RTS genre, those previous *Warcraft* games were sublime, solid hits and fan favourites too. So to drastically change from a very much loved and successful genre to a vastly different one was questionable. It would be like Rockstar Games announcing that *Grand Theft Auto VI* is going to be a Metroidvania-like platformer. You'd just scratch your head and ask, 'why?' Intriguing? Yes, perhaps. Confusing? Possibly. Disappointing? Most certainly.

But at the time, the RTS genre was losing ground and just not as popular as it had been several years previously. Plus, the whole *Warcraft* franchise was getting a bit long in the tooth, close to being a decade old at the time. Sometimes you just need to change things up to avoid becoming stale and outdated. Sometimes you need to evolve. That's really what it was, just a natural progression and the next evolutionary step for the franchise. Then there was *EverQuest*, another MMORPG released in 1999 that the team at Blizzard had been playing. *EverQuest* was proving to be very popular and Blizzard wanted a taste. So, for the development team, it just seemed right to switch genres, partly to keep things fresh and partly because they really wanted to deeper explore the world they had created back in 1994 with *Warcraft: Orcs & Humans*. Chris Metzen of Blizzard recalls the change of genre when he spoke to Eurogamer:

> "It felt like a natural progression. We had been working on *Warcraft III* or different iterations of it for a couple of years at the point when we really started to think about *World of Warcraft*, and a lot of the creative vision really translated from the *Warcraft III* experience."

Still, jumping from one genre that a team are very well versed in, over to another brings all sorts of issues. An MMORPG game is a vastly different genre to build over an RTS. The team often felt lost as the magnitude of the game soon became apparent, a far more complex and bigger in scope title that would require learning a whole new programming and design skill-set from the ground up. Then there was the setting, for a while Blizzard had no idea exactly when to set *WoW* within the rest of the franchise. Originally, the idea was to set it far into the future, the wars between the orcs and humans would've long been finished, paving the way for a whole new style and tone. Blizzard's art director, Sam Didier recalls some of the changes and ideas they had early on:

66 OF THE MOST IMPORTANT VIDEO GAMES EVER! (ACCORDING TO ME)

"We'd been trying some different things. We were pushing it a few years ahead, into the future of the world, or rearranging the way that some of the characters would look, and it just wasn't biting for a lot of people. It's like changing Darth Vader from a big scary death knight in the future into a small child. Oh, never mind, sorry, they did that already.

Basically, what happened was that one of the artists on the team just took the Gnoll character from *Warcraft III* and made it look good at the camera angle that we were using. He kept the same proportions, the same bright colours, the same silhouette with the exaggerated features, and we all looked at that and said, yes, this is what *World of Warcraft* is going to look like. Then he proceeded and did the Kobold, and from then on, that was... Well, it was like, why are we trying to reinvent this thing? Everyone loves *Warcraft*, let's just make this *Warcraft*. We don't need any futuristic spin on it, or scary versions of this character, compared to the *Warcraft III* one. Just make it *Warcraft III*, that's what the fans are going to love."

With the lack of experience in making an MMO title, Blizzard had to look for some new and much more experienced talent. Enter Tom Chilton, who had previously worked on *Ultima Online*, one of the first-ever MMORPG titles, and certainly the one that popularised the genre early on. Right from day one, Chilton installed certain philosophies and staples for what *World of Warcraft* should be. Using his past experience and knowledge of early MMO games, Chilton was the man who really wanted to correct some of the sins that previous MMORPGs had committed. He wanted to make it easier to get into and understand, which would (hopefully) attract a bigger audience. He wanted to make the game more quest driven, structured and focused to keep the player engaged, over something like *EverQuest*, which had a much more free-forming and basic 'just kill enemies for experience points' style.

Quests soon became the backbone of *World of Warcraft*, the simple and basic component that the entire world could be crafted around. Designed specifically to keep the player immersed as they played, the proverbial dangling carrot. It also gave Blizzard the perfect excuse to expand the game beyond its initial concept. Quests mean stories, stories mean writing, and writing means expanding. Of course, *World of Warcraft* would become famous in the gaming industry for its many and massive expansions, expansions that are still being made today. The latest of which, *Shadowlands* was released in November of 2020. That's pretty impressive, right? A game released in 2004 that is still being updated and added to seventeen years later... And still attracting millions of players daily too.

For me, this is what makes *WoW* so damn important. Just how the development team have built on it over the years. How it still amasses millions of players today. How it just keeps growing and growing. Even more impressive is despite more than a decade and a half since its original release and numerous updates, it still has that 'easy to get into' feeling that Tom Chilton insisted on being in the game early into development. As I said at the start of this chapter, I had never played *World of Warcraft* before, but I gave it a go for this book. Despite not liking MMO games at all, I found it stupidly easy to fall into and understand from the off. I fully understand just why millions and millions of people find the game so attractive. Again, the game is seventeen-years-old as I write this, yet it doesn't feel like it. That's some genius designing right there.

World of Warcraft is also a game that has attracted a lot of celebrities over the years too. I don't mean bottom of the barrel, z-lister, reality show 'stars', I mean genuine celebs. Elijah Wood, yes that kid famed for playing *Wild Gunman* in *Back to the Future II*, is an avid *WoW* player. Hollywood starlet who played Sarah in *Santa with Muscles*, Mila Kunis, is another. Apparently, Henry Cavill was so busy playing *WoW* that, when Zack Snyder called to offer him the part of playing Superman in *Man of Steel*, Cavill missed the phone call, causing Snyder to ring back when the future Superman wasn't so busy on a raid. Plus many other major names are self-confessed *WoW* fans. There's something about that which made this game, and indeed games in general, feel more mainstream and acceptable as a form of entertainment. For that, you really have to applaud *World of Warcraft* and doff your cap in respect.

66 OF THE MOST IMPORTANT VIDEO GAMES EVER!
(ACCORDING TO ME)

LEGO STAR WARS: THE VIDEO GAME
DEVELOPER: TRAVELLER'S TALES
PUBLISHER: EIDOS INTERACTIVE
PLATFORM(S): PLAYSTATION 2 & XBOX
RELEASED: MARCH, 2005

The Lego video games, there are loads of them now. From hugely popular franchised IPs like Marvel, DC, Jurassic Park, Harry Potter, Indiana Jones (and many more) to original licenses and ideas. Going back to 1995 and the very first Lego video game with *Lego Fun to Build* on the Sega Pico (only in Japan), the brand has grown and grown to epic proportions. Now, a lot of those early Lego games were a bit 'questionable' (read: shit), to say the least. Varying in quality from okay to just outright terrible. A cacophony of games all from various developers that just didn't seem to know what to do with the Lego license in terms of video games. Enter Traveller's Tales, a small British development studio with a bit of experience under their belts already, especially with licensed games. *Mickey Mania: The Timeless Adventures of Mickey Mouse*, *Toy Story*, *Muppet RaceMania*, *Sonic R*... oh and *The Weakest Link*. All well-known IPs and characters with various titles made by Traveller's Tales. But, it was when Traveller's Tales obtained the Lego licence and made the first 'proper' Lego game in 2005 with *Lego Star Wars: The Video Game*, when magic was created.

At the time, Lego had already built (no pun... Okay, a little bit of a pun) a great relationship with the Star Wars brand when they produced several Lego sets based on the massively popular film trilogy... And the not as popular first prequel film back in 1999. The first rumblings of a possible Lego Star Wars game about in 2002. Lego had set up their own software publishing label with Lego Media in 1997, renamed to Lego Software in 2001... Then re-renamed it to Lego Interactive in 2002. However, after several talks, the Star Wars game idea fell apart, Lego ended up moving away from video games and ultimately closed down Lego Interactive in 2004.

Yet, despite the closure of the video games label, ex-members and management of Lego Interactive, Tom Stone and Jonathan Smith, just could not let that Star Wars game idea go. Shortly after closing down Lego Interactive in 2004, Stone and Smith founded Giant Interactive Entertainment and restarted work on their Lego Star Wars game concept once more. Once they had worked out a concept that could be built on, Giant Interactive approached Traveller's Tales and offered them the chance to develop their Star Wars Lego title. Working closely with Lego in Denmark, as well as with Lucasfilm in California. While Giant Interactive and Traveller's Tales were both based in England, the game became a real international team up due to Lucasfilm being on the other side of the planet. Oh, it was also one of the first games developed via the internet as its main means of collaboration.

Covering all three of the prequel trilogy flicks, *Lego Star Wars: The Video Game* was a smash hit with adults and kids... And adults with kids. The game had a real universal appeal. Perhaps what was strange about the release of the title was the fact that it came out several weeks before *Star Wars: Episode III - Revenge of the Sith* hit cinemas. Seeing as the game featured levels based on *Revenge of the Sith* as well as a few plot points, elements of the film were spoiled in the game. Still, can you really spoil a film that is a prequel to another film which was released in 1977? Let's see... Vader is Luke's father!

The gameplay of *Lego Star Wars: The Video Game* wasn't really that remarkable, it was pretty standard hack 'n slash stuff, to be honest. Kill bad guys and get to the end of each level kind of basics. Aside from hitting Droidekas and Battle Droids with a lightsaber, you could use force powers too. Levels consisted of this kind of scrolling beat 'em up thing, with a few little Lego-based puzzles to solve along the way. You could use Lego bricks to build platforms and basic structures that would open up new areas. Different characters had different powers and skills, oh and there were fifty-six characters to unlock too, including fan-favourite Jar Jar Binks. Then, the levels would mix things up a tad, throwing in some vehicle-based action to keep things fresh. Podracers, Starfighters and more, all usable and helped to vary the game as you played through all three prequel films in Lego form. Each of the levels represented a major scene from each of the three prequel films. So yes, you could re-enact that awesome Darth Maul flight, in Lego... Or just keep killing Jar Jar Binks over and over.

66 OF THE MOST IMPORTANT VIDEO GAMES EVER! (ACCORDING TO ME)

Not only did the game recreate the more famed moments from the films via the levels, but the in-game mini-movies also acted out familiar scenes, all topped off with a wonderful sense of humour. One of my favourite things about every Lego game from Traveller's Tales is that sense of humour. Jonathan Smith talks about the comedy of the game with GameSpot:

> "Well, we take humour very seriously! There are lots of different games, and there are lots of different ways of making games, and people want different things out of a gaming experience. For us, we find we do our best work when we're really enjoying ourselves, and we enjoy ourselves most when there's humour involved."

All of the Lego games from *Lego Star Wars: The Video Game* onwards all have this distinct and unique funny bone that is tickled just right with every game. There really is this amazing feeling of family entertainment where adults get just as much of a kick out of the game as kids do. If you ever want to introduce your young children to video games, then playing *Lego Star Wars* with them is a fantastic way to start. Those Lego games from Traveller's Tales all feature that wonderful family feel to them, but it all started here in 2005 with *Lego Star Wars: The Video Game.* This is pretty much why I included it in this book, the way it brings parent and child together through gaming is unmatched. Often seen as 'kids games' but for me, that's a gross fallacy. Or as Jonathan Smith once put it:

> "I think that a game that is made for children, which children genuinely enjoy, will also be enjoyed by older players as well, because it will appeal to the child in us all. The more you make games for an 8-year-old boy, the more you'll make a game for everyone. That's what we found with *Lego Star Wars*. Everything that we did in that game that we did for children we enjoyed ourselves as well. This took us in directions where, as gamers and designers, we found ourselves creating new things, which older players, set in their ways, overexposed to conventions may not notice. Children, who are fresher, with new eyes, more impatient, and with better things to do, are great guiding lights for innovation. I think childishness can be a good thing."

The Traveller's Tales Lego games are everywhere now, the franchise is still going strong after sixteen years. Following the success of *Lego Star Wars: The Video Game*, we've seen *Lego Star Wars II: The Original Trilogy*, *Lego Star Wars: The Complete Saga* and more Star Wars games. Then there has been *Lego Indiana Jones: The Original Adventures*, *Lego Batman: The Videogame*, *Lego Harry Potter: Years 1–4*, *Lego Pirates of the Caribbean: The Video Game*, *Lego The Lord of the Rings*, *Lego Marvel Super Heroes* and so many more famed franchises all given that distinctive Lego game treatment. With *Lego Star Wars: The Skywalker Saga* being the latest released in 2021, which will bring together all nine main films in the Star Wars saga in one huge game and a game that has been completely redesigned from the ground up.

Even now that I'm in my mid-forties, I still have a major soft spot for those Lego games and I'm currently trying to get my 4-year-old daughter interested in them too. Hopefully, they will soon become our 'thing' and we can bond over this pastime that I enjoy so much.

66 OF THE MOST IMPORTANT VIDEO GAMES EVER! (ACCORDING TO ME)

WII SPORTS
DEVELOPER: NINTENDO
PUBLISHER: NINTENDO
PLATFORM: WII
RELEASED: NOVEMBER, 2006

Now, I've been gaming since around the late seventies or very early eighties. I can't remember exactly when I first played a video game or even what my first game was, but I do recall my dad coming home with an Atari 2600. Back then, gaming was a bit of a taboo. Buying 'game programs' (that's what they were called back then) for the 2600 wasn't easy because gaming wasn't mainstream and it was seen as rather seedy.

We didn't have dedicated gaming shops then, or if we did, they were very few and far between, miles away in another city. There used to be a hobbyist shop about two miles from where we lived at the time, one that sold Airfix model kits, model train/railways and the like. They began stocking Atari 2600 games, but the games were never on the shelves, sitting proudly on display next to the Focke-Wulf Fw190s and the Supermarine Spitfire Mk.1s. Oh no, the 'game programs' were kept behind the counter and you'd have to ask to see what stock the shop had in. It felt like trying to buy hardcore porn, as you leaned over the counter and gently whispered to the shopkeeper that you were interested in seeing his Atari 2600 wares. Hoping that none of the anoraks in the shop, who were browsing the model train section shelves, desperately looking for a Wainwright D Class Southern Lined Maunsell Olive Green 4-4-0 Steam Locomotive, overheard and gave you a dirty look as your filthy habit risked being exposed. Just where is this trip down memory lane going and what does it have to do with *Wii Sports* you ask? Trust me, the point is coming at the end.

Anyway, right from the off, Nintendo specifically designed their Wii console to appeal to anyone. But, creating a more accessible console was one thing, you need the software to go with it. Shigeru Miyamoto himself described *Wii Sports* as the console's flagship title, a game that would appeal to gamers and non-gamers alike. Early in development for the title, the iconic *Super Mario Bros.* characters were used as the avatars in the game. That idea was dropped in favour of people creating their own avatars, or Mii characters as they became known (based on Japanese kokeshi dolls), to help the player feel much more engaged and connected with the game itself. As for the sports in the game (tennis, baseball, bowling, golf, and boxing), they were chosen for their simplicity and ease of understanding. Everything about *Wii Sports* was designed with the idea to make it fully accessible from the start to any and everyone.

Even earlier in development, even before the Wii console itself had reached its finalised design, various Nintendo game programmers were given prototype Wii controllers. They were asked to design and create tech demos purely based on the controller alone. One such programmer was Keizo Ohta, who came up with the idea of using the Wii remote as a tennis racquet and so, the idea for *Wii Sports* was born. Ohta also went on to become one of the directors of *Wii Sports*. Originally, the game only featured three sports, tennis, golf and baseball. Nintendo soon realised that baseball is not very popular in Europe and worried that we Europeans would only find the tennis and golf games appealing, making *Wii Sports* feel rather empty overall. For a while, there was a battle between adding either bowling or boxing to the title to give the game more value. In the end, Nintendo just added both of them anyway as they both showed off the Wii's motion controls in different ways.

Wii Sports was first shown prior to E3, 2006 in an exclusive Nintendo press conference. Game designer, programmer, producer and all-round gaming legend Satoru Iwata introduced *Wii Sports*, showed off a video presentation of the game as well as a playable demo. What's interesting about that presentation/demo is that all of the previously mentioned sports were shown, but in specially designed and separate demo units. So there was *Wii Sports: Tennis*, *Wii Sports: Baseball*, *Wii Sports: Bowling, Wii Sports: Golf* and *Wii Sports: Boxing* and not as one singular title. But there was something else shown, another sport not in the released game, *Wii Sports: Airplane*. The demo shown featured an airplane (surprise) being flown around an island. The player held the Wii remote kind of like a paper plane and used it to dip and tilt to control the plane, to fly through rings. Very similar to the Nintendo classic, *Pilotwings*. Now, while *Wii Sports: Airplane* never made it into the final

66 OF THE MOST IMPORTANT VIDEO GAMES EVER! (ACCORDING TO ME)

version of *Wii Sports*, it did get reworked, refined and included in the sequel, *Wii Sports Resort*. Just as a little added titbit for you, the island featured in the airplane game is called Wuhu Island, which has popped up in numerous Nintendo franchises like *Super Smash Bros.*, *Mario Kart*, *Pilotwings* and others over the years. Nintendo does enjoy making little nods and references to their previous games. Did you know that the courses on the golf game in *Wii Sports* are actually 3D remakes of the original 1984 *Golf* game on the NES?

When it was released, *Wii Sports* was met with 'favourable' reviews. It didn't blow critics away or anything, but it was noted for its ease of use... Which was key and exactly what Nintendo wanted. *Wii Sports* went on to become the biggest selling console game ever, at the time, with around eighty-two million copies sold, now that is impressive. The reason for such high sales was mainly down to the fact that the game came bundled with the console itself, at least outside of Japan. So when the Wii console became a huge seller, so did *Wii Sports*. But even in Japan where *Wii Sports* was sold separately, it was still the best-selling Wii game.

Wii Sports' massive popularity is impressive, it even made it into TV shows, movies and more. Like the 80th Academy Awards where the tennis game was played in an amusing little skit on the huge screen that usually displays the faces of the privileged Hollywood elite. Perhaps one of the more entertaining stories attached to *Wii Sports* involves a drugs bust. Back in March of 2009, police in Florida stormed the home of Michael Difalco, a well-known drug dealer. Officers found several large quantities of illegal drugs in his home, packaged up and intended for sale. As the police searched Difalco's home and discovered the drugs, along with various weapons, they also found a large screen TV, Wii console and a copy of *Wii Sports*. The officers then conducted a nine-hour search of the property, often stopping to play bowling on *Wii Sports*. But how were they caught slacking off during a drugs bust? Well, the drug dealer in question, Michael Difalco, actually set up a security camera that caught the whole thing, even the supervisor of the drugs bust stopped to play instead of telling his officers to get back to work. At one point in the video (easily found with an interwebs search), one of the police officers jumps for joy after scoring a double strike instead of searching the home of a known drug dealer. It's hilarious, *Wii Sports* appealed to everybody, even drug busting police officers.

That story is a testament to the appeal of the game and a testament to its ease of use too. *Wii Sports* went on to be used in care homes to keep dementia sufferer's brains active and provide pensioners with some easy to do exercise too. Boxer, Albert Liaw, suffered a stroke, which led to a brain injury and left him wheelchair-bound. He was treated at Canada's Glenrose Rehabilitation Hospital and after four months, Liaw was out of the wheelchair and back on his feet. The hospital used *Wii Sports* to keep Liaw active and motivated. In fact, there are dozens and dozens of stories from all over the world where *Wii Sports* has been used and credited as helping a great many people to recover a variety of medical conditions. If a game that can quite literally help with mental health and physical pain recovery can't be considered important, then I don't know what can.

Just to finish and going back to my off-kilter introduction to this chapter, they really were the dark times of gaming. Skulking around hobby shops, trying not to be noticed as you attempted to buy a new Atari 2600 game. And yet we went from that seedy feeling of being a gamer, to octogenarians playing tennis on a Nintendo Wii in care homes or stroke sufferers making full recoveries due to the game. I'm still really amazed at just how far gaming has come over the years that I have been alive and gaming. I'm far more impressed with just how accepted the pastime is now than any technological advances in gaming to date. *Wii Sports* really is one of the most important games ever made for breaking down many of the barriers and taboos that have been attached to gaming for decades. It has helped make games more accessible and accepted in the world today by so many.

66 OF THE MOST IMPORTANT VIDEO GAMES EVER!
(ACCORDING TO ME)

BATMAN: ARKHAM ASYLUM
DEVELOPER: ROCKSTEADY STUDIOS
PUBLISHER: EIDOS INTERACTIVE
PLATFORM: PLAYSTATION 3 & XBOX 360
RELEASED: AUGUST, 2009

"I'm not going to kill you. I want you to do me a favour. I want you to tell all your friends about me."

Ahhhhhh, Batman. The Dark Knight, The World's Greatest Detective, The Caped Crusader... Bruce Wayne (SPOILERS!). He's had a right old chequered past in terms of video games over the years. Some good games, some downright awful games. No matter the quality of the titles themselves, there was always this issue with them where you never really felt like Batman. Basic side-scrolling beat 'em ups, platformers, puzzle games, and so on. They were really nothing more than games that just had Batman in them as opposed to being true Batman games.

In the spring of 2007, Eidos had managed to secure the rights to publish Batman games, and they asked the relatively little-known Rocksteady Studios to come up with some ideas. A concept was drawn up, tinkered with, then presented to Eidos and tinkered with some more. Until in September of 2007, full production on that concept began. DC Comics asked famed Batman writer Paul Dini to come up with a story. Dini quickly came to realise that previous Batman games had mostly been based on movies or TV and he saw a gap where an original story could be told, as Dini recalls when he spoke to The Telegraph:

"It sounded very intriguing to me because at that point most of the Batman games weren't original. I think there were like, a handful, that did not owe their existence to a movie or a TV show or something like that. DC really wanted to create something right from the ground up, but build it around very familiar Batman elements. So they asked me; 'if you were writing a Batman movie or a brand new graphic novel, that was designed for gameplay, how would you go about it?' So I talked to DC about it and I met the team over at Rocksteady Games and we found that we were all on the same page with where we wanted to take the story."

S. L. PERRIN

The game and story were developed alongside each other. This idea allowed the title to feel much more authentic and also ensure that Paul Dini's story didn't overreach whatever limitations the game's mechanics would have due to the hardware. Aside from various Batman comic book stories from the likes of Neal Adams and Frank Miller, a few notable video games also helped shaped the direction that *Batman: Arkham Asylum* would head in. The likes of the massively overlooked *Eternal Darkness: Sanity's Requiem* as well as *The Legend of Zelda* and *Metroid* (of course) all helped create the mould that *Arkham Asylum* would be made in. The game's director Sefton Hill talks about those influences with Gamasutra:

"Like the rest of the design world, I'm a big fan of *Zelda* and *Metroid* games, going back for years. They were definitely big influences. I like that sort of approach to design, giving you a number of different gadgets and abilities that you can use and combine in different ways, and the way that combines and the feeling of being in this complete other world. Those games were definitely a big influence. I played *Eternal Darkness* and I really liked that. Those guys did a great job with that. They had a sanity system in there that freaked a lot of people out. It was a nice idea.

We were also really fundamentally influenced at the start with the character himself. We had a combination of fans in the studio, and some people who were more mainstream Batman fans who were only aware of Batman through the films. Something that happened throughout the studio was that we realized how much depth this character really had, and I think everyone in the studio came to really love him. I think that's really unusual when you're in a studio working on a project. People just got more and more into Batman, and more and more excited by Batman. They devoured more and more of the Batman lore and universe. That was great to see over the course of two years. We really started taking those facets from the character in the comics directly, and said, 'These are the things that are Batman.' We wrote those things on a board and said, 'We have to make a game that really exaggerates these things and brings them to the fore'. We left those there."

That was another major key of the game, being influenced by the Batman character himself. Yeah I know, it sounds stupid, but as previously mentioned, other games just didn't do that, they were games

66 OF THE MOST IMPORTANT VIDEO GAMES EVER!
(ACCORDING TO ME)

that had Batman in them as opposed to being actual Batman games. What the team at Rocksteady and Paul Dini did between them, was to craft a Batman character that relied on the use of iconic aspects of the Batman mythos, right down to the voice actors. Dini was well known among Batman fans as to being one of the writers of the much loved *Batman: The Animated Series*. On that show, Kevin Conroy voiced Batman with Arleen Sorkin as Joker's girlfriend/sidekick Harley Quinn. And rounding off the cast was Mark Hamill as Joker himself... Greatest Joker ever! So of course it was a no-brainer to get the cast to reprise their roles for *Batman: Arkham Asylum.* Yet, even with those connections to the animated show, the game was still treated as a very different and separate entry to the Batman lore.

The idea to set the game solely in Arkham Asylum came about as to restrict just what Batman could do. No outside help, no police. Just Batman on an Alcatraz-like prison island, trapped with some of Gotham's worst criminals. While the game featured a really strong rogues' gallery of some of Batman's most infamous adversaries, some didn't quite make the cut as Paul Dini recalls with The Telegraph:

"There were few that, great as they would have been, just didn't fit either the game or the story in the game. Mr Freeze, for example, would have been wonderful to have, but he didn't fit. Mr Freeze is motivated by different things. He doesn't really have that much of an axe to grind with Batman. Batman is an irritation and an impediment to him, not an enemy that he hates. He doesn't have the hatred that the Joker has for Batman. He's not like the Riddler who is obsessed with proving that he's smarter than Batman. Freeze is off in his own universe; he has what he wants to accomplish and he rarely even cares what the other villains are up to. If Batman gets in his way, he'll take him out, but Freeze doesn't really fit as part of this game.

Mad Hatter is another character we talked about, one of the ideas I pitched was a garden maze that you could wander around in which could've been a good location for Poison Ivy, she could make the maze grow in different directions, but in the centre, there would be this bizarre tea-party that the Mad Hatter was hosting for Batman. Ultimately, it didn't really fit the tone of the game so we left it out."

One of the best and most satisfying aspects of *Batman: Arkham Asylum* was its free-flow combat. It's beautifully brutal and very rhythmic once you get the hang of it. Seeing Batman punch, kick and even break the bones of his enemies just felt so heavy compared to other games that used similar fighting systems. I mean, go play some of the *Assassin's Creed* games that were around at the time, take out a few bad guys, then play some *Arkham Asylum* and see how much more rich, varied and deep the combat feels and looks. However, that amazing combat action had to go through a few variations before the one in the game was settled on. One early idea was to make the combat work like a rhythm action game. Think something like *Rock Band* where you press a certain button in time with symbols on the screen.

Even now, twelve years since its release, *Batman: Arkham Asylum's* combat system is the best ever used in a game, only bettered by its own sequels. Button mashers could make their way through the game, but if you actually took the time to learn the game's simple counter and gadget-laden mechanics, you could really pull off some visually impressive and extremely satisfying fisticuff-scuffles.

What's funny is, that looking back at when *Arkham Asylum* was first teased and announced, no one cared. That first trailer was shown and it pretty much got a collective 'so?' from the majority of the gaming press at the time. It was not only seen as just another Batman game, but also just another superhero game too, which gamers didn't particularly care about. Plus, licensed games were not exactly held in high regard then... Mostly still not today either. Then, of course, there was the fact that this Batman game was made by a studio that were still pretty much unknown at the time. Rocksteady's only other game before *Batman: Arkham Asylum* was the very average and awfully janky *Urban Chaos: Riot Response*. Gamers and gaming press were just not expecting anything other than another boring and all to mediocre title from an inexperienced game studio. But then when it was released, everyone was proven wrong.

Batman: Arkham Asylum was not only the definitive Batman game, but it put in place the extremely high standard all superhero games would be measured by ever since... With most of them falling well short. *Arkham Asylum* managed to capture the feeling of being Batman almost perfectly. From the first moment you picked up the controller, right up until you

66 OF THE MOST IMPORTANT VIDEO GAMES EVER!
(ACCORDING TO ME)

saw the end credits, it was clear that everyone involved in the making of the game really had a passion for the Batman lore and the Batman character himself. This was no 'thrown together to make a few quid off the name' game, *Batman: Arkham Asylum* was a title made by fans for fans. A mesmerising melding of not only Batman's brute force, but also his guile and cunning as a detective, along with his penchant for hiding in the shadows and scaring the hell out of his enemies. With plenty of amazing gameplay and game mechanics surprises thrown in too. Just compare this story of a Warner Bros. and DC Comics (Detective Comics Comics... it just doesn't sound right) backed game to the *Superman 64* one. Do you know what the difference was? The suits actually just let Rocksteady Studios get on with it and make the game their way. The end results speak for themselves.

Oh, and I've just invented a new drinking game too. Re-read this chapter and take a shot every time you read the word 'Batman'.

S. L. PERRIN

ANGRY BIRDS
DEVELOPER: ROVIO ENTERTAINMENT
PUBLISHER: ROVIO ENTERTAINMENT
PLATFORM: IOS
RELEASED: DECEMBER, 2009

I am really not a fan of these mobile, tappy-tap games. They usually offer greatly watered-down versions of already successful and much-loved titles. Or they are just plain crap shovelware. Finding a truly great mobile game is like searching for the world's tiniest needle in a massive warehouse crammed full of giant haystacks. The main issue seems to stem from the fact that anyone with even the bare basic knowledge of game design/programming (or in many cases, not) can fart out a game and get it on your nearest app store with relative ease, all with barely any quality control. Mobile games get released so frequently too that most of them are forgotten about days or even hours after release. Then you have all of those endless clones of games that have been somewhat popular, from talentless individuals trying to cash in on someone else's successful ideas. As I said, I'm not a fan.

Finnish video game developer, Rovio Entertainment, were spit-balling ideas for new games in early 2009. Game designer, Jaakko Iisalo, showed off a simple bit of art that he had knocked up. It was nothing more than a little round bird-looking character with no wings, no legs, but a very angry look on its face. The little bird-thing was moving across the ground with dust clouds being kicked up behind it. It looked like the birdy-thing heading towards a pile of blocks… And that was it. There was no description of what the bird-like character was or what it was doing, just that single picture. Still, everyone in the room really liked the character, so a game was designed around that bare basic concept.

Just having an angry-looking bird was not enough to make a fun and engaging game though, so an enemy was thought up. At the time, the 2009 swine flu pandemic was in the news and pigs were not seen as very likeable, so the enemies for the game very quickly became evil porcines. Another inspiration came from the physics-based mobile game, *Crush the Castle*, a simple game where you used a medieval catapult to knock down the walls of a castle with people inside. Okay, so maybe not so

66 OF THE MOST IMPORTANT VIDEO GAMES EVER! (ACCORDING TO ME)

much 'influenced' as *Angry Birds* pretty much ~~stole~~ 'borrowed' the concept and gameplay mechanics. Anyway, what makes *Angry Birds* such an appealing game is its simplicity. I'm taking *Tetris* levels of simplicity here too. Anyone can pick up and play the game with ease and understand it quickly. You fire little birds at makeshift buildings that house pigs, to try and knock down the dwellings, via the use of a slingshot… That's it. Just like *Tetris'* arrange falling blocks into neat piles, it's the simplicity of the game that works.

Angry Birds was a smash hit and it really paved the way for mobile gaming from that point on, love it or hate it. In many ways, *Angry Birds* is the *Pong* of the mobile market. Rovio's CEO, Kati Levoranta talked about the game's appeal and impact when she spoke to GamesIndustry.biz:

"*Angry Birds* enabled us at Rovio to expand our business beyond mobile games and into other types of entertainment. We transformed from a gaming company into a games-first entertainment company. We kind of showed the way that a global brand can be born out of mobile games. A mobile gaming brand is not limited to just mobile games, you can make different forms of entertainment with that brand. Of course, that requires innovation and the mindset that you want to do and be something more than just mobile games. I think *Angry Birds* has shown that this is definitely possible, and you can even go as far as making a feature film."

'Brand' is the exact word to use too, *Angry Birds* exploded way beyond the game that started the whole brand. I mean, there have been multiple movie tie-ins with the original game including, *Rio* (the 20th Century Fox Animation), *Star Wars* and *Transformers*. Plus numerous other spin-offs and *Angry Birds* variants, including a sequel. As I write this, there have been twenty-one official *Angry Birds* titles… Twenty-one games released in the twelve years since the first game's release! And people say studios like EA and Ubisoft milk their franchises.

Now, branding is nothing new in gaming. I mean, go back and look at *Pac-Man*, the original gaming mascot. But *Angry Birds* is on a whole other level compared to any other game ever made. Merchandise everywhere, multiple TV shows and two hit feature films. That's on top of all the games too. *Angry Birds* is (perhaps) the world's first world-famous IP born from mobile gaming and proof that mobile gaming can be a serious contender when handled right. As I sit here writing this, *Angry Birds* is the most downloaded game app ever, as a franchise. It's still going strong too with the most recent game and movie both released in 2019. It's a phenomenon. Donny Kristianto of app analytics site App Annie had this to say:

> "*Angry Birds'* initial success was due to a number of factors, but most notable was its mobile-centric design. Being one of the first games in mobile to truly leverage the possibilities of smartphones with touch and gesture control that translated into instant feedback, innovative yet simple gameplay. Rovio built on this success with content updates and multiple titles with different themes."

Angry Birds as a game, pretty much created the entire mobile gaming craze. Then look at the studio that created *Angry Birds*, Rovio Entertainment. They have evolved from a small and unknown Finnish studio making simple tappy-tap games, to a world-famous production company with their fingers currently in a lot of different pies. *Angry Birds* has been spun off into multiple gaming genres like racing, RPGs and even pinball. Rovio Entertainment itself has bought out and opened new studios as they continue to expand and build on what they have created. And it all started with that simple bit of static artwork that Jaakko Iisalo showed with a little round bird character running toward some blocks.

**66 OF THE MOST IMPORTANT VIDEO GAMES EVER!
(ACCORDING TO ME)**

RED DEAD REDEMPTION
DEVELOPER: ROCKSTAR SAN DIEGO
PUBLISHER: ROCKSTAR GAMES
PLATFORM: PLAYSTATION 3 & XBOX 360
RELEASED: MAY, 2010

As Will Smith once eloquently proclaimed back in 1999:

> "Wicki-wild wild.
> Wicki-wicki-wild.
> Wicki-wild.
> Wicki-wicki.
> Wild Wild West."

Classic! The American frontier, the Old West, or the Wicki-Wicki-Wild Wild West is a fantastic setting for video games, and yet it's a setting that's just not really been used very much or well when compared to other historical backdrops. There was the Capcom arcade game *Gun.Smoke*, Lucasarts' massively overlooked and utterly brilliant *Outlaws* and the (even more) overlooked *Gun* from Neversoft. Oh okay, I'll throw in *Outlaw* from Atari too. Yeah, I know there have been more games set in the Old West, but it's still a vastly underused historical period for video games. Yet, it was Rockstar Games and more specifically, one of their many studios, Rockstar San Diego, who managed to make the Wild West just that little bit wilder.

Strangely enough, the origins of *Red Dead Redemption* can be traced back to that previously mentioned Capcom arcade game, *Gun.Smoke*. See, *Gun.Smoke* was designed by Yoshiki Okamoto and Okamoto was approached by a small development studio called Angel Studios. The team at Angel wanted to make an updated version of Okamoto's arcade classic, *Gun.Smoke* called *S.W.A.T.* (Spaghetti Western Action Team). Long story short and Angel Studios got to work on their Wild West game, while being overseen by Capcom, things didn't work out and development on the game ground to a halt as Stewart Spilkin, producer on the game recalls with Polygon:

S. L. PERRIN

"It got to a point where they [Capcom] were just like, 'We don't really want to hear your ideas; we're just going to tell you what to do and we just want you to do it.' You know, these are all really smart, talented guys [at Angel Studios]. And part of the enjoyment of spending so much of your life making games is, you get to exercise some creative freedom. When you're in an environment where you can't do that, it becomes stifling."

The relationship between Capcom and Angel Studios broke down and their *S.W.A.T.* game, now renamed *Red Dead Revolver*, died. In 2002, Rockstar Games bought Angel Studios and renamed it Rockstar San Diego. Dan Houser of Rockstar got to see the unfinished build of the game and loved what he saw, he thought it would really work well as a Rockstar game and set about getting it finished for a release. Dan Houser talks about saving the very first *RDR* game with IGN:

"The one that always caught our eye was this cowboy game that looked very good. For the time it looked visually spectacular, but also speaking to the management guys there, it was a complete mess. It didn't really exist as a game. Capcom were prepared to walk away from it, so we said we'd finish it and all they ever wanted was the rights to publish it in Japan if we ever did finish it, which they never thought it could be. Our focus was to get the thing done and get it out to a level that we thought that was worthy of coming out. We knew it wasn't going to be completely designed the way we would have done it if we were doing it from scratch, but that doesn't mean there weren't some good ideas there that couldn't be made into something that was fun and interesting in its own right."

So, the newly named Rockstar San Diego finished the game, under the guidance and experience of Rockstar Games and so, *Red Dead Revolver* was released in 2004. Still, as happy as they were with the title, Rockstar knew that it wasn't quite what they would've done if they had built the game themselves from the ground up, instead of just taking over a dead project and finishing what was already there. In 2005, Rockstar Games got Rockstar San Diego to work on a new game, a sequel-ish/follow-up game that, while it wouldn't be a direct story continuation of *Red Dead Revolver*, it would exist in the same universe. *Red Dead Redemption* had begun...

66 OF THE MOST IMPORTANT VIDEO GAMES EVER! (ACCORDING TO ME)

Telling the story of the very charismatic John Marston, an ex-outlaw now working for the government, trying to track down his old gang members. Set in 1911, just as the Old West was beginning to die out and the modern world was on the horizon. The team at Rockstar drew inspiration from classic Western flicks such as *The Wild Bunch*, *High Plains Drifter*, *Unforgiven* and *The Proposition* to name a few. Setting the game at the end of the famed Wild West era gave the team the chance to break away from the typical cowboy fiction and tell a rather unique story. Dan Houser talked about the game's time-frame and setting:

> "From a game design standpoint, it gave us a big toolset to play with. With this, we wanted to give ourselves all of the strengths of the West, horses and stagecoaches and lassoes and lots of things you couldn't really do in a *GTA* game, but also give ourselves as much modern stuff to play with like trains and explosives and so on. From a story perspective, it felt more interesting. Doing a classical 'we are conquering this wilderness' story didn't seem very interesting to us. But having this interface and period of great change between this savage, horrendous world with delusions of nobility evolving into modern society it seemed very interesting, more interesting than some deluded settler, subduing savages in their mind. That seemed like it would be excessively limiting and not something we would agree with the politics of."

Playing as John Marston in *Red Dead Redemption* is one of my all-time favourite gaming experiences. It's up there with playing *Doom* for the first time, getting the proper ending in *Metroid*, seeing *Dragon's Lair* in the arcade and so many other gaming experiences which have been burnt into my memory. *RDR* was Rockstar's finest piece of storytelling and really showed how the team had grown up. It was wonderfully thematic, dramatic and it felt very authentic too. You really do feel like you are in the midst of the dying years of the American Frontier, there was a sense of foreboding stitched through the entire story. All of which led to one of the finest finales to a video game ever. Still now, eleven years since the game's release, I've never felt such a personal draw to a game. That ending left a lasting impression on me that no other game has ever managed to do before or since. An ending I still think about today too.

S. L. PERRIN

It always annoys me when people describe *Red Dead Redemption* as just being *Grand Theft Auto* on a horse, because it is so much more. *GTA* has always been for more 'cartoony' in its approach, a broad satirical stab at American culture, celebrity, capitalism, living the 'American dream' and so on. *GTA* has always been hyper-exaggerated and played up for laughs, even when it's pretending to be serious. But *RDR's* writing, approach to storytelling and characterisation is much more 'grown up' and grounded. Yeah, the basic template and structure of a typical Rockstar open-world game are prevalent in both, but it is *Red Dead Redemption's* deeper respect for the player that really sets it apart from the *Grand Theft Auto* franchise if you were to ask me. For want of a better phrase and to quote The Mad Titan, Thanos for a second, *Red Dead Redemption* is 'perfectly balanced, as all things should be'. Dan Houser talked of that balance with IGN:

> "The challenge with a western is that we didn't want it to turn into something that's very camp. But equally, we didn't want it to be very pompous and so finding a balance between those was certainly a tonal challenge."

For me, *Red Dead Redemption* is Rockstar's opus, the best and most important game they have ever made... And ever likely to make too by the looks of it. It really scratched an itch with me that struck a very specific spot. The setting, the characters, the story, the pacing are all perfect. So perfect as a game it is in fact, that Rockstar themselves couldn't better it with the sequel (prequel).

66 OF THE MOST IMPORTANT VIDEO GAMES EVER! (ACCORDING TO ME)

MINECRAFT
DEVELOPER: MOJANG
PUBLISHER: MOJANG
PLATFORM: MICROSOFT WINDOWS
RELEASED: NOVEMBER, 2011

Whenever people talk about *Minecraft*, it's often referred to as a 'kiddy's game', one so simple and basic that it attracts a much younger audience. It does attract a young audience, there's no denying that. But it also attracts old-timers like me. Yup, I like to play *Minecraft* and I'm perfectly content about that too.

Markus 'Notch' Persson used to develop games for King Digital Entertainment, the studio behind the massively popular tappy-tap game, *Candy Crush Saga*. While working at King, Notch learned several different programming languages, which he would use to develop his own games in his spare time. One such title was the unfinished *RubyDung*. The game was going to be a kind of isometric base building game inspired by *Dwarf Fortress*, which itself was a roguelike construction game. There was another title which Notch had started too, it was going to be a *GTA: Chinatown Wars* meets *Left 4 Dead* mash-up kind of thing (as he described it), which never had a title. But this untitled 2.5D zombie game was when Notch began to experiment with 3D texture mapping for the first time.

It was in 2009 when Notch left King Digital Entertainment. He began to feel stifled and wanted to make his own games his own way. It was around then when he also discovered *Infiniminer*. A competitive online multiplayer game where you worked in teams to excavate precious metals from a mine to earn points to win. It was this simple mining game that led to the birth of *Minecraft*, as Notch himself recalled on his Tumblr blog:

"I found *Infiniminer*. My god, I realized that that was the game I wanted to do. I played it in multi-player for a while and had a blast, but found it flawed. Building was fun, but there wasn't enough variation, and the big red/blue blocks were pretty horrible. I thought a fantasy game in that

> style would work really, really well, so I tried to implement a simple first-person engine in that style, reusing some art and code from *RubyDung*."

Taking assets from his unfinished *RubyDung* game (the grass and stone blocks in *Minecraft* came from this) and adding a first-person mode using his knowledge of 3D mapping from his untitled zombie game, Notch created a very early prototype which he uploaded to YouTube called *Cave Game Tech Test* (very easily found on the YouTubes if you wish to see it). It's really nothing more than just a first-person camera, jumping around on grass and stone blocks. It was that simple tech test that pushed Notch to create a new game, one that blended his base building idea from *RubyDung*, with the 3D texture mapping he had been playing around with for his untitled zombie game, to then finish it all off with the mining elements of *Infiniminer*. Only, Notch didn't want to make a competitive multiplayer mining game, he wanted to make something more adventure-RPG-ish.

I guess that technically, *Minecraft* was first released in May of 2009. It wasn't the proper game, but a private alpha-early build which Notch used to gain valuable feedback from those who played it. From that feedback, Notch kept updating and releasing improved versions of the game through 2009 and 2010. It was around mid-2010 when Notch co-founded his own video game company, Mojang, and by late 2010, *Minecraft* officially went into beta testing. By then, the game had already been updated and added to several times. New blocks, items, monsters (mobs), several changes to the game's behaviour (water flow, mob reactions, etc) and a survival mode was added too. It was this survival mode where the game really came to life. Before then, *Minecraft* was pretty much just a game where you mined and built blocks, a chance to be creative. But survival mode added so many more gameplay elements and allowed Notch to really push the RPG-adventure angle he wanted from the start.

As the game grew, so did Mojang as a studio as more people were hired to work on *Minecraft* and help build it from its early concept, to a more robust and complete game. More updates and bug fixes followed and the game was eventually released proper in November 2011. Then on the 1st of December, 2011, things changed. Notch stepped back as *Minecraft's*

66 OF THE MOST IMPORTANT VIDEO GAMES EVER!
(ACCORDING TO ME)

principal designer/developer and Jens 'Jeb' Bergensten took full creative control of the game and it just exploded from that point on.

Very much like the previously covered *World of Warcraft*, *Minecraft* is still being updated today. The *Pretty Scary Update*, *Horse Update*, *The Update that Changed the World*, *Exploration Update* and *Village & Pillage* are just a few of the many updates *Minecraft* has had over the years. The latest one (as of writing), *Caves & Cliffs*, is due out later in 2021. That's the beauty of *Minecraft*, it'll never be finished, continually added to and being built upon for years. But it is not the game's never-ending and constant expansion why I chose to put it in this book. Nor is it the fact that it was largely, at first, the work of just one man and went on to become such a monumental sensation in gaming. Nor is the fact that Notch sold his shares in Mojang and the *Minecraft* IP to Microsoft for 2.5 billion dollars, a pretty decent paycheck eh? No, the reason *Minecraft* is in this book is because of its mass appeal and staggering usage.

As I said at the start, I'm an old-timey gamer and *Minecraft* is often seen as 'kiddie' game by so many. Yet, myself in my mid-forties, am a big fan. I just love the fact I can create pretty much anything my imagination can muster with the many various blocks in the game. It really takes me back to being a kid and playing with Lego, clicking those plastic blocks together to create whatever came into my 8-year-old mind. Playing *Minecraft* relaxes me, if I've had a particularly rough day, if I'm feeling highly anxious, stressed or depressed, if I feel my mental health is not at its best (issues I do genuinely struggle with), messing around with *Minecraft* calms me down like no other game can. It gives me a sense of serenity that just helps me to relax. Of all the games in this book, this is perhaps the most personal pick for me because it really helps with my mental health issues and state of mind.

But, then there is the massive creativity that the game offers too. I've played *Minecraft* for years, yet when I do build in the game, I'm usually pretty basic with what I do. I love exploring the randomly generated maps, making a house and expanding it, building a farm with crops and animals, etc. I keep things pretty much basic for what the game offers. I look at my farm with separate pens for cows, chickens and the like. I admire my sugar cane, wheat and pumpkins as they grow and I'm happy with what I've created. All while that calming, melodic music plays in the background. Then I look at what other and far better *Minecraft* players have made on the interwebs and I'm in complete awe. Space shuttles, the Acropolis, the USS Enterprise, the city of Chicago, King's Landing, a working computer with RAM and so much more. Truly amazing constructions and creations which really leave me gob-smacked. *Minecraft* really is an open-source for those with the most vivid of imaginations and quite frankly, it's really fucking impressive what people can do when they let their imagination take over. Especially given that the game is basically a digital version of Lego.

But there's still more. *Minecraft* is being used for educational purposes too. In fact, there's even a dedicated *Minecraft: Education Edition* specifically designed to help students and pupils learn valuable life skills, to teach kids about history, enhancing reading & writing. Aid with problem-solving, maths and so much more. This simple game for 'kids' is helping to educate and encourage the next generation, all backed up by worldwide educational bodies. The following lengthy snippet is from Thierry Karsenti, a Professor and a Canadian Research Chair in Technologies and Education:

"My team and I adopted an exploratory research design to highlight the main uses of *Minecraft* in a school setting and to identify any benefits of using *Minecraft* at school. We developed a program called *Minecraft Master* where students had to complete more than forty different tasks. Tasks were closely linked to the school curriculum; for example, students have to create a navigable map, making use of language, mathematics and spatial design, something we asked them to do with *Minecraft*.

With the support of a program facilitator, students worked individually and in teams to digitally build structures such as impressive houses, a soccer stadium, a spaceship, a railroad track to the Titanic and the Titanic itself.

Researchers also attended some sessions. We studied the main impacts on learning to investigate how gamified learning interventions may increase student engagement and enhance learning. We used a

66 OF THE MOST IMPORTANT VIDEO GAMES EVER! (ACCORDING TO ME)

combination of data collected from surveys, interviews,'think aloud' protocols (where students speak their problem-solving strategies out loud), journals, tracking of student progress and digital footprints. Using these various methods allowed substantial data triangulation and validation.

The educational impacts we found were encouraging. The students showed a heightened motivation towards school, stronger computer skills, greater problem-solving skills, expanded reading and writing skills, a development in creativity and autonomy and increased collaboration with classmates. The results of the studies we conducted confirm that *Minecraft* has real educational value."

There are multiple reports from various reputable sources that have carried out studies and discovered just how beneficial to a student's learning that *Minecraft* really is. What *Wii Sports* did for the medical profession, *Minecraft* has done for education and an entire generation of children. As I now reach the end of this book, looking back on this lengthy journey from *Pong* in 1972 up to *Minecraft's* proper release in 2011 and even other games released today, that's almost fifty years of important games covered right here. We've come a long, long way from two sticks and a square ball simulating tennis to entire worlds being created, and gaming now used to educate the next generation of children and that is most definitely important.

S. L. PERRIN

HONOURABLE MENTIONS

Now, I know they'll be readers of this book wanting to scream and shout at me about the exclusion of a game or seven. As I said right from the start, and as the title of this book suggests, these are the most important games, (according to me). This has always been a very personal book and list of games. I didn't choose these games because they were big sellers, critically acclaimed, fan or even personal favourites. They were chosen by me because I felt each of the games in this book are important to the gaming industry in one way or another, or because they impacted me in some way as a gamer.

As I was writing this book, the list of games changed several times. While the main core titles were there from start to finish and remained throughout, other games were added, removed, added again, removed once more. Some made the final cut, others didn't, as I worked on the multiple drafts over time. Why certain games didn't make the cut really is down to various reasons. Still, I did spend time researching and even writing full chapters for several games now not appearing in this book. So with all that info I had collected, I thought, why not just do an honourable mention thing at the end. So here they are, the games I will happily admit that are certainly important... But perhaps just not quite important enough to be full chapters... (according to me).

SPACEWAR! (1962)

I already mentioned this game in the *Pong* chapter right at the start. I guess it would be foolish of me to write a book on important games and not include *Spacewar!* in some meaningful way, even if just a quick honourable mention like this. Still, I did give my reasons why I didn't give the game its own chapter in that there *Pong* opening. *Spacewar!* is often considered the very first video game and I guess it really was (if you ignore *Tennis for Two* from 1958 that is). It just didn't have the overall impact that the other games which managed to make into this book did. To me, *Spacewar!* was the doorman of video games and it stood there right out front and held the door open for so many others to walk through.

66 OF THE MOST IMPORTANT VIDEO GAMES EVER! (ACCORDING TO ME)

BREAKOUT (1976)

This block-busting arcade classic is often overlooked in favour of some of the more popular games of the era. I guess this could be summed up as an update to Atari's classic *Pong* really, just given a new slant. You still control a paddle and have to hit a ball, but instead of going up against another paddle in a simple version of tennis, you have to destroy the blocks at the top of the screen. Did you know that *Breakout* actually had a plot? I didn't until I wrote this book. Anyway, the paddle you control is meant to represent a prisoner and the ball is a ball and chain that said prisoner is hitting against the wall to 'breakout' of prison. Now the title makes sense.

COMBAT (1977)

I often get asked what was the first video game I ever played. The truth is that I'm not exactly sure. I mean, I often forget what I had for dinner the previous day or why I walked into a room. So, trying to remember the first game I played forty-odd years ago is tricky. Still, I do remember us, as a family, having an Atari 2600 as our first games console. That wood finished beast was bundled with a copy of *Combat*. A mighty twenty-seven game modes packed into one 'game program'... All pretty much had you shooting the crap out of the other player in a variety of military vehicles. So I tend to credit *Combat* as being my first game and the one that started my love for gaming that I still have today.

ASTEROIDS (1979)

Another arcade classic and this was one of the first games I wrote a chapter for, and it stayed on the main list for at least three drafts or so. But it felt less and less relevant the more I wrote about other games. The shoot 'em up genre had already (pretty much) been created with *Space Invaders*, and the backstory to that game was just slightly more interesting to read (and write) than the one for *Asteroids*. Still, this game had amazing vector graphics at the time that were quite revolutionary. *Asteroids* also has some truly great and massively inspiring fast and frantic gameplay. *Asteroids* is a game that most definitely helped to popularise arcades, shoot 'em ups and gaming as a whole in those early days. It rightfully should be considered among the all-time greats, even if I don't feel it quite as important as others.

MISSILE COMMAND (1980)

Another one of those all-time arcade classics that didn't quite make it into my main list. A shoot 'em up with a difference, a game that showed you didn't have to destroy alien life to entertain. A game that actually played in the fears of the whole Cold War thing, the political tension it bought and the severe concerns over nuclear war breaking out. Having to defend cities from the bombardment of missiles that rained down was some top gameplay action for sure... If a little too close to certain political threats at the time. Plus those trackball controls were something very different at the time.

KUNG-FU MASTER (1984)

Released as *Spartan X* in Japan and inspired by the Jackie Chan flick, *Wheels on Meals* (also called *Spartan X* in Japan), with perhaps a little bit of Bruce Lee's original concept for *Game of Death* thrown in too. Despite it being based on the Jackie Chan flick, it really has no connection outside of character names. *Kung-Fu Master* is said to be the first-ever side-scrolling beat 'em up. But as you know, I've corrected a few similar claims in this book already. As far as I can tell, it is. So *Kung-Fu* Master paved the way for the whole scrolling beat 'em up genre. *Double Dragon*, *Final Fight*, *Streets of Rage*, et al, all owe a little something to this game. Besides, there aren't too many games where you can punch midgets (non-pejorative) in the face.

GHOSTS 'N GOBLINS (1985)

Capcom made some absolutely blinding games in the arcades back in the eighties. *Ghost 'n Goblins* was no exception either. A scrolling-platform-shooter with a dark/horror edge. Zombies, ogres, demons, cyclopes and more devilish monsters are trying to stop you from rescuing the princess. The plot was paper-thin, but the gameplay was amazing. Rock hard difficulty sure, this was my generation's *Dark Souls*. But, this well crafted and beautifully realised game kept us coming back for more. Plus, Arthur running around in his undercrackers is one of

66 OF THE MOST IMPORTANT VIDEO GAMES EVER! (ACCORDING TO ME)

those iconic gaming images. While I'm on the subject, just what the feck was going on at the start of the game with an almost naked Arthur, the princess and a graveyard?

GRADIUS (1985)

Before Konami became famed for making pachinko machines, they made fantastic arcade games. *Gradius* (*Nemesis* outside of Japan) was a brilliant side-scrolling shoot 'em up. Some of the most iconic shooter gaming images ever are in *Gradius*. From the instantly recognisable Vic Viper ship you control, to the many enemies you have to blow up... those Easter Island-like heads spring to mind. Then there is the power-up selection the game offered. Pretty much all scrolling-shooters took many cues from *Gradius*. But, as great and important the standards set by the game are, that's not the reason I wanted to give it a mention. This is... Up, Up, Down, Down, Left, Right, Left, Right, B, A. The Konami code as it became known. A cheat code so famous that it has not only been used in multiple Konami games, it now has a life outside of not just Konami games and gaming, but life in general. The code has been used in music, TV, films... even kids toys. Seriously, I've got a Fisher-Price, pre-school game controller for my kids and if you put the Konami code into it, it plays a hidden tune. To be honest, the code was not in the original release of *Gradius* and was first used in the NES port of the game from 1986. But hey, we wouldn't have that NES port or the code if not for the arcade original. How many gaming cheat codes do you know that have their own legacy both in and outside of gaming?

LITTLE COMPUTER PEOPLE (1985)

I did cover *The Sims* in the main part of this book, but I have to wonder if that game would have even existed if not for *Little Computer People*? Also known as *House-on-a-Disk*, this title was *The Sims* fifteen years before it even existed. Basically, *Little Computer People* saw you maintaining the life of a little digital person perceived to be living inside your computer. You couldn't 'win' and the game was viewed as a kind of cutaway doll's house. A little person would move into the house and you would have to care for him/her, using the keyboard to direct them to perform everyday tasks. As I said, this was *The Sims* a decade and a half before *The Sims* existed. Funny story time, I had a copied version of this on my C64 and didn't know how to play it. So I went to Toys 'R Us and found the game, took out the instruction manual from the game's case and slipped it into my pocket. Yup, I stole the game's instructions (not the game). Thirty-three years later and Toys 'R Us went bust... related?

OREGON TRAIL (1985)

Very much used as more of an educational tool than a game really. But still, *Oregon Trail* certainty holds great importance to the industry. Now, it was originally released as a text-based game in 1971, but it's the more famed graphical version from 85 for the Apple II computer that people know best. If you don't know what this game is, well it's a kind of an adventure-survival game that taught people about the 19th-century and pioneer life. Travel, hunt, trade and more. See how far you can make it along the famed *Oregon Trail* before you die from a multitude of causes such as diseases, animal attacks to the classic, dysentery. A very early example of a survival game and one that many games in the genre are still influenced by today.

CASTLEVANIA (1986)

See, this is another one that was in and out of the final list a lot. How could I include *Metroid* but not *Castlevania*, especially when the portmanteau sub-genre of gaming, Metroidvania, is one of my faves? It was a tough call, but *Castlevania* just didn't quite cut it for me. It's a great game and I do love the Dracula/horror setting... But I've always felt that the original *Castlevania* lacked 'something'. Some of the sequels were far better, including the awesome *Castlevania: Symphony of the Night*. So I had to at least give it an honourable mention due to its importance in half creating the Metroidvania sub-genre and the fact that some of the sequels are amazing. But I honestly didn't feel that any of the games in the franchise are singularly important in and of themselves.

FIST II (1986)

Unless you owned one of the popular microcomputers of the eighties, then you've probably never even heard of this one. *Fist II: The Legend Continues*, to give it its full title, was the sequel to the massively popular

66 OF THE MOST IMPORTANT VIDEO GAMES EVER! (ACCORDING TO ME)

The Way of the Exploding Fist. But, whereas the first game was a very typical one on one beat 'em up, this sequel dared to be different. It was a side-scrolling, free-roaming adventure game, almost *Metroid* like in fact. Given a large map to explore, you have to fight off bad guys, solve puzzles and discover the secrets of the world you are in. Think of this as a very early version of *Shenmue* with its open-world kung-fu style of gameplay. *Fist II* really was quite revolutionary at the time, critics hated it when it was released, mainly as it was something so new and the fact that it was very different from the first game. However, it has picked up a lot of love over the years and gone on to become a bit of a cult classic in gaming. People now finally see its influence and importance after thirty-five years.

DUNGEON MASTER (1987)

RPGs were not new in 1987, but they all pretty much suffered from the same problem. They were slow, turn-based, slogs that were bogged down with awkward controls. Then along came *Dungeon Master* and changed everything. This game had a first-person view, it featured real-time combat as well as, what is known as, a paper doll interface. This new feature had a simple 'paper doll' cut-out of your character that you could just drag and drop inventory and equipment to, a feature pretty much all RPGs use today. *Dungeon Master* made RPGs easier to play and understand, it did away with the stifling and stiff elements of other RPGs of the day and made the genre much more approachable.

SID MEIER'S PIRATES! (1987)

The pirate era, such a wonderful world to make a game in, yet hardly any (great) pirate games exist. *Sid Meier's Pirates!* was such an amazing game that I still scratch my head over why no one seems to want to make pirate games like it since it was released. Set in the Spanish Main during 16th, 17th and 18th centuries, you could play as a pirate, a privateer, or even a pirate hunter. There was a main story to follow, that being, trying to find your long-lost family. But the gameplay was very open-ended. You could form alliances with various governments, attack ships and towns, look for buried treasure, trade with the various cities and so much more. *Pirates!* was kind of like a piratical version of the classic *Elite*, a wonderful open-world game where you were free to be as good or as bad as you wanted, with plenty of various gameplay options along the way. There was a remake called *Pirates! Gold* from 1993... Which itself was updated in 2004. *Gold!* is definitely the best version of the game to play full of fantastic enhancements. Still, I'd love to see a much more modern remake made today.

HOSTAGES (1988)

This'll be another one of those games that not too many are aware of. It's also a rare example of a game being based on a real-world event that isn't a world war. It was the 30th of April, 1980 when six armed men stormed and took over the Iranian embassy in South Kensington, London. The siege lasted six days, on the last day a hostage was killed and their body thrown out on the street. That was when the Special Air Service (SAS) launched 'Operation Nimrod' to save the other hostages being held. *Hostages* is based on that very event. You take control of several SAS members in this game that is split into three different gameplay styles. First, you have to position three men around the embassy while dodging searchlights and use cover to avoid being shot. Second, you snipe the windows of the embassy to take out any visible terrorists. Finally, you breach the embassy to take out any remaining terrorists and rescue any hostages. The game was not only based on a real-world event, it was also the first to feature a snipe rifle... Oh, and it can also be credited with being one of the early games that created the tactical-shooter genre.

CATACOMB 3-D (1991)

If *Doom* is considered the daddy of the FPS genre and *Wolfenstein 3D* is the granddaddy, then *Catacomb 3-D* must be the great-granddaddy. Also, from id Software is this FPS game that most people seem to forget about. While still not the first FPS game (there was Hovertank 3D... also from id as well as quite a few others), *Catacomb 3-D* is definitely an ancestor of the genre and a game that set the ball rolling at id Software to go on and make the games and create the massive impact they eventually would. The *Rage*, *Quake*, *Doom* and *Wolfenstein* franchises perhaps would never have existed if not for *Catacomb 3-D*.

66 OF THE MOST IMPORTANT VIDEO GAMES EVER! (ACCORDING TO ME)

LEMMINGS (1991)

Puzzle games come in all sorts of shapes and sizes. *Tetris* really started a trend when it was released. Then, when DMA Design came up with the idea to base a game on suicidal rodents (an erroneous rumour started by Disney), the puzzle genre had a new master. The premise is devilishly simple, take your lemmings from one end of a level to the exit. However, you never had direct control over the little green-haired blighters. Instead, you had skills that you could assign to the lemmings to guide them to their goal. *Lemmings* featured a beautiful difficulty curve that really drew you into its truly awesome gameplay. Still one of my faves.

SUPER MARIO KART (1992)

I was thinking about putting the SNES classic, *Super Mario World* here. The fact that there are already a lot of Mario platformers in the book kind of made me change my mind. Then I remembered this classic. One of the first kart racers, the first being Sega's *Power Drift* if you're asking. I have a lot of fond memories of late-night sessions playing *Super Mario Kart* with my brother and friends on the SNES. But the real reason it has made it into the honourable mentions is due to its influence. While not the first kart racer, *SMK* was the one that got the sub-genre noticed. The use of the SNES' Mode-7 graphics, a colourful collection of characters and one of the best multiplayer games of its day. *Super Mario Kart* was a pure joy to play and put karting games on the map.

DONKEY KONG COUNTRY (1994)

Yeah, I know, more Nintendo, but this one is a tad different. While licensed by Nintendo to use one of their original IPs, *Donkey Kong Country* was actually developed by Rare. It was the ground-breaking 3D graphics that really made me want to give this game a shout. Even today, looking at screens from the game, it's kind of hard to believe that the game was running on a 16-bit SNES console. The fact it was a fantastic platformer with a lot of charm to boot helped too. Plus this was one of the 'rare' (pun fully intended) times that Nintendo allowed one of their beloved IPs to be handled by another developer... let's not mention those CD-i Zelda games.

S. L. PERRIN

TAMAGOTCHI (1996)

I actually debated including this as it's not technically a video game, but I can't really ignore how much of an impact the *Tamagotchi* has had in terms of games. I knew quite a few people that had these too, I hated the fucking things. The annoying beeping when it needed feeding and so on. I mean, this was 1997 (when they launched outside of Japan) and I was 21 at the time. I'd be down the pub with my mates having a beer or seven... then that annoying beeping would sound off and several of my friends would start patting down their pockets, desperately searching for their digital pet to give it some food. Several twenty-somethings all worried their few pixels on a tiny key-chain screen was going to die. Still, as much as I detest these things, they have had a positive impact on gaming. I'm pretty sure some, if not most, survival games owe something to *Tamagotchis* in some way. Plus, Peter Molyneux used the virtual pet idea for his game *Black & White*, which also led to the creation of *Fable*.

THE LEGEND OF ZELDA: OCARINA OF TIME (1998)

When I came up with the idea for this book, I honestly had no idea that it would contain so many Nintendo games. I guess that's just a testament to how great the Big N were at making games. This didn't quite make it onto the main list because I honestly felt that *Majora's Mask* was just more important due to how it really changed things up so much. Still, *The Legend of Zelda: Ocarina of Time* deserves a mention because it was so utterly brilliant and set the standard for action-adventure games for years. Plus, as I covered in that *The Legend of Zelda: Majora's Mask* chapter, if not for *Ocarina of Time*, then the sublime *Majora's Mask* never would've happened.

ASSASSIN'S CREED (2007)

This spin-off from the *Prince of Persia* franchise had a rather bumpy start. The first game was a hell of a great looking title back in 2007. The setting and story were amazing too. But the game itself leaned a bit too much toward the repetitive. The first sequel is one of the greatest game sequels ever and *Assassin's Creed* really got me into researching all sorts of history. *AC II* (and its spin-offs) especially made me fall in love

66 OF THE MOST IMPORTANT VIDEO GAMES EVER! (ACCORDING TO ME)

with Italy, to the point where I took a holiday out there one year and specifically went on a tour around Rome, just so I could take in and experience the amazing architecture that I had seen in the games. I got to walk around Castel Sant'Angelo and it was just like in the game. Beautiful. I should've climbed it.

ETERNAL DARKNESS: SANITY'S REQUIEM (2002)

Resident Evil really started something with its survival horror angle, there were a lot of very similar games that copied its formula. *Eternal Darkness* managed to stand out in the crowd with a rather unique game mechanic, sanity effects. A feature so brilliant, that Nintendo patented it. How it worked was, as your sanity dropped, various fourth-wall-breaking effects would happen. You would try to save your game, for the game to delete your file. The volume on your TV would be turned down. The game would 'blue screen crash'. Rather dark Edgar Allan Poe quotes would flash up on the screen. Your character's limbs would fall off. Your inventory would just disappear. The game would abruptly end, telling you it would be continued in a sequel. Plus many, many more other visual and audible effects that played on your senses. Sadly, it's a concept that's not really been built on and used much since (save a few brilliant moments from *Batman: Arkham Asylum*). Still, the fact that the sanity effects thing hasn't been used a lot really makes *Eternal Darkness* rather unique in a genre that is rather over-bloated.

FORTNITE (2017)

Okay so, this particular title has been in and out of the main list more so than any other. I've honestly really struggled with deciding to include this or not, right up to the very final draft... Obviously, it didn't make it, but why? Well because, I just don't think of it as being important, or at least not important enough. People claim that *Fortnite* kick-started the whole e-sports thing, not really. As mentioned in the *Doom* chapter, it was id Software's seminal FPS that really got e-sports underway. Then there's the claim that *Fortnite* created the battle royale gameplay idea, very debatable. *PlayerUnknown's Battlegrounds* beat *Fortnite* to the market by a few months. But even so, I can't be the only person who used to have multi-player sessions on *Super Bomberman's* (SNES) battle mode. You know, a mode where you had to kill everyone else, and when time ran out, the game map would get increasingly smaller until only one player remained... sounds familiar. So *Fortnite* certainly wasn't the first to do anything that other games hadn't already done before, but I still feel I should give it a shout out because let's face it, *Fortnite* is gargantuan in terms of streaming right now.

RED DEAD REDEMPTION II (2018)

I never knew it was possible to both love and loath a game as much as I do with *Red Dead Redemption II*. As I said in the *Red Dead Redemption* chapter, I think that is the best game Rockstar have ever done or ever will do. So of course I was looking forward to the sequel (prequel). After being burnt by *Rise of the Robots* so many years ago, I didn't get swept up in the hype of the game, but still really looked forward to playing *RDR II*. Initially, when I first started playing it, there was this wave of euphoria as I made my way through the snowy mountains of the game. Yet, as the game wore on, I began to find it too much of a chore to play over it being a joy. I'm not going to sit here and claim that *Red Dead Redemption II* is a bad game, cos it's not, far from it. But to me, *RDR II* felt way overproduced and was crammed with filler ideas that really didn't need to be there. Honestly, I got bored of the game long before it ended and the way that epilogue dragged on and on at the end, Jeebus! But, I still needed to put it in this book because of the rich and textured world in the game. Quite easily the greatest open-world environment I've ever seen. I've lost count of the number of times I would be riding around on my horse just admiring the scenery. The level of detail was and still is astounding. *Red Dead Redemption II* is such a stunningly beautiful title, despite being a disappointment to me. Even though I don't think much of the game overall, I still sometimes load *RDR II* up just to enjoy the world in which it exists. An overly drawn out story, plenty of needless filler, terrible pacing, but beautiful to look at. *Red Dead Redemption II* is the *Zack Snyder's Justice League* of the gaming world.

SONIC THE HEDGEHOG (1991) & FINAL FANTASY VII (1997)

I honestly don't think these two games are important, but they are just here at the end to shut certain people up... Annoying pricks that they are. Happy now?

**66 OF THE MOST IMPORTANT VIDEO GAMES EVER!
(ACCORDING TO ME)**

THANKS

First up, I have to praise and thank my family and friends. Even though I've not seen most of you for over a year now due to this pandemic and all, I still know you're there and hopefully one day soon, we can meet up for a BBQ and a beer or seven. Especially given recent family events.

Very special thanks to my ever-loving, better half and mother of my children, Louisa. It's been a very rough ride recently, but we're still going strong and your support is very much appreciated and needed. Plus my two little monsters, whom I do any and everything for. A smile and a hug from my kids keeps me going when I'm not necessarily feeling my best. And I can't forget our dog Monty for keeping me company whenever I sat there alone tapping away on my laptop.

A huge, massive, gargantuan sized thanks to Lord Badger Nimahson over at Stoffel Presents. Thanks for all the kind words. Thanks for all the interest and support with my writing. Thanks for the chats we've had recently too. And thanks for introducing me to *HyperParasite*, the best game I've played in a long while. If you come up with a catchy quote for this one, let me know. I hope you enjoyed the book fella.

The crazy usuals at Digitiser Gamers and Geeks on Facebook for always managing to put a smile on my face. Hopefully, at least some of you will buy a copy. Got to give a mention to Tezz Williams specifically.

Dave Corn and everyone at Lockdown Gaming (name subject to change... again). Enjoy the read folks. You'll have to buy a copy now too see that you've been thanked...

Any and everyone connected to any of the games mentioned in this book. It's your hard work and dedication to the industry that has made these games my personal picks of *66 Of The Most Important Video Games Ever! (According To Me)*.

Thanks to you for buying and reading my book too. I really do hope you enjoyed it. Having a grateful and entertained audience makes me want to write more and more. I've already started on the next one.

S. L. PERRIN

SOURCES

1Up.com, 8bitdigi.com, activision.com, altarofgaming.com, amigareviews.leveluphost.com, angrybirds.com, animationcareerreview.com, antstream.com, arcade-history.com, arcadeattack.co.uk, arcadingonline.com, arstechnica.com, atariage.com, atarigames.com, atarihq.com, atariprotos.com, bbc.co.uk, blog.playstation.com, bloody-disgusting.com, britannica.com, bullfrogproductions.fandom.com, businessinsider.com, c64-wiki.com, canonn.science, carthrottle.com, cbsnews.com, censorship.wikia.org, classicgaming.cc, combineoverwiki.net, computinghistory.org.uk, cracked.com, dampfkraft.com, destructoid.com, digitalcommons.law.uga.edu, digitpress.com, doomwiki.org, education.minecraft.net, elderscrolls.fandom.com, engadget.com, esrb.org, eurogamer.net, ew.com,factor-tech.com, fandom.com, flickr.com, forceforgood.co.uk, frgcb.blogspot.com, funstockretro.co.uk, gamasutra.com, gamespot.com, gamexcess.net, gdcvault.com, ghettogamer.net, glitterberri.com, gonintendo.com, gran-turismo.com,gran-turismo.fandom.com, greenmangaming.com, guinnessworldrecords.com, hackaday.com, iconeye.com, ign.com, indieretronews.com, insight.ieeeusa.org, inverse.com, jordanmechner.com, kotaku.com, libertygames.co.uk, lucasfilm.fandom.com, magweasel.com, mauronewmedia.com, menshealth.com, metroactive.com, minecraft.gamepedia.com, miyamotoshrine.com, mmo-population.com, museumofplay.org, nfornerds.com, nintendo.com, nintendoworldreport.com, notch.tumblr.com, npr.org, nytimes.com, oldschoolgamermagazine.com, onceuponatari.com, onlysp.escapistmagazine.com, openstem.com.au, pcgamesn.com, phys.org, pixelatron.com, playclassic.games, playercounter.com, pocketgamer.biz, pocketgamer.com, pong-story.com, polygon.com, princeofpersia.fandom.com, qz.com, raregamer.co.uk, readonlymemory.vg, rebelscum.com, redbull.com, researchgate.net, retrodomination.com, retrogamer.net, retrojunk.com, ringsandcoins.com, rockpapershotgun.com, shacknews.com, shmuplations.com, siliconera.com, simcity.fandom.com, slashfilm.com, snopes.com, statista.com, streetrodonline.com, super-play.co.uk, swos.gazchap.com, syndicate.lubiki.pl, techcrunch.com, technologyreview.com, telegraph.co.uk, theconversation.com, thegamer.com, theguardian.com,

66 OF THE MOST IMPORTANT VIDEO GAMES EVER! (ACCORDING TO ME)

thekinsie.com, thelatenightsession.com, theweekly.co.uk, thexboxhub.com, thezorklibrary.com, thezorklibrary.com, thinksetmag.com, threefieldsentertainment.com, time.com, todayifoundout.com, twingalaxies.com, twitter.com, unseen64.net, usgamer.net, variety.com, venturebeat.com, videogamehistory.fandom.com, villains.fandom.com, web.archive.org, wired.com, worldofwarcraft.com, youtube.com, zelda.com, zelda.gamepedia.com

One of my biggest sources. My own memoires of being a gamer for the last four decades or so.

S. L. PERRIN

www.ingramcontent.com/pod-product-compliance
Lightning Source LLC
Chambersburg PA
CBHW071351210526
45465CB00001B/58